The Bermuda

Fundamental Financial Planning Primer Series

BOOK ONE

The Dawn of New Beginnings

Your Personal Back-to-Basics
Financial Review to Dramatically
Improve Your Lifestyle

Written Specifically for All Bermuda Islanders
By Bermudian Martha Harris Myron, CPA JSM
Master of Laws in International Tax and Financial Services
Content Editor: Julie A. Hendrickson-Simons, BSc. AAPA QFA

Copyright

Bermuda 1610

Bermuda - 1610
Map drawn by Sir
George Somers

Part 1- History of Bermuda

Listen to Ralph Richardson,
Mariner Extraordinaire,
Author of the Bermuda
Boater, Owner of Winsome
Tours & Consulting, Past
Commodore - the Royal
Bermuda Yacht Club

https://tinyurl.com/yhbbcdqo

Dedication

We Commemorate our Legendary Bermuda Pilots

Bermuda is a beacon, a tiny island situated on a defunct volcano in the middle of the Atlantic Ocean.

Settled since the year 1604, Bermuda has had a marine history of astonishing proportions to her size and population.

For more than 400 years, Bermuda sailors have roved the high seas. Our forebears built highly desired internationally renowned fast sloops, earning skilled reputations for danger, daring, and dedication.

By the early 1700's, Bermuda maritime commerce contained more than 700 merchant fleet vessels in the technically, innovative and highly influential for that time, the fast Bermuda rig sloop - used for fishing, whaling, trade, plundering, smuggling, and privateering.

Historical research has established that local Bermuda shipwrights built more than 4,000 Bermuda sloops, sold, traded in the Grand Atlantic triangle to British, French, American navies, and commercial seafaring companies. Bermudian seaman played auxiliary roles from our strategic Atlantic Ocean location during the French Revolution, Napoleonic Wars, and the English and American War for Independence. They ran crucial supply blockades (more than 1,800 visits) during the American Civil War and provide troop support in the World Wars They rescued many sea faring souls, some deliberately, some inadvertently, ship- wrecked off our coasts.

How Bermuda's speedy sloops joined the Royal Navy by Dr Edward Harris, Royal Gazette, Sep 1, 2012.

Among these ancestral sailors were the legendary mighty men, our fearless Bermuda pilots whose original navigational tools consisted primarily of their own innate skills, the sea, stars,

A large Bermuda sloop, built for the British Royal Navy, about 1750, with typical raked mast and fore-and-aft Bermuda Rig: the greatest invention in sailing technology after the European "Square Rigger": Dr. Edward Harris

and sky. It was not until 1805 that the first chart, Heathers Improved Chart of the Bermudas was published, documenting and adding to their traditional knowledge.

Piloting in Bermuda was a respected, stressful occupation demanding intuitive planning, great physical and mental strength. In early days, a crew rowing at full speed might easily surpass twenty nautical miles in the race for the first right to pilot a ship, the most lucrative nautical prize. The job required ingenuity and intuitive observations of our ever-changing marine environment.

A Bermuda Pilot's expert guidance and ocean risk management experience brought vital commerce through ruthless reefs and treacherous shoals into Bermuda's calm safe harbours. Their legacy has been an extraordinary contribution to the building of the economic infrastructure of our country.

We honour these pilots of old (these original maritime planners) with archival photos sourced to us by the Bermuda Maritime Museum. View the superb commemorative book, Bermuda Piloting, celebrating Bermuda's brave mariners and written by Elena Strong, Jane Downing, and Adrian Webb.

The contemporary piloting/navigating text book, The Bermuda Boater, authored by Ralph Richardson, past Commodore of the Royal Bermuda Yacht Club (2008 - 2009) and former Chief Pilot with Enterprise Submarine with 700 hours underwater as Pilot and Trainer, is a fascinating, technical amplification by Bermudian, Mr. Richardson, with his navigational expertise of the skills required to navigate Bermuda's unique marine environment.

They that go down to the sea in ships, that do business in great waters…

In Bermuda, the primeval influence of the sea is everywhere. It is part of us, not easily separated from us. It is the salt in our blood; the spray on our faces; the essence of moisture in our lungs. Our ocean is never far away, less than a mile from any homestead. It penetrates our being; it assaults our senses and shores with intimidating towering ferocious rollers in storm driven surf. It is euphoric on blissful sunny days, glittery, sparkling rainbow lights dancing on azure waves. In dawning pink- blushed tranquillity, it elevates our souls.

The sea has been our perpetual conduit for commerce and discovery. For centuries, it was our only access to the outside world. For we islanders were, and still are, dependent upon the sea for our livelihood. It is our one constant, always there - surrounding this tiny isle in the fourth most remote spot on earth.

Bermuda's marine influence still has far reaching significance

Today, our Bermuda's international finance centre is home to some of the largest financial risk managers in the world.

With information crossing all borders, intellectual reefs and shoals still exist, still dangerous yet far more complex, while digital obstacles have become the new challenge.

Physical trade by sea and by air will continue conventionally.

Physical world boundaries will always exist, but our stratospheric world has expanded electronically.

More than ever, we need to understand our faster-than-the-speed-of-light world, our finances, our goals, and our place in life.

The consequences of ignoring financial planning in our sea-faring, now electronic world, may mean not only the difference between financial success and failure, but the blink-of-an-eye liquidation of one's entire financial resources, perpetrated by resourceful predatory digital thieves.

We Bermudians know
the sea – very well.

References

Dr. Edward Harris, MBE, JP, PhD, FSA Director Emeritus National Museum of Bermuda (1980-2017). Inventor of the industry standard archaeological system (1973), the Harris Matrix, Author of Principles of Archaeological Stratigraphy, Bermuda Heritage Matters and numerous major historical fortification and early Bermuda period narratives.

The Bermuda Boater: Ralph Richardson, Commodore of the Royal Bermuda Yacht Club (2008 - 2009) and former Chief Pilot with Enterprise Submarine, navigator/ pilot for multiple cross-Atlantic yacht races.

Elena Strong, Director, National Museum of Bermuda Johnson Savage, MD. Drawings from the 1800s Donated to National Museum of Bermuda. In the Eye of All Trade: Bermuda, Bermudians, and the Maritime Atlantic World, 1680-1783, Michael J Jarvis.

Part 2
Listen to
Ralph
Richardson

https://tinyurl.com/ygvtqqf3

> Sailing is how we were discovered, how we survived, and how we have thrived.

Bermuda Pilot Boat
Nineteenth Century

The graveyard of shipwrecks surrounding Bermuda is testament to the island's perilous encircling reefs and complicated channel systems. On the ocean floor lie the remains of French, Spanish, Dutch, Portuguese, English, Danish, Italian and American vessels—the victims of Bermuda's extensive reef network and 500 years of material evidence documenting Bermuda's interaction with the Atlantic World.

Local knowledge, navigation charts, lighthouses, signalling stations, beacons and buoys have all aided in the safe passage of incoming and outgoing ships but the expertise of local pilots has been of paramount importance. Once an incoming ship was spotted, a conch was blown, and the pilot crews rushed to launch their boats in the water and raced each other under oar or sail to the sighted ship, as far as 50 miles from shore.

Enslaved pilot James 'Jemmy' Darrell performed an exceptional maritime feat for the Royal Navy that led to his eventual freedom and being appointed a King's pilot—the highest ranking pilot on the island entrusted to bring in the Admiral's flagship.

In 1795, Darrell successfully navigated Lord Admiral Murray's flagship HMS Resolution safely through the reefs to a safe anchorage on the East end of the North Shore (now called Murray's Anchorage). "With great coolness and presence of mind… he had the vessel's sail shortened, backed her through the more intricate part of the channel…and then proceeded by the usual course."

Pilot Darrell's home in
St. Georges, Bermuda

JAMES DARRELL
Who died 12th April 1815 aged 66 years.
In his publick life as a servant of his country
he obtained the general approval of his talents and worth.
In his private walk as a member of his community
his name will long be remembered
for his usefulness and integrity.

Excerpt from grave memorial

St.George's Harbour scene about 1835, a year after the Emancipation of slaves in Bermuda. Several Bermuda sloops are afloat and the women in the rowboat appear to be possibly taking bananas for sale to ships in the Harbour (Dr. Johnson Savage Collection, National Museum of Bermuda).

A small Bermuda sloop with the classic "Bermuda Rig" (fore and aft sails) used by most modern yachts and invented in Bermuda before 1674 (Photo takenabout1910).

Courtesy Dr. Edward Harris, retired Director Emeritus, National Museum of Bermuda

Modern Bermuda Pilot Boat with a Replica of the Famed Pilot Gig. The Pilot is holding a commemorative wreath to be laid in memory of Bermudian pilots lost at sea, sponsored by the Bermuda Guild of the Holy Compassion.

"Oh, they that go down to the sea in ships, that do business in great waters; these see the works of the Lord and his wonders in the deep." Psalm 107.23

PILOTS

Contents

Covid Commentary

Dear Readers: this has been an abrupt, serious and to far too many, tragic challenges to your personal lives!

We grieve for all lives lost and express sincere condolences for their families.

How are you handling your finances, worries, health, and mental attitude during our worrisome, shelter-in-place, social distancing environment?

While many of you are no strangers to another economic downturn after experiencing the 2008 sub-prime market collapse and financial recession, that time was truly a never-before- experienced survival of the fittest financial endurance test.

This time is different.

This time it is your health and your finances at risk.

This time, governments, including ours, were able to put some mandated impediments to social contact in place to limit communities' health exposures, devastating personal losses, and provide some temporary financial support.

This time forced decreased demand in services and products has impacted home values and sales, rental lease terms and occupancies, wages and the possible availability of jobs, tourist and business vitality, and led to sparse retail commerce on thinly trafficked sidewalks.

Thousands of individuals and their families are reporting job losses, while some have never fully recovered from the last recession.

Resources are running low. Even so, relentless inflation marches on without skipping a beat, continuing to exact its toll on islanders with increases in cost of living products and services.

What more can you do now?
We cannot control change, but we can plan to put ourselves and our families into the best possible position, financially and healthily to weather adversity.
No matter what, life does go on. Enjoy the little things, the everyday wonders in life: a child's smile, sparkling seas, sunsets when we know we will rise again in good health to meet the challenges of another day. Blessings to all of you.

Martha Harris Myron August 2020

Mission Statement

Welcome to The Bermuda Islander Fundamental Financial Planning Primer Series, a much- needed comprehensive guide to be published in digital format (FlipBook/PDF), written about Bermuda's financial environment specifically for Bermudians, Bermuda residents and expatriate guest workers, living and working in our Bermuda's international financial environment.

Designed to start with Series One - Your Back-2-Basics Personal Financial Review, the Series builds upon the basic platform first, then, is followed by further components of financial planning in seven more digital eBooks to fully arrive at a comprehensive understanding of all things financial in Bermuda.

Please see introduction below for full details on Series One through Eight.

Any proceeds earned from the BIFFPP Series will be donated to the Bermuda Salvation Army in memory of our mother, Clarine Harris and our father, Cecil E Harris, the Sewing Machine Man of Wesley Street, Hamilton, Bermuda.

As a long-term (February 2000) financial columnist for the Royal Gazette, Bermuda, it is my hope that this series will provide relevant useful, financial information to help Bermuda Islanders understand the complexity of the relationships between their domestic financial interests and their international connections to better manage their finances.

Why would I do this?

Background. Bermuda and our people possess a proud and unique history. For more than four hundred years, Bermuda and our people have commanded a strong, viable position in global trade, inconceivably inversely proportionate to our tiny island and small population.

From the arrival of our first shipwrecked sailors, Bermudians have always lived in an open society with fiercely independent survivalist instincts.

Never much constrained by physical frontiers, as well as possibly to relieve the restrictions of life contained within 21 square miles, Bermudians have acquired legendary reputations as some of the world's foremost mariners, traders, and explorers.

Our forebears, in 1610, delivered the US Jamestown settlement from starvation in the Bermuda-built HMS Deliverance (from scavenged nautical wreckage and native cedar); have joined just causes (and other countries' armies), with some fighting the ultimate battle for world peace, liberty and justice for all. Families have emigrated to far off nations, assimilating new cultures and relationships in the quest for commerce and discovery.

Centuries, generations, and decades later they have returned to Bermuda bringing with them the trappings of international living, cosmopolitan thought, multiple extended family nationalities, while possessing assets and conducting business in other jurisdictions.

This Global mobility (rock fever) of our people is indicative of the reality that every country and its residents now live in a time of constant change: people, money, goods, intellectual property, innovation, and ideas literally encompassing, circumventing the earth in continuous movement.

In tandem with these migrations, Bermuda, our country, transformed itself from a relatively simple cash society (fishing village style) where everything moved slower; where business was conducted on a trusted handshake and a cash-count-those-bills deposits and bill payment structures; where the economy was closed - operating in a comfortable, stable, unexciting financial environment.

Bermuda's People are a microcosmic polyglot of nationalities, races, languages, religions, and cultures all derived from various origins from immigrating, emigrating across the globe to and from Bermuda. Some arrived involuntarily as slaves, and indentured servants. Others were merchant seamen, share-holders, governing bodies, politicians, and freemen settlers. Among the most influential familial and business connections are the United States, United Kingdom, Canada, Azores (Portugal), Ireland, Europe, Australia, New Zealand, and the Caribbean: Barbados, Turks & Caicos, Jamaica, Trinidad & Tobago, St. Kitts & Nevis, Anguilla, Barbuda, Tortola, and others related.

This plethora of international personalities, businesses, countries of origin, residency, domicile, immigration rights, and taxation assertions presents enormous complexity in the financial lives of every-day Bermuda residents. Keeping up with these changes is a tremendous challenge for individuals across the Bermuda spectrum, particularly in today's 24/7 business environment, when most people's first focus is on work, family life, faith, and community.

Just as our ancestral seafarers derived their origins from many domiciles, locally, it is highly probable (and often verifiable) that the majority of Bermuda residents:

- possess more than one passport;
- own assets in various other jurisdictions;
- embrace more than one culture;
- speak more than one language;
- be related to citizens of other countries;
- have relatives, responsibilities, and connections to more than one jurisdiction;
- be employed in more than one jurisdiction, and
- have both foreign and domestic beneficiaries.

Further, Bermuda's good fortune is that Bermuda's international finance centre today is a financially sophisticated, dominant force in the global marketplace of insurance, reinsurance, investments, banking, trust administration, fintech, marine and aviation commerce. It is endemic of this environment (and the clients that we serve) that local financial institutions routinely offer money market funds in more than nine major currencies, while foreign currency exchanges take place in a matter of minutes electronically or at a local bank teller window.

But what of the ordinary resident of Bermuda, whether well-off, or not-so-financially successful?

More and more responsibility for our own future financial security is being placed squarely on our shoulders.

- We are overwhelmed with financial data. Electronic media have plugged us into the 24/7 global arena, a complex and ever evolving world.
- We are working harder and longer than ever before.

- We know we need to pay attention to our finances, but when we are really stressed, it is far easier to plan for a great vacation.
- With the constant pressure of spiralling living and housing costs, Bermudians and expatriate residents alike face a bewildering, daunting array of financial choices for managing their family budgets.

Why are term deposits so low?

How can we manage the ever-increasing cost of living here?

Health care affordability is an increasing concern to us.

What type of investments and in which currencies are most suitable for us?

Have I made the right choices for my pension?

How much education funding is needed for our children?

How much will I need to retire; when should I retire: and should I relocate?

What are the ramifications of losing my job?

How can we ever manage not making our mortgage payments? Will we lose our home?

I'm a dual-citizen of Bermuda and another country - what are we going to do about estate planning for our multi-national family?

Our children are living in multiple jurisdictions - should we consider relocating, and what citizenship will be our primary?

Financial complexity and difficulty in finding information relevant to our Bermuda economic environment abounds. It can be far more challenging than any homework.

But, it shouldn't be.

Why the focus on financial Knowledge?

The level of your future financial success is directly related to the level of your financial knowledge

Becoming financially savvy is having the courage to understand and control your entire financial environment by,

- Developing a personal financial mission statement for personal success
- Branding yourself to move up the career ladder
- Managing your cash, both income and expenses
- Accumulating assets by appreciating your net worth and decreasing your good debts
- Utilising all employee benefits offered to you in real money terms
- Investing in yourself and your children with continuing education
- Preparing for all contingencies with risk management protection, insurance, and prudent risk decisions
- Learning about Investments available in our complex international environment
- Understanding your financial behaviour and working on positive modifications
- Choosing a qualified experienced financial advisor, or do-it-yourself investor
- Living and adapting to Bermuda's AA+ economy – an expensive place to live, work, and retire
- Refining lifestyle changes: relocation, revitalisation, retirement, investment asset allocation, annuities, drawdown risk and monitoring your pension contributions.

- Minimising domestic and international tax issues
- Wending your expatriate resident / Bermudian international connections through the off-shore/onshore financial and cross borders' maze
- Coping and managing the human element: the effect of finances on relationships, careers, and serious life events
- Organising your ultimate passing: When you die and the role of estate planning, trusts, business succession, stamp duty, and multiple jurisdictional oversights.

Readers, take the challenge - to figure out what you have, what you can do to use your resources to make a personal financial plan that works for you.

This series will help you accomplish your plan. Sensible, practical, and doable — all designed and engineered for you.

Now it is up to you.
"Change your Life for the better."

Martha Myron introduces the First Primer in the Bermuda Islander Financial Planning Series: Book One - The Dawn of New Beginnings. Your Personal Back-2-Basics Financial Review to Dramatically Improve Your Lifestyle.

https://tinyurl.com/yfwdjkhu

Introduction

The Bermuda Islander Fundamental Financial Planning Primer Series in eBook Format.

The Bermuda Islander Fundamental Finan- cial Planning Primer Series (the BIFFPP Series as they will be referred to further) is written for all Bermuda Islanders and their globally mobile families, their Domestic Affairs & their International Connections across the Great Atlantic Pond.

The BIFFPP Series will be featured across the next two years in published Flipbook/pdf down-loadable Segments, available on the Royal Gazette

Website Resource Library

https://www.royalgazette.com/bermudaislander/

the Bermuda Islander Pondstraddler Perspectives website.

www.pondstraddler.com

These eBooks will be issued in electronic format, updated from time to time to reflect changes in our investment world: Bitcoin, blockchain technology, cashless societies, global trade impacts, and so many more disruptive elements introduced to the global investment marketplace that impacts us all locally and globally.

A couple of notes.

These eBooks will not be fancy, and the formatting will probably not be perfect, but some will be completely free, or at a tiny minimal cost to you. Any proceeds will go directly to the Bermuda Salvation Army, a non-profit Bermuda registered charity.

Each eBook written specifically for Bermuda residents living in the Bermuda financial environment, represent the culmination of the author's experience with clients, readers of the Royal Gazette and knowledge derived from more than thirty-five years as both a United States and Bermuda international tax and financial planning services practitioner.

These eBook Series provide references, materials, links, hypothetical composite cases, anonymous reader feedback, complied from presentations,

white papers and, Moneywise, the acclaimed weekly Personal Finance column for The Royal Gazette followed by thousands of readers since February 2000.

The eight primers will cover: cash management, investments, risk & insurance, retirement & pensions, taxation, estate / legacy, Bermuda's economy, and the challenges of international cross border planning.

Building Your Brand

SCOTT STALLARD PHOTOGRAPHY

Laying the Nets at Dawn

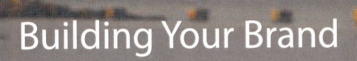

Step One - Branding

Building your brand.

How can you be successful if you don't value yourself?

It used to be called 'making a statement'.

Watch anyone today, anywhere, anytime. We all send subtle (sometimes not so) signals about what we stand for, what we want, who we think we are, and where we'd like to be seen in our social strata. We think that we are completely individualistic - choosing to do our own thing – but, whether making that selective choice to be a loner or star of the evening, we are conforming to a pattern of expected behaviour.

For most people, it is an unconscious thing even though great care may have been taken to dress a certain way with a certain hairstyle, choice of shoes, jewellery, body ornaments and so on. While the statement may say - look at me - there is no real 'sale' of value, or is there?

Aren't we all subliminally selling our personal value, confidence, ethics, and integrity to compete for our standing in a community? Moreover, aren't we trying to deliver on that value every single day of our lives?

Take the concept one step further and your statement becomes the selling of you, your personal brand. The positioning of your brand is only half of the equation – the other half is building the relationship with the buyer(s) so-to-speak of your brand. Instead of 'just making a statement,' you are now in the full-time business of managing all kinds of relationships, work, home, extended family, peers, community.

Image is not everything – but it certainly is the First Perception of You.

What makes someone a positive standout?

Trite question, but you know what I mean. Take any group of people. There are sure to be one or two who are complete standouts, for various reasons (mind you, not always good ones) but wherever the assignment, conference, or work group, these people are in the forefront. The rest of us will remain in, perhaps prefer, the background: not speaking up, working away in a corner cubby even though we dress professionally; say the right things, do the right things and finish the right things on time. But, we aren't standouts - we'd like to be, though wouldn't we?

Why Brand Yourself?

"Visibility is far more important than ability," according to Peter Montoya, author of "The Brand Called You."

Just a little secret – it is the key to outstanding personal success. Conversely, why not brand yourself? It is a far more positive action to take than letting others define who you are.

If you (and only you) control the personal image message to others that you are an professional of integrity and profound work ethics, surely personal satisfaction in knowing who you are and financial success will follow.

This branding concept is what makes the perception of some of us more far more than we really are. Why? Because we humans are uncomfortable with the unknown.

Branding begets familiarity.

Yes, we still struggle with that primitive fear of the unfamiliar. Even if familiarity breeds contempt, familiarity in foods, households, clothes, politicians, processes, destinations is highly preferred.

At least, you know what you are getting! Brands are familiar, even bad familiar brands are purchased time after time before good unknown retail products, for instance. Brands are always about emotions, drawing powerful feelings in yourself and others. When you display an expensive coveted handbag, for instance, what does it say about you and to others: envy, confidence, familiarity, success?

Nothing is more effective than a Personal Brand that says, "I'm the one to get it done for you!" If being a brand equals unparalleled success, how do you brand yourself in your workplace for ultimate recognition where there are for instance, numerous mechanic technicians, teachers, electronic sales, financial advisors, insurance brokers, chefs, accountants, politicians, lawyers, front-line salespersons, etc.?

- By setting out a formulated time frame and a consistent message that brands you.

- By being visible! According to Peter Montoya, "The Brand Called You! Visibility is more important than ability."

That's right, accomplishing a superb job on a car repair, legislative bill, a top line sales month, a gorgeous restaurant meal, a technical renovation, excellent customer services, an innovative spreadsheet program won't get you anywhere if no one knows about it. While ability is extremely important, unknown ability is never recognised. If you are interested in becoming a brand, you should carefully assess your current working environment and key into an area where you can become a standout. You may find that:

- you have a particular analytical talent,
- you are good at a particular type of sales,
- you are an innovative problem solver,
- you are willing to take on projects no one else wants,
- you are adept at client relationships,
- you find it easy to display a consistent positive attitude,
- your knowledge filter is always on the cutting edge of industry changes.

Gear yourself to being the problem solver; the can-do person; the trusted person who can discretely handle every client issue; the person with high integrity who always finishes the project while making everyone feel good about his or her role; the go-to-industry knowledge expert.

Then, you have to tell people about your competence, without boasting. This is the stickiest part. No one likes a braggart, so your competence message must be subtle and sincere, but it must be disseminated every single time you have a professional success.

Brand Yourself. Hone in on that; concentrate on that; have a phrase that labels you that you can use whenever you work with other people: "I'm a seriously inspired service salesperson named Mr. Solutions or another example, No matter the time or day, I always responds to my client's finance questions."

Deliver the goods. Whatever it is, use your brand label every single chance you get and deliver the very best job possible. If you are the best mechanic, IT specialist, banking professional, etc., people will remember and trust you. Nothing is more effective than a Personal Brand that says, "I'm the one to get it done for you!"

You will become a brand!

Be genuine. Branding will not reap any rewards if you are not sincerely genuine. Constant negativity, competitiveness, phoniness, and superficiality in dealing with others are absolute killers, no matter how talented you may be.

You make the difference. Assess yourself in a personal review every morning. "Am I more worried about how I look, or how I am performing? You must focus on the clients' need to feel trust, by being consistent, real, expert, flexible, talented, and unafraid of failure (hide your fears, we all fail). Display absolute integrity, mentor those who are learning, perform consistently at a high level, show positive energy at all times, and always give credit for performance when due to your peers and team workers. Making them look good will always make you look good.

Neutralise the negative stereotype thinkers, become a Personal Brand and financial success will follow.

Listen to Reasons to Value Yourself

https://tinyurl.com/yeuyk2js

Listen to Fast Facts Becoming Your Brand

https://tinyurl.com/yetmm5nv

References & Resources

There are many Self-help branding media, articles, and books available.

Just GOOGLE!

Don't forget that many books (print and digital) can be purchased used for a fraction of the price of a New book! Some of these references are ageless because the secret of personal success is within you. Use that power.

The Brand Called You, by Peter Montoya, the original recognised leader in Personal Branding, out-dated now, but still incentivising. Published 2005

Influencer,

Building Your Personal Brand in the Age of Social Media, by Brittany Hennessy. The blue-print book to manage and monetise your influence as a content creator. Published 2018

Born to Win Find Your Success. Zig Ziglar. One of the greatest salespersons of all time. His successes and quotes are as valid today as ever.

- "You were designed for accomplishment, engineered for success, and endowed with the seeds of greatness."

- "If people like you, they'll listen to you, but if they trust you, they'll do business with you."
- "Your attitude, not your aptitude, will determine your altitude!"

7 Ways To Build A Brand With The New Class Of Black Creatives, Contributor, Forbes, March 06, 2019

Goldie Chan, "I'm known as the "Oprah of LinkedIn." I'm a top LinkedIn creator, digital strategist, and personal branding expert. www.goldiechan.com

1) Believe in your worth.
2) Study your craft.
3) Make your own experience.
4) Be yourself.
5) Build your village.
6) Always show up prepared.
7) Be consistent, professional, and on time.

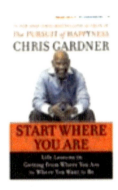

Chris Gardner's remarkable transformation from homeless single father to millionaire was chronicled in his number one New York Times bestseller The Pursuit of Happyness and in the movie of the same name, starring Will Smith.

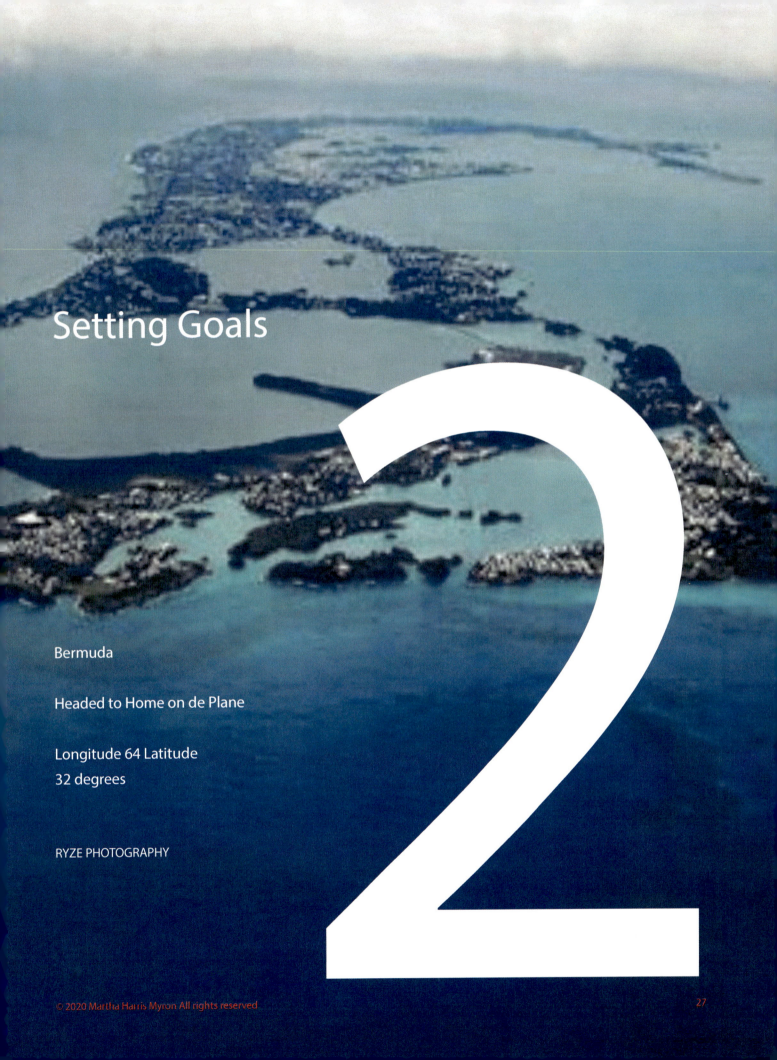

Setting Goals

Bermuda

Headed to Home on de Plane

Longitude 64 Latitude
32 degrees

RYZE PHOTOGRAPHY

Step Two - Setting Goals

Setting motivating goals is easy.

Changing old habits is hard.

You will need Motivation

Only you can decide that!

How can you motivate yourself to get going – to achieve any goal?

Have a reason. What matters MOST TO YOU!

Your goal must something you want to do just about more than anything else.

- Make it your first priority
- Commit to achieving your goal
- Become relentless and disciplined in that commitment
- Write your plan down

Yes, life obstacles may slow you down. So, return to your goal as soon as you can.

One individual had a little goal book that at the beginning of every year – she planned the goal for the year – I want a promotion to a manager! At the end of the year, she reviewed her progress – if not quite there, she wrote the same goal down again.

Overcoming Old Habits

If the COVID health economic issues have taught us anything

It is this, forced change is tough, especially if you are used to:

- complacency
- sameness

- just going along to get along,
- it is just not easy.

Because now, you have to challenge and motivate yourself to change your old habits

Change means developing new goals.

What should your goals be?

Only you can decide that!

It does not matter what the goal is – the end game here is to help you get to the finish line. That means putting financial $$ Dollar figures on those goals, then figuring out how to get them. Some may take a month, six months, a year, five, ten, twenty years.

Ask yourself if you have the tenacity to stick out these determined time frames?

Goals may be anything that is highly desired and relevant to you, plus a goal is not always about acquiring things:

- becoming healthier, a vivid reminder of COVID impact
- rebuilding a relationship
- just getting control of your finances!
- owning a home
- obtaining a graduate education for yourself, or for your children
- starting a long-term successful business

- jewellery, timepieces, electronics
- a vehicle
- a new career
- relocation
- a fabulous vacation.

One family wanted to buy a home – MORE THAN ANYTHING ELSE!

Every month they cut out new pictures of the home they wanted, pasting the pic- tures every-where in their rented home.

Then they counted their savings each time they added to the pot.

Setting a personal goal(s) for yourself?

There are only a few steps. Imagine.

1. FIRST, PLAN, PLAN that when you are setting a financial (or any other goals) that YOU HAVE THE ABILITY to achieve them, no matter the obstacles.

2. SECOND: Make changes in your personal fi-nancial habits to:
   a. Reorganize your thinking, if health focused,
   b. put a progressive plan in place,
   c. motivate by research and
   d. Layout progress on your monthly calendar

3. THIRD, become very financially focused by figuring out the cost of the goal and divide by the number of months, or years, you think it reasonably could take to reach the savings goal.

4. Work with your spouse, partner, or family for motivation to stay on track.

5. Use the Internet for motivation, too. Mil-lions of websites exist for goal setting, e.g. www.goalbuddy.com

Take Action.

You have to believe in yourself and your ability to change, absolutely.

Remember, achieving goals will take time

Be persistent and consistent

Use motivational incentives to keep that goal top of mind – remember the home pictures

The personal satisfaction of achieving a goal can-not be underestimated!!!

What about our lady with the goal book? When I met her, she still used the same worn goal book twenty years on.

And she had made multiple promotions in her career.

She motivated others to succeed!

 Listen to tips for Setting Goals

https://tinyurl.com/yhqaplrk

 Listen to tips for Increasing Your Human Capital

https://tinyurl.com/yfovr9v9

References & Resources

GoalBuddy: The Complete Guide to Goal Setting. The Goal Buddy System

This free system was developed by two Bulgarian entrepreneurs, and is designed for working independently, or with the mutual support with a goal buddy. Well worth exploring for confidence, motivation and defining what you want out of life!!

These templates are to be used in the goal setting process and are part of the "GoalBuddy" system.

They are free and accessible to everyone according to GoalBuddy. Download them, no email registration needed.

https://goalbuddy.io/goal-setting/

The Start - Goal Setting Step I, The Confidence Fuel Tank

Goal setting templates

https://goalbuddy.io/templates/

A. The What I Want Manifesto - The idea is to help you figure out what you want from life

B. The Vision Game Plan - The purpose of it is to choose a vision and then examine it from different perspectives until you reach an effective action goal.

C. The 90-day Activity Focus - Print out the template and fill it out with your visions and action goals every three months as part of the process of setting the next 90-day goals.

Goal Setting Guide

The Complete Guide To Goal Setting. Start Here

Goal Setting Quick Start Guide

Download the Goal Setting Templates

Step 1 – The Confidence Fuel Tank

Step 2 – The True Goals Discovery Process

Step 3 – The What I Want Manifesto

Step 4 – The Vision Gameplan

Step 5 – The 90-Day Focus

Step 6 – The Goal Buddy Support System

Step 7 – The Goal Buddy Meetings

Embracing
Change

The Spirit of Bermuda
Scott Stallard Photography

3

Step Three - Embracing Change

Embracing Change.

Make No Mistake, It Is a Challenge

The 5 Key Stages of Change

Stage 1	Stage 2	Stage 3	Stage 4	Stage 5
Pre contemplation	Contemplation	Planning	Action	Maintenance
Haven't considered the idea of change / resistant to change	Considering how change can affect us	Preparing for the new change S.M.A.R.T goals ensure a plan is effective	Implementing the plan with "doing" based actions	Maintaining the change as a new long term behaviour

Relapse

Relapse can take you back to any stage during the process of change and can be caused by:

- **Internal Pressure** (The voice in your head that says the change is too hard)
- **Social Pressure** (Often lack of support by family and friends)
- **Special Situations** (A combination of internal & social pressure)

Do you want to change?

This is your decision. You may need to modify your financial behaviour to achieve your goals.

And, that is a very hard thing to do!

Because it means changing what and who you are now.

Change means taking risks.

Change means you could fail and feel foolish.

Change may mean losing personal relationships – if you decide to say, cut back on expensive partying nights out, or going on a diet (to save on groceries), or changing other personal habits that no longer will match those of your friends, your significant other, or your family.

Change may draw criticism. You may be called stingy, cheap, and lots of other snide (really envious) remarks.

See the Key Stages of Change chart above used in setting a Savings Goal. The path is not a straight line. The key, even if you relapse, is to just keep going!

We are all afraid of change.

We hate to get out our comfort zone, even when we are not the least bit happy in that zone.

Example: The Fives Stages of Changes to Establish a Savings Plan.

1. You may feel you are not ready to make a change, or that your situation is just too tough to ever resolve.

2. Then, the more you think about the goals, the more determined you become to start, but you are still not sure if you want to take the challenge on.

3. A bit more thinking, you are not sure, but then, you decide to layout an action plan.

4. The biggest stage. You start to change your financial behaviour to increase your savings.

5. You are elated. You have changed and put savings plan in place. You will need to continually work on maintaining that positive can-do attitude.

Change is constant. Nothing - outside of your mind – ever stays the same. The pace of change in business today is so fast, it is almost frightening to think about.

Even if you don't want to change, eventually you will be forced into changing your behaviour, your financial habits, and your life.

You cannot stop progress!

Here is a little secret. When you are forced to make changes – you have no control.

Wouldn't you rather make the decision yourself to positively change to achieve your goals, not let someone else's decisions dictate your future?

Change means progress. If you keep doing the same things over and over, you are going to get the same old results and end up with the same old frustrations.

"You were born to win, but to be a winner, you must plan to win, prepare to win, and expect to win." Zig Ziglar

Embrace change in your life. Let it take you to new heights of success.

Listen to tips for Becoming an Agent of Change

https://tinyurl.com/yeudt4k4

References & Resources

Reference source for the Five Stages of Change originally came (according to Google) from two researchers, Carlo C Clemente and J O Prochaska to assist psychologists.

The model displayed above has been adapted over the years to help motivate anyone wanting to change their behaviour (lifestyle), ranging from physical and mental health, financial habits, relationships, dietary, workouts and more.

Wikipedia: Transtheoretical model

ExperienceL!fe. The Whole Life Health & Fitness Magazine

www.experiencelife.com

There are hundreds of change-type and experience websites - just GOOGLE!

Listen to Shantel Deshield, CEO, Pocketchangebda, an agent of change for young adults teaching them to manage their finances.

https://tinyurl.com/yzjstqag

4

Making An Action
Financial Plan

Step Four - Making An Action Financial Plan

Making a doable financial action plan.

These are the critical components needed to become financially successful.

- Following through on implementing your personal goals as outlined above.
- Manage (invest) your cash flow and live within your means.

This is the hardest challenge for most people because it means delaying gratification. Our society has culturally conditioned us to want instant happiness, (however temporary).

- Increase knowledge to plan for the future.

The compounding effect of relentless knowledge building upgrades your intellectual skills, brands and positions you to capitalise on opportunities in the workplace, harmonises your personal relationships, and is a sheer catapult to lifelong personal and financial success.

What does it mean to make a financial action plan?

To understand how the elements that comprise financial planning fit together, we need to go back to the good old days in Bermuda when life was simple, mostly pure cash transactions (some of us remember the little brown pay cash envelopes)? Bills were paid in cash; purchases were made in cash; savings were often hoarded in cash in the proverbial cookie jar, or under the mattress.

There was little to no conscious structured future planning by Bermuda islanders; it was just plain survival common sense.

If cash was not available to buy goods, or, in inclement weather, the latest supply ship did not come in from Australia with butter, mutton, a few frozen foods, etc. then people resorted to barter. Of course, I oversimplify, one ship does not a fleet make but the sense of isolation was there.

However, if I assign a manpower value to fixing your roof, then fair enough, you can buy my labour for a boatful of fish. A lot of fish (and whatever else was native) was eaten back then, but disliking fish, you might sell to a neighbour for a cash profit, ingenuity being every Bermudian's middle name!

Or you might trade the fish for a cow, sell the milk, grow the herd, and invest in farmland, possibly build a home - assuming that in a perfect world, your herd remains healthy.

So, if your survival instincts helped you to not only eat but earn surplus cash, you might actually try to plan for more than a subsistence level in the future: acquiring other assets, starting a business, arranging some protection for your family, perhaps, even some formal retirement planning with a pension - something that was relatively non-existent for most folks, back in the good old days.

This was the instinctual beginning of financial planning.

How Can You Plan? Should You Do-It-Yourself?

Yes, you can. Ask three simple questions

1. One. Where am I now?
2. Two. Where do I want to be - in one year, two years, five years, ten years, etc.?
3. Three. What to I have to do to get there?

A very, very simple financial plan, taking one goal at a time, can look like this. For instance, you are constantly trying to catch up on your credit card debt, and consequently, do not have any cash reserves for a rainy day. Take some solace in knowing that you are not alone. A 2017 survey by US bank-rate.com indicated that more than 60% of US households could not afford a $400 emergency expense.

Illustrative Simple Plan Example:

Review All Your Finances. Increase Your Income. Monitor Your Spending.

Build a Cash Reserve. Reduce Credit Card Debt. Manage Your Risk Contingencies.

A. Review your current and future income projections
B. Seriously, review and monitor your spending.
C. Set up an easy to use budget.
D. Build your cash reserve account by watching the small stuff.
E. Open your cash reserve savings account even if only $50 a month, use the rest of the extra income and expense savings each month to apply to your debt. Ask your employer if an extra 1% or so can be withheld to increase your new reserve savings account.
F. If your credit card debt is out of control, schedule an appointment with a local debt counsellor to see if you can consolidate your debts into one interest rate and monthly payment.
G. Pay every single penny - as much as you can over the minimum credit card payment required every month - working on the highest interest rate card first, or the credit card with the smallest balance. You must feel incensed to continue by watching these balances decrease and then, disappear!
H. Then, use your card sparingly or not at all. Pay the monthly balance on time or before the due date to avoid any late penalties.
I. Better yet, stick to your debit card. Knowing your cash account will be depleted immediately is a good BRAKE STOP.
J. Review your remaining financial positions: employee benefits, pension balances, investments, insurance, basic estate plan, other debt payments, etc.
K. Motivate yourself and your family to save for a specific goal - that is the reward.

Does Everyone Need a Plan?

Some in the industry would say, yes, others would argue definitely not always. Sometimes, a full financial plan is overwhelming in length, depth, and time to implement. It becomes such a hurdle that nothing ever gets done. Focusing on one aspect of a plan at a time can be more appealing and achievable.

How will you know whether you need (or don't) a plan?

Start with the trigger questions below, and if you answer yes to more than a couple, you should think seriously about putting a simple financial action plan in effect.

Ignore the more complex issues for now as they are included by topic in each Series Primer to help with long-term planning.

Significant Life Event Financial Action Plan Triggers:

Are you experiencing significant changes, such as any of the following life happenings?

- Little to no idea where your ATM cash and other little cash expenses go
- Credit card or other debt out of control
- Redundancy and need for emergency cash
- Retirement looming and just not ready
- Significant changes in lifestyle creating demands on all finances
- Goal achievement, e.g. purchasing a home, car, college, etc.
- Divorce, marriage, widowed, extended family support issues
- Serious disability, special needs, or illness in family of child, breadwinner, etc.
- Business viability, loss of partner
- Annuity distribution decisions, domestic, foreign pensions
- Beneficiary of an inheritance
- Proceeds from sale of, or investments in, real estate, securities / investments
- Mortgage finally paid-off!

- International / domestic tax connections and liabilities
- Property investments abroad
- Obtaining another citizenship, e.g. United States, Canadian, UK,
- Lump sum Settlement of a insurance policy, lawsuit, lottery winnings, bonus
- Investment knowledge upgrade, choosing an advisor
- Starting a business, incorporating, selling a business
- Organising an estate, making a will, settling a trust,
- Emigration to another domicile
- Personal relative Eldercare, and accompanying long-term maintenance of real property

A Sample of a Simple Financial Wellness Action Plan

- Take a look at this Outline of a Financial Action Plan
- Set your Most Important Goal and time frame, incentive to fulfil this goal!
- Increase savings
- Diversify currencies
- Increase life insurance
- Implement personal plan to increase salary
- Work on prepaying mortgage principal
- Update wills, including living and medical care directives
- Assess estate, and death tax issues
- Start a globally diversified capital preservation portfolio investment
- Re-allocate pension assets to fit your risk profile / change pension beneficiaries

Once accomplished, the satisfaction of a working plan means Peace of Mind!

- The Pieces fit
- Your Finances are in harmony
- Update your plan as it keeps working, year after year!

Listen to tips for Making a Doable Action Plan

https://tinyurl.com/ygcmaxvn

References & Resources

Here are a couple of websites to help you get started with your own financial plan. These can be used for inspiration along with the ideas promoted above.

REMEMBER! These are no Bermuda planning websites, so you will need to ignore some of the topics such as taxation, investment products and so on.

Keep in mind also that these are suggestions only and that the author, Martha Harris Myron does not endorse or support in any way, help listed websites and references.

8 Steps to Creating a Smart Financial Plan

Ten Steps to Creating a Solid Financial Plan for Yourself

By Bola Sokunbi. Published on January 24, 2020

Savings for Rainy-Days and Contingency Planning

5

Step Five - Savings for Rainy-Days and Contingency Planning

Starting Your Budget Plan

Control the Small Stuff Slippage First.

To Budget is to Control Your Money in order to acquire peace of mind (and some luxury).

So Why is it such a challenge working with a budget?

The word budget has negative connotations for most people, on a conscious and subconscious level. The thought of a developing a budget immediately brings forth visions of constant denial of what we want, guilt about spending too much, or represents just one more thing to do at the end of the day; let's face the truth, we hate it.

We also tend to think on a short-term basis, thoughts heightened incrementally faster and faster given the overall social/business media expectations for 24-hours a day of every conceivable information sound-byte. It is much harder for most people to consider a goal, then focus on that same goal for days, weeks, months, and years.

We have become more attention deficit with each new generation – my opinion only, of course!

Yet, all statistics being on scale, some individuals manage just fine financially without a planned budget, while the rest of us may have problems just keeping track of the last ATM withdrawal.

Why is this important part of our financial lives just so easy to ignore?

Daniel Kahneman, PhD, 2002 Nobel Memorial Prize in Economic Sciences, in his research on the psychology of human judgment, financial decision-making, and behavioural economics, found that we have certain biases toward money choices. We tend to compartmentalise spending decisions by placing unequal values on the same sum of money - say $600.

We do not perceive a difference in choices, but there is actually quite a difference.

We won't hesitate to purchase a new designer bag or make a credit card down payment on a finely tuned timepiece or jet off to a Las Vegas vacation.

Yet, when it comes to using the same amount - $600 – for groceries, we agonise over every item in our food basket. Yes, food is costly in Bermuda. All the more reasons to be sure you are getting your nutritional food's worth for every dollar you spend.

Other examples:

We treat ourselves to takeout lunch, sometimes breakfast and takeout dinner, too – on bad days and good days both. Costs can run upwards from $20 plus per lunch dine alone, ignoring the fact that two slices of bread with an inexpensive filling (egg salad, cheese, peanut butter) costs a fraction of that lunch and far less time.

We will whine about the price of one loaf of bread ($7+/-) or commercial popcorn offerings, for instance, without considering that an entire five pound bag of flour (costing about same or less) with water, a bit of sugar and yeast produces at least eight to ten loaves of bread, home made - no artificial ingredients or preservatives. One-half cup of Popcorn popped by hand at home completely fills a 4-quart pot for an incredibly lower cost. No butter, of course.

As investors, we can be subject to huge emotion-based decisions in reaction to volatile price swings in investment markets - the proverbial "sell at the low, buy at the high price" impulse. Individual investing is detailed in BIFFPP SERIES Three Tacking & Turbulence The First Bermuda Investment Primer coming soon.

Our erratic money decisions simply mean that we are human, not perfect.

It is true. None of us, whether we have cash flow surpluses of millions or just a few dollars left at the end of the week, enjoys disciplining ourselves to live within our means.

It is just not that easy!

We need to develop a positive attitude to our personal budget, treating our personal finances as a business, with a profit motive, rather than thinking of it as dreaded homework.

Because when we are in control of our finances, that uncomfortable feeling of having to live up to out-side expectations will no longer subliminally influence how we perceive ourselves.

And, that is a good feeling!

Before you even begin to undertake setting up a formal budget, let's fight the frustration of not getting ahead by starting small, easy-to-achieve financial goals.

Small Stuff Savings (Instead of Frittering Cash Away)

$ DOLLARS SAVED per month	Type of Cost Savings
8	Subscribe online to magazines rather than newstand purchase.
40	Hang eight laundry loads outside instead of dryer @5.00 per load
40	Drink filtered tap water instead of 30-40 cans soda per month @1.00 per can
128	Take the bus/ferry twice a week – @ 6.00 round trip per trip over parking and driving each day $22 per day minus $6 = $16 per day savings = $20 TIMES 4 = $80 and HEALTHI
24	Serve one meatless meal each week @ 6.00 per pound average
64	Pack a homemade lunch, twice a week i.e. egg salad/apple/banana savings 6.00 per lunch over purchased lunch varies between 9.00 and 15.00 = 12 TIMES 4 = $64
50	Shop Thrift stores for books, school uniforms, jeans, party dresses, children's toys, DVD's, tapes, etc. per month
20	Buy groceries on discount day Wednesday – 5% on $400 = $20
20	Pay BELCO before discount date 5% on balance of 400
80	Cut back on cigarettes, two packs a week @ 10.00 = 20 TIMES 4 = $80 **better yet, QUIT!**
140	Avoid afternoon snack break - coke, coffee, chips, candy @ 7.00 for 5 working days a week = $35 TIMES 4 = $140 this goes for KIDS, too!
40	Use prepaid phone cards – when they are gone they are gone each month Estimated Savings off bill - you figure out what you can save!
20	Grow your own flowers – take cuttings with permission – dip in Root grown @ 12.00 a jar savings over potted plants 2 - per month @ 10
12	Grow your own bananas – ask a friendly neighbour for a few roots savings Monthly - @ 3.00 per pound for 4 pounds
10	Grow tomato sets in pots or recycled coffee cans – average 12 tomatoes per pot @ 4.99 per pound 2 pounds a month
60	Buy washable workwear (made of polyester and triacetate blends) instead of drycleaning – women only, unfortunately – savings $60 per month and rayon/non-silk shirts
28	Buy men's high grade polyester/cotton shirts – iron at home or not, savings per week One hour ironing @ 5 compared to 12 = 4 SHIRTS a week TIMES 5 TIMES 4 = $20
US$784	**Estimated monthly savings total, subject to price fluctuations**
	And you thought you could not save anything.

We didn't even discuss eating out less, drinking one less glass of wine, beer etc.
Bet you can come up with even more savings than this if you make this part of your goals.

$784 a month - NOT PEANUTS !

AT 50%. $392 a month - STILL NOT PEANUTS!

Things You Can Do Immediately to Increase Cash Inflow!

Control Small Stuff Slippage

Set up an automatic savings plan Increase your voluntary pension contri- bution

Take the cookie jar challenge Find a side hustle

1. Set small "stuff" budget savings goals. Just for a month, skip buying coffee, tea, soda, snacks, breakfast, and lunch out, cigarettes (yes, I know that will be difficult), drinks after work, etc. by putting that amount into your piggy-bank. See the estimated chart above and develop one for your lifestyle!

   Yes, a literal piggybank. Count up that small change at the end of week. Not so small now, is it?

   At the end of the month, Deposit this "small stuff" money in a statement savings account, or an accumulator small minimum investment account. No spending splurges now! Before you know it, you will be able to start an investment savings plan for the long term. A number of local investment firms offer start-up minimum investment accounts. More on those offerings in the Investment Section.

2. Set up an automatic savings plan through payroll deductions or standing orders. You won't miss a 1%-2% deduction, will you? There are numerous firms in Bermuda that offer this type of regular contribution to a savings or investment contribution plan. If your employer does not, be determined to place that 1% in the cookie jar, too. You can do this!

   2% of a $60,000 paycheck X 20 years, even with no interest earned is $24,000. And it could be significantly more!

3. How is your pension performing? Can you afford to gradually increase your voluntary contribution over time, at even 1% of your gross salary per year? Your pension is managed by experienced qualified internationally certified investment professionals with a mandate to appreciate your pension for the long-term. This savings won't go in the cookie jar, but you know it is there!

   20 years in your balanced* pension fund choice can potentially be an add- ed $19,500 or even more! * Based on average rate of return of conservative portfolio returning 3.5% annually.

Mortgage Payoff Success story.

He had an additional 2% of his gross salary withheld under the employee voluntary contribution offering for the Bermuda National Pension Scheme when the plan started in 2000. He is retiring in three years. His voluntary portion has grown substantially, so much so that he has accumulated enough to pay the remaining balance of his home mortgage.

Voila! He and his family will own their home, debt-free. He never missed that 2%, saying that he felt better investing in his house than frittered away on mindless consumption.

Source 123rf.com

4. Take the old-fashioned - cookie jar challenge. $5 per day for 30 days = $150; or if you feel particularly invigorated, deposit in the jar, the monetary amount of each numbered day of the month, e.g. $1 - day 1, $2 - day 2, $3 - day 3. This plan is harder, given the last week, $28 - day 28, $29 = day 29 and on = $465 in thirty days. Even half of that, each month is significant. Annual Accumulations. $150 a month times 12 months = $1,800

$465 a month times 12 months = $5,580 or half = $2,790

Will you really miss that money? No, because we waste money every day without even thinking about it, don't we? Source: SavingAdvice.com 30 Day Create a Money Saving Habit Challenge by Jeffrey Strain, 2015Jan08

5. Digital cash, in the form of Debit cards, credit cards, gift cards, and the like have almost replaced (fiat) paper and coin money in numerous countries. No problem!

There are numerous digital budgeting apps designed for modernistas. See NerdWallet in references.

More income producing ideas to increase your monthly cash inflow.

Searching income producing or cost savings websites reveals endless generic (and some very innovative) lists of income producing ideas, but what may work elsewhere may mean tailoring the product or service to our Bermuda environment.

Pessimists may feel that it just can't be done. Bermuda still recovering from prior tough economic times while set back again from unanticipated COVID protocols. People are still unemployed; or working in static little advancement current jobs.

However, there may be just as many of you hopeful for a better future and determined to become successful. Don't we all want to see better days ahead?

Truism.

I am ever the optimist; I firmly believe that you can take control of your finances. You just have to try no matter what to find your way out of your current financial position.

You need to be optimistic, too, by being alert to all opportunities. You want to be the one that provides that help and gets paid for it.

Fortunately, there are certain numbers of individuals still employed in our workplace (since our economy must still function). The price of having a job, though, is longer hours than ever - 60-80 hours a week - accompanied by lots of stress.

Career individuals may need some outside assistance to stay on track - say, from various service providers - due to the ever-present demands of their jobs.

Think about what these people need.

What they cannot do for themselves because of job priorities.

Take on a part-time job or start a new service.

Explore products or services that will make their hectic lifestyles a bit easier.

Use the five-cornered approach to earning extra income:

1. Do whatever the job needs doing.
2. Analyse and innovate - figure out what services / products are in demand, understand and carefully research your market for products that will sell again and again.
3. Be Consistent; quality in service delivery - above quantity
4. Be Persistent; never stop give up.
5. Have Confidence and Belief in yourself, your faith, and your destiny.

Here are some more ideas to make extra cash.

I've culled them from various resources and reader feedback and have only featured those that appear workable in Bermuda with a caution that other types are generally a consideration, but not workable in the current environment.

It won't be easy to do this, is it ever? But, you can!

- Bookkeeping, remote
- Baby sitting
- Eldercare relief for primary provider
- Home-prepared meals or novelty baking items
- Concierge services, anything and everything for busy families
- Tutoring, remote
- Personal Coaching, remote
- Word processing and graphic design at home, remote
- Personal shopper
- Caterer, specialty parties
- Crafts
- House sitter
- Salon nails
- Furniture, small household problem repairs (Mr/Mrs Fixit)
- Dog Walker
- Animal groomer
- Vendor stall
- Boat cleaning services
- Home cleaning and small maintenance
- Use e-Moo / other to sell unwanted items
- Shop yard sales for resale
- Rent your things: lawn mower, bicycle, paddleboard, sewing machine, and even work/attire clothes, shoes, etc. If Nordstrom's can do it, so can you!

- Rent a room, or Rent your home
- Internet consulting gigs of all kinds: website review/production, writer, graphics, book editor/formatter/translator, video/audio consulting, and so on
- Landscaping, garden design, stone wall creator
- Part-time jobs operate after regular business hours, i.e cashier, wait staff, gift shops, newspaper delivery
- Buy dividend-paying Bermuda stock positions and become a small investor. First, however, you need to have an investment portfolio account, and if you don't, you have to find the extra money to start one. Go Back to square one above to start your savings plan.
- Start up a side business.
- Leverage off existing jobs, but continuing education is key to that growth. Online universities and the Masters world is replete with free courses.** Take them.

Entrepreneurship is touted in Bermuda. Be your own boss; work your way from your bedroom to a major store front.

The key concept - give people what they want at reasonable prices with good service.

How easy is that?

Startups need planning, for both best and worst outcomes; not as easy they seem. Startups need cash, particularly, if you plan to sell merchandise. Know your client market. Little to no sales, no profit. Keep up with trends. Surf Instagram, Pinterest and other social medias for product ideas.

Look for retail or service niches that require little initial cash outlay. This concept is important as many self-starters fund costs for a new business right from their savings, then still have to borrow from the bank.

Start small, carefully, and conservatively. If you are close to retirement wanting to own your dream business - be extra, extra cautious. You may not have the resources to recoup your investment if the business does not succeed, thereby, impairing the quality of your retirement.

You never want to use your home as collateral for a business loan.

And, be sure to comply with Bermuda regulations for food preparation, vendor licenses / registration, payroll taxes, pension contributions, and so on.

More income producing and saving tips can be found at popular websites by typing "small stuff, frugal living, money savers, penny pinchers, etc. the list is unlimited. Use your imagination.

Talk to your elderly relatives - your grannies, gramps, aunties all, they know the value of extra income, cost cutting and saving! How do you think they managed to survive?

Keep in mind, too, that Bermuda still has numerous foreign workers employed in jobs where Bermudians do not have the current skills and / or may not feel they want to do the work. The answer, then, if you want to improve "your lot in life" as our elders often say, then you do have part-time work options to get ahead.

More ancient wisdom. "Some money is better than none."

Seriously consider taking that lower paying part-time job. It may not be the job you want, but it brings in extra cash, and while looking for a job, is better than unemployment. Learn those skills and then aggressively lobby for a job upgrade or find a new position.

Warning! Never leave your old job - until the new job is absolutely secured! You could lose your health insurance and other benefits.

Taking on, at least, temporarily a job that you normally would not want is a way to meet your goals:

- Build the cash cushion you need for the future.
- Get the education you want.
- Start the business you want.
- Acquire the home you want!

Small Savings Composite Success Story!

Composite case of a Bermuda Islander survivor. An incredible single mother who owns her home and raised two children through university. She advanced steadily in her primary position: loyal, dependable, no matter how tough the day, she was amazingly flexible at job performance, while very popular with clients and co- workers.

Just about every evening around 6pm she headed off - not home - but to her second job as a cashier.

"You see," she once said to me, "my second job is my safety net. It has provided the extra income to pay my mortgage down faster, educate my children through university, and it is a great meeting place for social contacts."

Small financial goals can be achieved, allowing you to dream of attaining your financial success.

Keep at it.

Setting up a Bermuda Rainy Day(s) Savings Ladder

Year and Estimated Interest Rate Breakdown

	amount	interest rate
less than one year savings a/c	accumulate up to $3,000 or more	0.01%
1-2 years term deposit	transfer 1,000	1.50%
3-4 years term deposit	transfer 1,000	1.60%
5 years term deposit	transfer 1,000	1.75%
second 5 year TD	transfer from the 1-year matured	?? 2.00%
third 5 year TD	transfer from the now matured 2-yr TD	?? 3.00%

How the savings ladder system works

a) Save as much as you can as soon as you can in a savings account and keep saving - this is your first go-to rainy day fund.

b) Assume your $3,000 is not needed in the second year

c) Transfer $1,000 into a 2, 3, 4, or 5 term deposits, supersaver, or other offering at your favourite local Bermuda bank.

d) Each deposit should be longer in years than the one laddered before to take advantage of higher interest rates.

e) As each term deposit matures, say the one year comes due and the cash is not needed, take the $1,000 plus a years interest and open another five years deposit.

f) Another year rolls by and your 2- year deposit plus interest matures. Open another 5-year deposit with the longest interest rate.

g) And on it goes, the 3-year deposit matures, roll that plus interest into the next 5-year term deposit.

h) And on it goes, you ladder and ladder and ladder. When you have enough of a rainy day fund for protection against redundancies and other emergencies, you can then start to allocate your regular savings into a starter investment fund, conservative to begin with, of course.

i) You can also allocate funds to different currencies than Bermuda Dollars where interest rates may be higher, but be aware of currency exchange fluctuations!

j) Keep in mind that interest rates will vary as years ebb and flow. Every Bermuda bank offers varying rates for their savings, e.g.Term Deposits, Super Savers, Quarterly Bonus, CDs, 5-Year Saver, Accumulator Accounts. Remember also that you may have savings amounts deducted from your salary directly into your savings account, depending upon your wage plan structure.

Finally, this sounds like a lot of work, and not as much interest rate as anyone would like, but the premise is based upon consistent saving. You only need to start to see your deposits grow. Numerous individuals over the last twenty years, who were incredibly motivated, have used this system and were not particularly comfortable with investment markets. Every bonus, every bit of extra income - not considered necessary for every day living was shunted into the Term Deposit Ladders. Now, at close to retirement, they have created their personal annuity fund - under their control - to enhance their basic government pensions. Some will continue to use the format of revolving maturity Term Deposits because the consistency pattern works for them!

Use every opportunity to save what you can!

© 2000 - 2020 Martha Harris Myron Pondstraddler Life™ Financial Perspectives

Saving and Building a Rainy Day (Ladder) Buffer

Buffer pain for long-term gain

A savings buffer is a rain-day plan, a safety-net cushion. Everyone needs one!

A buffer is not your credit card - to be paid off later - sometime don de road! You don't own that money. Someone, some credit card company owns you (and your assets).

We save because we must placate our fear of having no money at all. Everyone needs a safety net cash cushion. Having to seek financial help is a humiliating blow to human pride in self-sufficiency. If nothing else can, let those feelings motivate your decision to save something each month.

Figure out - what a good buffer savings amount for emergencies to cover living expenses is for you? How long would you need it for?

Take the FINANCIAL SURVIVAL QUIZ below!

Think redundancy, unemployed, hurricane disaster (such as Dorian), debilitating illness?

Would you need ready cash for how long?

- 3 - months?
- 6 - months?
- one year?
- two years?
- five years of ready cash? You have to decide thoughtfully, how long could your family last without a paycheque without cashing in everything you own.

How would you create a cash savings buffer?

See the Step Five Section on How to Save: Small Things Slippage, avoiding splurges, along with savings tips and the Cookie Jar Challenge

Other resources. You may also have other assets from which you can cash out/borrow short-term, such as

- Cash value in a life insurance policy assuming you can continue to make whole life insurance payments
- Consider selling assets that you can convert to cash, then move to your savings/term deposit account.
- Apply for The Bermuda Pension Commission Hardship Exemption as soon as possible - if you have a Bermuda National Pension Scheme account.

Take the Financial Self-Evaluation Contingency & Survival Readiness Quiz

Take the Financial Survival Quiz

1	Do you have enough cash that is easily accessible for the next three to six months of living expenses, including food, rent, transportation, electric, phone/internet, mortgage?	yes	no
2	If you don't have enough, can you borrow what you need from your bank, relatives or friends?	yes	no
3	If you borrow money, can you pay it back?	yes	no
4	If yours is a two person income family, can you survive on one income?	yes	no
5	Do you think your job is safe?	yes	no
6	Your tenant wants you to reduce the rent; can you absorb the difference?	yes	no
7	Is your employer's business showing healthy profit increases?	yes	no
8	If you were made redundant next week, do you think you could obtain another position in less than a month?	yes	no
9	Do you think your new job will pay the same salary?	yes	no
10	If you lost your job, could you afford to pay your own health insurance?	yes	no
11	Do you find that your credit card debt is decreasing?	yes	no
12	Have you been able to put extra payments on your credit card or your mortgage?	yes	no
13	Do you have any cash left just before the next payday?	yes	no
14	Are you paying all your bills each month?	yes	no

When bad financial things happen to good people.

Life happens to all of us.

We are trundling along, making plans for a vacation, thinking about a weekend get together, considering an advancement or a promotion in our workplace, buying that special pick-me up for the evening, children healthy, grandparents busy in retirement, everything seems just fine.

We feel somewhat complacent, did a bit of planning, perhaps not as much as we might have, but we know that we can get back to finalise things soon. Normal days, normal lifestyle. Better days ahead – wonderful thoughts!

Then, without warning, normal becomes something far different, our life changes, sometimes irrevocably. And as it has been so often quoted, "even the best laid plans, go awry." poet Robert Burns.

Some disasters: hurricanes, fires, and our now total pandemic immersion are collectively worse as they indiscriminately and brutally affect the whole community. The permanent loss of a loved one, disabling illness, redundancy, financial fraud, are so painfully personal they can barely be articulated.

Our Emotions React to Disasters

When an unexpected disaster happens, it can be a sudden shock, or at the least, a very delayed acknowledgment that life will not be the same.

Our emotions can run the gamut, figuratively, see-sawing through our psyche, making our innate logic ability harder to find any perspective.

We are everything and everywhere all at once; emotional reactions tend to follow stages

- Anguished and incredibly sad at the worst of life events.
- Angry and defiant at the world. How could this happen? Why me? Why my family?
- Anxiety and stress become evident as we cope with this new challenge.

  Sleep patterns may be interrupted. Interpersonal relationships may become strained, while unpredictable feelings such as boredom, and detachment increase.
- Decision Paralysis can set in, in concert with depression. Thoughts of why bother trying when you can't control anything? It becomes harder to make any decision – that is actually a way of handling grief, by shutting out reality.

All the while, financial undercurrents can cause additional stress.

Our Innate Resilience comes to the Fore as Time Goes On

Acceptance of the new Reality gradually evolves. And you start to cope with your situation – re-establishing your regular routines, going back to healthy behaviours: eating better, exercising any way you can, communicating with friends and relatives, getting adequate sleep, taking small actions initially.

You are Perfectly Normal

Individuals may feel guilty, too, for their behaviour so that they may appear irrational, unsettling, and anti-social.

However, behavioural psychologists know that every single one of these emotions are perfectly normal responses to such impactful, abrupt events affecting our lives. You are grieving for your loss, your family, yourself, and a possible complete lifestyle change.

Finally, you will Arrive Back to a New Normal Place to Take Action

Everyday living has to resume in a new normal. Children have to go to school, meals have to be prepared, we have to go back to work, support family members, community involvement resumes, bills have to be paid, assessment of current finances is needed, and planning for the future resumes.

Some Thoughts on What to Do If a Disaster Has Left Your Finances Short.

It is never, ever easy – coping with unexpected tough expenses in your own personal situation, let alone managing financial survival in a total community social distancing situation, never before experienced in our lifetimes. No one could have predicted with certainty, that the 2020 COVID-19 situation would have happened at this time in this community.

Use every means possible to bolster and protect your cash fund.

- Cash in savings – use sparingly, if possible
- Paycheque loan or an advance from an employer, if possible
- Borrow from relatives, friends, but formalise with signed promissory note – they are in the same situation and must be repaid, later.
- Home equity line – arrange ahead - if any sense of impending financial retrenchment, such as a company restructuring
- Ask for a temporary rent reduction from landlord
- Sell investments, assets, anything of value, in a worst-case scenario, sell home
- Arrange temporary mortgage payment abeyance, delay or reduction
- Borrow against life insurance if available
- Consider Social media funding
- Get a job, any job, or obtain a second job, understanding that it may not be as easy to procure in a bad economy

- Barter with your community, especially, if you are trying to keep your emergency fund intact – no cash changes hands, no reduction in cash cushion, but the opportunity to establish new relationships!

- Seek Government assistance, that is what governments are for – to protect and help those disadvantaged. This is what our combined taxes are meant to do, to support our community.

The Aftermath of an Unexpected Catastrophe

You've been able to raise enough cash to see you through the worst of these times, however?

But, what if you cannot save enough going forward because you lost your job, you become ill, your spouse has passed, you go through a divorce, you have a fully dependent adult child?

You are now in the financial survival mode.

Time for some very tough questions and answers from the Survival Quiz above!

What You Can Do Now to Prepare for the Unexpected Contingencies in Life

We are focusing on the real-life challenges associated with redundancy, but this section can apply to any contingency life planning!

Warning: Life (and your finances) can change without notice. The recent redundancies in late summer and fall in Bermuda 2019, and the long, wearing shelter-in-place COVID pandemic shutdown are again a reminder that in job markets today, a job can dissolve overnight, no one has a job for life, no one can become complacent, no one should ever, ever think that they are irreplaceable (regardless of talent and expertise).

Are you financially and emotionally prepared to survive abrupt life changes?

Results of your self-evaluation quiz listed above?

How did you Do? More no answers than yeses means that you will need to do more in building your rainy-day fund. Ideally, you want to build as big a buffer against tragedy that you can: savings that can carry you a year or more, until you get back on your feet.

Job redundancies happen for myriad reasons: political expediency, economic conditions, relocations, technology improvements, outdated skills, pandemics, or pure personality clashes - the last are referred to in company vernacular as 'not buying into the new company vision.'

In 2003, for the first time, my Personal Finance column in the Royal Gazette commented on the Bermuda redundancy environment during the history-changing event of the Bermuda Bakery facility closure.

It was a shock, a loss I personally felt keenly - that heavenly smell of fresh bread wafting over Hamilton every day since all our childhoods, gone forever. A significant loss, too, in so many ways for many: employees, vendors, owners, consumers all, one less local product produced locally by local people in Bermuda - gone forever.

Is your job at risk? Why it pays to keep your eyes open, Martha Myron, Published Mar 12, 2011 in the Royal Gazette.

Time moves on.

In the decades since, global capital markets experienced another boom, Bermuda coped with a damaging recession in 2008 - that was the first recession ever experienced in our Bermuda lifetimes, regrettably, Bermuda's economic recovery has been very, very slow.

Those of us who were in denial back then as our local recession has dragged (and has yet to return to the glory days) - still imagining the Bermuda money faucet would never turn off, now realise that Bermuda was (and is) very vulnerable to world economic drag.

And we need to be prepared.

When cutbacks and redundancies occur, the general public perceives employers to be greedy and heartless.

Some are. We read every day about those self-absorbed individuals-in-charge who have taken their firms down, all in the name of more - for them and only them.

There are more decent, caring employers who just have no choice.

For their own companies' survival, they must implement economic triage to place their capital in the most profitable areas, those that will generate the best return for shareholders. No company or CEO, in their right mind, can operate altruistically (and unprofitably) because the final catastrophic alternative is to go out of business.

Then no one has a job. Is your job in jeopardy?

Is your internal radar sending intuitive messages? Pay attention to what is going on in your work environment; keep your eyes open to subtle body language and your ears tuned to oblique comments. Network more vigorously with your co-workers.

Time to switch to survival tactics.

One professional associate told me that she knew her job was going when her manager stopped looking directly at her (as if she no longer existed). If you pay attention, a change in company operations should not come as a surprise.

Anticipating changes allows you to put your redundancy survivor tactics in place.

Triage Planning: What to do if you think your company might be announcing redundancies:

- List all critical bills due, particularly, rent/mortgage utilities, phone, car payments and gas.
- Review your finances to assess if you have enough cash right now for at least three to six months of living expenses to cover these critical bills and food.
- No cash cushion? Start saving as if your life depended on it. It does.
- Sell what you do not absolutely need. Yes, this means those extra designer bags, electronics, and expensive car, etc. Find a cheaper car, pay cash for it and get out from under those large car payments. All cash adds up.
- Radically cut back on all non-essentials. In order to save, you must temporarily stop spending on everything that is superfluous and unnecessary: cell phone use, eating out, special snacks, new shoes, leisure clothes, shopping sprees, vacations, little expensive electronic treats.
- Cut your food budget down to plain, practical small portion meals. You'll lose weight in the process.
- Shop locally where possible - for those essentials. We are in an island consumer- interlinked daisy chain. Our local businesses' futures are as dependent upon us as we are on them. You can be sure that if they fail, someone in our related families will also be adversely affected.
- Make credit card charges a complete no-no. Reserve your cards for absolute emergency use only. The psychological effect of coping with large credit card balances can create tremendous stress. Pay the minimum balance for now because you must keep ready cash available, until you can arrange to reduce principal (in the future) to a manageable level.

Do not skip a payment!

- Home equity line - if you are a two income earner family and own your home, arrange to have one put in place now. You cannot borrow money if only one of you has a job, and you don't have to use it unless you absolutely have to.
- You may (or may not) want to talk to your mortgage officer. If cash is going to be tight, discuss procedure for a short-term interest only payment plan. However, there is caution here - because if you are listed jointly on your mortgage (and now only one of you has a Job), your mortgage officer may reclassify your loan - possibly with higher interest rate or a restructuring of the loan itself. Investigate and read carefully the terms and conditions of your mortgage loan document before approaching your banker.
- If you rent, talk to your landlord - you may be able to negotiate a lower fee, or look now for a less costly rental.
- Get your CV updated immediately and start quietly networking with friends, business acquaintances, and family contacts.
- Step up your personal grooming. This is not the time to let your appearance slip, no matter how miserable you may feel. Indeed, this is one area where you will need to spend, but don't go overboard, such as purchasing

a $1,500 suit and $500 shoes! In your job search, you must look like an absolutely confident, poised, polished intelligent professional at all times.

The first impression is the only impression. And remember, then you have to deliver on your appearance!

- Be proactive - do not act like a deer frozen in car headlights. If you think you can handle it, and you are sure the company is downsizing, be one of the first to ask your current employer for a separation package. Those who volunteer themselves out the door first, often walk away feeling very financially fit.

Warning, do not attempt the separation move without reviewing your personal finances and the available job market first. You must be absolutely sure you can/ have obtained another position.

Increase your athletic activities. Do not let yourself go. Work out that stress and uncertainty on the fastest walk or run you can. Picture that mental image of a confident, poised, polished professional. No one can define who you are, except you.

- Operate in this survivor mode until you know for certain that your job is still intact, or that you have attained another.

Now, none of this may come to pass for you personally, but look what you have done.

You are a changed professional. You just may find yourself receiving a promotion and a brand-new career. The sceptics think I am kidding, but it happens all the time.

You have also accomplished building a successful rainy-day fund. Now, keep adding to this fund – the better prepared you are, the less stressful any outcome may be.

- Reinvention (of yourself)
- Renewal (of your educational aspirations)
- Resourcefulness (in the face of adversity) promotes
- Resurgence of interest in you and what you can contribute to your employer's bottom line. You will become the employee everyone wants.

Change is inevitable.

You become the change agent; embrace it and use it to your advantage.

You will remain the person in charge of your life.

So, your worst fears are realised. You are redundant. What now?

- Do not badmouth your prior employer.
- Get rid of the anger (and the bitterness). Do not show it during the exit interview or afterward. What goes around comes around; if the business picks up, you could be first hired back.
- At the very least, you must ask for a really good reference.
- Negotiate the best termination package you can. If you are allowed to stay for another couple of weeks, a month, do it. Use that time (and their equipment) to network with everyone you know.
- Get an extension on your health insurance coverage if you can.
- Update your CV if you have not done so already using their resources, following the being proactive guide above.
- Ask if you can stay on as a temporary worker. The object here is to keep working (and a paycheque) until you can find another position.

What to do immediately to protect yourself and your family.

- Prepare yourself emotionally and mentally, being made redundant is a terrible blow to your pride and psyche.
- Count your cash, literally. Any extra cash that you have, allocate to buckets or envelopes: food, rent/mortgage, transportation, etc.
- Pay your rent / mortgage ahead now, first. You need to assure yourself of a roof over your head without having to think about scrounging for the money.
- Be realistic, what about that expensive car and those large monthly payments. If you don't have the cash to meet the loan payments, your only method of looking for another job will be taken away from you with a foreclosure.
- See if you can find a second-hand car, then sell the superslick model and get out from under that debt.
- You must have a family meeting and lay out the facts. Do not try to hide this from everyone. Present a united front and tell them that you are all in this together, you will survive.
- Don't have enough cash to put aside, talk to your family and make arrangements for shared temporary accommodations, and other support if necessary,

- Use all of the hints above, except do not notify your mortgage officer regarding the change in mortgage on your home. You do not want to have your loan reassessed based upon one income-earner instead of two, because you will get back on your feet.

It has happened, accept it, be proactive, put the rest of your emergency plan into action, get out there, network, interview, educate yourself, do not sink into apathy. The longer you delay your reaction the harder it is to find another job.

You have just been hit hard, now use every single bit of your personality, your faith, and your family support to fight back and win, yes, win yourself another job.

Listen to tips for a Savings Buffer Safety Net

https://tinyurl.com/yhx9mkth

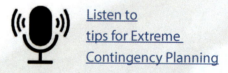

Listen to tips for Extreme Contingency Planning

https://tinyurl.com/ye2ma4m8

References & Resources

MONEYWISE
Is your job at risk? Why it pays to keep your eyes
open, by Martha Myron, Published Mar 12, 2011

The Survival Questionnaire Listed above.
Laid off? 10 Steps to Manage Post-Redundancy
Blues, Mel Fisher Nov 27, 2017

The Guardian/money
How to Recover from losing your job, Lisa Bachelor, September 4, 2009

How a Cash-Only Budget Can Help Your Finances
Using cash to pay for purchases
BY PAULA PANT Updated May 27, 2021

Atypical Finance
Electronic Cash-Only Budgeting

Nerdwallet
Goodbudget Review: A Hands-On Digital Envelope
System
Lauren Schwahn, Laura McMullen Feb 4, 2021

Setting Up Your Budget Trackers

6

Figure 1

Simple Monthly Bermuda Budget Worksheet

Family of 3

Money In	
Wage -1	5,000
Wage -2	3,000
Additional income	0
Total income	**US$8,000**

Money Out	
Housing (Rent or mortgage)	3,500
Groceries	1,700
Transportation	400
Utilities	400
Communication	250
Medical	500
Entertainment	100
Daycare	?
Property / auto insurance, annual cost /12	?
Land/property tax, annual cost /12	?
Education	?
Total expenses	**US$6,850**

Money Left Over	
Income minus expenses	US$1,150

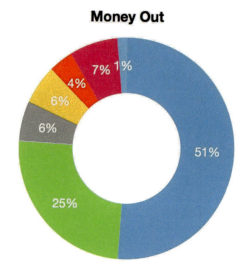

Money Out

- Housing (Rent or mortgage)
- Groceries
- Transportation
- Utilities
- Communication
- Medical
- Entertainment
- Daycare
- Property / auto insurance, annual cost /12
- Land/property tax, annual cost /12
- Education

Figure 2

Budget versus Actual Monthly Expenses

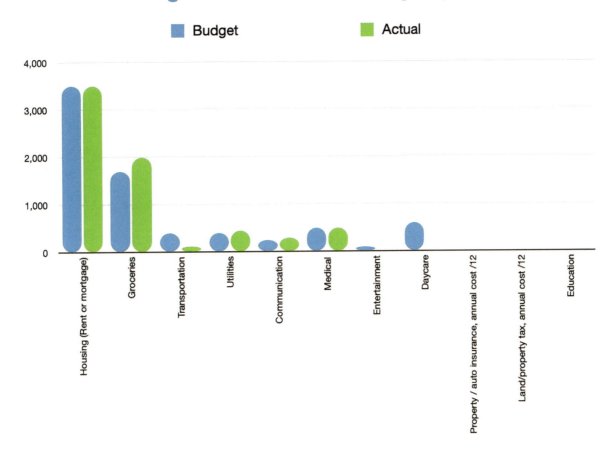

Summary by Category

Category	Budget	Actual	Difference
Housing (Rent or mortgage)	3,500	3,500	0
Groceries	1,700	2,000	(300)
Transportation	400	120	280
Utilities	400	450	(50)
Communication	250	300	(50)
Medical	500	500	0
Entertainment	100	0	100
Daycare	600	0	600
Property / auto insurance, annual cost /12	?	0	⚠️
Land/property tax, annual cost /12	?	0	⚠️
Education	?	0	⚠️
Total	US$7,450	US$6,870	US$580

Step Six - Setting Up Your Budget Tracker

Review Your Finances,

Set up Your Basic Budget Tracker

There are two simple steps to the method of managing your household costs and your budget:

- Monthly (or quarterly) Track Actual in- come & expenses, the monetary things that happen in real life.

- Then, define your budget - you determine what you would like to receive in income and what you want to control in allocating your spending each month. Many of these are fixed costs: rent/mortgage, utilities, transportation, school fees. You have to pay them. However, you are planning ahead as well for those once-a-year cash hits, vehicle registration, vacation, land tax, house or tenant insurance, education, etc.

It is very seldom that these two - actual and budgeted are the same. Close to - is good enough!

See the two charts ABOVE again.

In Fig. 1, We assume that you have completed the simple tracking income / expense chart for Actual inflows and outflows of cash for the first month.

In Fig. 2, you can see the sample two column worksheet:

- Budgeted amount - enter the budget- ed amounts, those costs that you have defined as how much you would like to spend. Note the section to show annual costs of car,

house insurance etc. divided by 12 - even though you haven't spent the money, the budget needs to show that the expense will be covered.

- You are encouraged to set those projected amounts aside in your emergency savings fund.

Truthfully, many people find the two-column budget-to-actuals just too hard to keep up with. They prefer to simply track income and expenses monthly, hopefully making sure that there is always a surplus of positive cash at month end, however small.

There is one serious problem with simply tracking income and outflow. We all know what that is - the unexpected, unplanned for annual/semi-annual expenses to license the car, property insurance, special condo assessment, co-pays for dental braces, medications, an accident, and so on.

These unplanned for items can throw a simple monthly cost plan into disarray.

My suggestion always is to set up a budget, and an actual by itself, as a reminder of those annual expenses, then use the single tracking method of Figure I for your real income / expenses each month.

Starting Your Plan by Reviewing Your Finances!

Try not to feel overwhelmed initially, just start!

Your monthly bank statement - or online transaction activity is a good place to begin.

Yes, it is time-consuming. It may take you a day, a couple, a week, or a month to go through at least one-three months of bank transaction activity. Additionally, if you are at the start of a New Year, then it is a good time, a traditional time for review because you will be receiving all of the year-end reports that show cumulative activity: your cash and credit card accounts, investment and pension accounts, insurance if you have variable life, or cash value build-up, your expenses and the recognition that what " I spent that amount on that?

What was I thinking!

It is true that the number of people who find this exercise tedious, boring and over-whelming are many, measurable by their complaining, procrastinating, just finding any excuse to put the chore off.

Uh, you don't want to do this, I know you don't, however, as your Moms used to say, "**It's good for you!**"

There are three reasons (rules) to review your finances once a month, or quarter, or more, if needed:

1. No one, but no one, can manage your money the way you can.

2. If you don't manage your financial affairs, you haven't a clue where you've been, where you are, or where you are going.

3. Neglect your finance review, when something goes badly wrong because your identity was scammed, you were overcharged, you will never know — until it is too late.

Will you only have yourself to blame? FORGET BLAME, just resolve to do better!

Figure 1 Tracking Your Income - Expense Numbers

Start with the Illustrative Bermuda Simple Monthly Income-Expense Tracker Worksheet at Fig.1 above, or you can try other budget math tools that I've researched for you.

Electronic and manual tracking spread-sheets - See links in reference section.

The Do-It-Yourselfers can use a generic electronic spreadsheet. There are countless downloadable templates that you can tailor for your personal use. Free spreadsheet software is available from open sources: Apache Open Office, LibreOffice, Excel, Mac Numbers, Google, and many others. Search for the free ones and experiment in learning.

- Use a commercially set up budget planner (also free) such as Open Office or Vertex42 - easy to find in Google search, just search free budget planners.

- Use Our Simple Budget Worksheet featured in the accompanying chart – tailored for the Bermuda environment. Fig.1 above and in Resources End of STEP.
- Manual Tracking the old-fashioned way is sometimes just as easy, by hand, using legal or two column 8/11 inch lined paper and copying the format of Fig.1 or 2. Use one page for each monthly set of income/expense categories. You don't even need electricity!
- Add the totals up manually each month on a calendar type planning book then enter on your Master Income/expense sheet for the month. You can also create one for the for the year.

FIG. 1 INPUT Your Net Cash Inflow in the Money In Section

Enter your monthly gross income before any bottom-line adjustments. This is so that you can see your real net pay - the amount that is left after your payroll deductions for payroll tax, health insurance, life insurance, 5% pension match, old age contributory pension, etc.

Then, before you enter any other income (or expense) received jump down to enter the deductions (expenses) listed on your paycheque. Notice how the numbers are negative red - denoting subtraction from your gross paycheque. The net amount left should be the net paycheque listed on your bank statement.

It is important to enter the amounts this way because your bank statement does not show your health care deduction, pension, etc. yet they reduce your pay - as you well know. Plus, it gives you the real picture of all your expense outflows.

Then, Still on Money In, add any cash income from part time jobs, interest or dividends, rental unit(s), pension annuity payments (if retired), and so on, all listed on your bank statements. Don't forget to include other cash payments you may earn on side hustles - that are not accounted for on your statement.

Remember you want your complete financial picture for the month. You can't plan for anything, if you don't know what your resources (cash and assets) are!

Don't list things like inheritances, lump sum payments, or even bonuses - they are not a monthly cycle item. In fact, they are "surprise" gifts. They require different spending / saving decisions.

FIG. 1 TRACK Your Cash Out- flow in the Money Out Section

Categorise your spending habits using the MONEY OUT column in Figure 1.

This is the toughest, most annoying section of this exercise. How on earth are you going track all the little items? Heck, you sure know what your mortgage or rent payment is - to the penny while groceries, electricity, cable/phone/Internet, transportation (gas for bike/car) are fairly predictable.

The rest of that spending - especially the ATM withdrawals will be challenging – since the informal rule on spending is this: The smaller the cost of the items, and the larger the number of cash withdrawals, the harder it becomes to remember just exactly what it was that you did buy. Especially on those days when you're harried and everything in your life seems out of sync.

The Just Don't Know Where the Money Went!

Take the attitude of no moral philosophising, such as were these expenses necessary or just regretful splurge items? Simply designate all those items in the Just Don't Know category.

This is the hardest category because most of it is cash slippage; that is, it just slips through your fingers every day.

> You must get control of the Just Don't Know cash spent.

You may be appalled at just how much cash has slipped away. If you don't ferret out those unidentifiable expenses every month, you will lose control of your budget very quickly.

Credit card payments. Yes, it sounds like duplicating costs. However, if you bought that "stuff" months ago, you still have to pay it back. Your goal is to have zero balance credit card each month.

Other expenses – the catchall list. Some people like to set aside money for holidays, birthdays, vacations, etc. However, in Figure I, we are tracking Actual cash spent, not items that will be paid for in the future.

Figure 2 will demonstrate how to plug and plan for those future annual (or semi-annual) costs by theoretically setting aside the Budgeted number amount each month.

You get the point.

Now, you have input all Money In and Money Out for the month. Where are you with the actual income/expense tracker? Anything left over?

Can you consider starting a Small Stuff Savings account? Review STEP FIVE again.

Figure 2 - Set up the Budget Estimates using what you actually spent for the month - but only as a guide.

Note that all numbers used in the budget chart Figure. 2 are the author's GUESSTIMATES. Only you know what your realistic numbers are.

EXAMPLE: I've used a family of three, with gross combined earnings of $120 thousand a year – for two employed parents and a small child. Just about anywhere in the world, these salaries would be considered super fabulistic, but our island is a different expensive challenge - as we all know.

Two parents earning $60,000, annually, their combined gross salary is $10,000 per month but take a look at the deductions to arrive at their net pay. Hardly anything left at month end to save!

Your budget is trying to set limit guidelines on various items to help you control random spending. So, for instance, you would specify just how much you are willing to budget - for those Just Don't Know Items so that you can plan to avoid hurtling over that number again.

First, list the necessaries. The bills you must always pay first and the monthly estimated amount:

- rent/mortgage, these don't vary that much - if at all.
- food, decide on your budget limit - see if you can stick to it
- utilities, use a good estimate - not too low, not too high by reviewing your prior bills, easily accessible online
- transportation, car, bus, ferry, bike
- phone/cable /internet, same thing - set a limit - track your prior usage and arrive at a happy medium cost for the whole family
- personal health care, this category can be a fixed cost - or variable if you elect to DIY, say nails, hair etc.
- day care, the cost is the cost, not much flexibility
- entertainment, other activities
- clothing / shoe purchases. How many outfits do you really need?

Next, the out-of-the-blue surprise bills that you completely forget about because they happen once a year. Divide those costs by twelve (or by six if semi-annual or 4 - if quarterly) - as you only pay these intermittently, but you need to allocate money for them each month. Remember how we mentioned avoiding those awful, big ticket surprises?

- car/bike insurance,
- car/bike/boat registration,
- land tax,
- life insurance,
- house insurance, etc.
- others?

Then, list credit payments, if more than one card, catchalls, and the just don't know expenses like ATM withdrawals, expenses paid in cash, etc.

- Credit card payments
- Catchall: birthdays, holidays, vacations
- Just Don't Know expense items, ATMs etc.

Now the reckoning, comparing actual costs to budget estimates

Expenses - remember the first column is your budget expenses, these are the estimated costs you want to control not what you are spending on each item currently. The budget and actual expenses may be different to start with.

See Fig.2 chart!

Do you have any cash left over? Is your month ending number - positive or negative?

Yes, surplus to put aside for your rainy-day fund. Yay!

No, decide what can you cut back on, or alternatively raise extra money. See beginning of Budget section for small stuff slippage and income-raising ideas.

Your budget should include a monthly savings amount – that once you establish a controlled budget is the first thing you do.

There. You have Your Simple Bermuda Budgeted to Actual Worksheet set up.

I've input some GUESSTIMATE numbers, now you input your real income and expenses, then you decide what percentage you will try to save.

Repeat every month - simply track your actual income and expenses.

Then compare your actual costs to your budget amounts.

The budget amounts won't change be- cause you have now defined a limit on your spending for the year.

The goal is to see how close you can bring your actual costs to your budget amounts! Each month!

Can you see a pattern? You can resolve these unknown expenses by setting up a simple necessary budget using your real numbers to filter out and control the random spending.

Feeling bad that your net monthly savings numbers aren't better?

Don't forget that you are saving - if you are currently employed!

Your Bermuda National Pension Scheme is putting away 10% of your gross salary every single month, every single year, unless in 2020, you temporarily elected 6%. Monitoring your pension accumulation to-date (covered further under Employee Benefits) is another opportunity to manage your finances going forward.

Many Bermuda families, way back when, never had a formal budget, but they knew the value of money!

Heads of households who worked two jobs:

the day job for someone else, the night job for the family. The extra income went immediately to reduce their mortgage principal balance and other debts.

Families who built their homes themselves - after working all day.

They didn't save with bank deposits; they used any extra cash above their living expenses (and a small cushion) to buy building materials. Some months, there was only enough cash for a few boxes of tiles.

Bermuda Homes overlooking StGeorge's Harbour & an old shipwreck Scott Stallard Photography

But, they persevered.

These are not just stories; I have met some of these determined individuals.

It took years to build by saving and budgeting, but! They finally owned a home, a wonderful appreciating asset.

[Listen to tips for Making a Basic Budget](https://tinyurl.com/yfhc59z6)

https://tinyurl.com/yfhc59z6

[Listen to tips for a Simple Budget to Track ALL Income and Expense](https://tinyurl.com/yesfpnre)

https://tinyurl.com/yesfpnre

References & Resources

Budget Calculators, Spread sheets and Motivational DIY Websites

There are thousands of budget websites, charts, and DIY help. Just type budget into a Search engine, what a huge surprise - take your pick

Here are some websites I like, just type names into your favourite search engine:

360 Degrees of Financial Literacy Home Budget Analysis

www.Vertex42.com calculators - these are free, designed for the more experienced individual who has worked with spreadsheets, etc.

There are just as many or more websites, blogs, Facebook, Instagram person accounts of managing a budget

Jamila: Journey to Launch to Financial Freedom - Budget Boot Camp. I like Jamila for her personal touch and motivational webinars, meetings, and podcasts! She has been featured on CNBC, Buzzfeed, Money, Business Insider and more.

NEFE Financial Literacy. The National Endowment for Financial Education from high school to adulthood, NEFE has worked hard for more than thirty years to promote, teach and motivate Americans to become financially successful. www.Nefe.com

Debt Conflict of

Wants
Versus Needs

7

Step Seven - Debt. Conflict Of Wants Versus Needs

Debt: The Conflict Between Wanting

Versus Really Needing!

The Deceptively Deceitful Allure of Debt

Debt is easy money. So is a lump sum payment, upfront cash, easy to justify, easy to spend. Trouble is, what you bought with it, what you used it for - like propping up the HomeFront Budget - is not yours, not until you pay the cash back.

Personal debt is a personal burden, almost turning one into a financial slave.

You are not your own complete person when someone, a company, or a government can control your financial dignity and destiny.

No matter the financial circumstances or the persuasive asset acquired, the decision to borrow money is an emotional and mental strain.

Debt is never an investment in the future, no matter how eloquently stated, or how firmly the belief is held. Instead, debt resembles a giant poker game bet with all moves predicated on future performance.

Debt is borrowing money with a promise to pay the principal sum back - with interest to the lender - because who in their right mind would lend cash to receive the same amount back years later.

The future promise to repay for the individual, even in contract form, is an intangible uncertainty.

Why?

Because we assume that there will always be a job, a revenue generation for income, expenses and the like to support the repayment of principal and interest - in the future - but will there?

Now, you can understand why I dislike debt - always preaching that every family purchasing a home should reduce their mortgage debt as quickly as they can, particularly, if any family member is close to retirement.

If you own your home outright, you can manage on very, very little.

Debt has to be a means to an end, not an end in itself, using short term debt to meet cash flow shortages. Where is the capital asset there?

Long-term debt is and should be used to purchase assets that will appreciate over time, long after the debt is repaid.

Borrow only the amount of debt that you can safely cover, even in bad financial times.

What is dangerous here, even with the use of good debt for appreciating assets, is the inability and reluctance to understand that debt must have a ceiling beyond which the borrower cannot trespass.

Otherwise, at the mere hint of hardship or a reduced income stream, there will be little to no ability to meet debt payments. It is too easy when times are booming to feel confident that your compensation scale will always be the same or better.

In a competitive global economy, there is no such thing as always.

A few of the many kinds of debt.

Plain unadorned long-term fixed rate debt (mortgages) repaid in an amortisation schedule over time is well known to most goal-focused individuals.

Credit card debt - the second worst lifestyle enhancer is borrowing from others to live beyond one's means and on borrowed time.

Credit cards carry the highest rates of interest, while Credit card debt purchases generally never represent appreciating assets.

Unfortunately, many are using credit cards for basic necessities, food, treats, and trips. That cute bag you bought may take five years to pay off, long after you are interested in displaying it at your job.

Ever look at the back pages of a credit card bill? Almost no one reads the 16 pages of fine print in the debt encumbrance section. Credit card companies will take your first-born child in their relentless pursuit of repayment.

Why shouldn't credit card companies want to be repaid? You've had a high old time dining out, picking out that special designer bag, traveling, or acquiring more electronic gadgets. Credit card companies sell successful lifestyles with their soothing media message of how to acquire the finer things in life with no money down. They know that even with thousands of debt default- ers they are turning great profits.

- Leveraged debt, one of the worst types of debt for the small investor, is called by any other name but borrowing. CDOs, subprime, margin accounts, credit enhancers these are all terms used by the investment industry to describe borrowing against securitised assets, or in an uncollateralised form to in- crease yield and capital gains. These are big no-nos for small investors - be careful, some- times this leveraged debt is buried in the small print of a 150-page investment fund prospectus, or a high return hedge fund, for example. Read all of the fine print be- fore you invest! Keep in mind that leveraged debt in the form of Collateralised Debt Obli- gations (CDO), Collateralised Mortgage Obli- gations (CMOs) and other forms of these es- oteric securities were largely responsible for the 2008 global market investment crashes - even as they were rated investment grade -right to the end.

  ### They were not!

- OPM, Other People's Money - borrowed.
- Individuals, with no ethics, can be crassly careless with the use of OPM. Debt to them is the same as cash, their cash, not anyone else's cash. They feel entitled to have what everyone else is perceived to have. Debt becomes a game to see how much can be leveraged without any responsibility for re- payment.

And, when they've had enough, splurged enough, or acquired enough (this impulse is never curbed in those careless with other people's money), they walk away from the debt, and the commitment to repay.

After all, it isn't their money, so why should they pay it back!

Guess who picks up the tab again?

The rest of us, those ordinary citizens, the ones the ultra-social climbers look down on, the mid- dle class that does the right thing, working, sav- ing, voting, living life by actions applied respon- sibly. The middle class that represents the back- bone of a country, once again, get to shoulder this collective country debt, along with our own personal loans - for the rest of our lives.

We have to get our personal debt under control, and so does our government. Using we, the peo- ple, as a revolving credit card machine is not an investment in our country.

Personal loans,
credit card debt and
mortgages: there are
differences

A Refresher on Loans 101

Investor.com defines a loan as follows: an arrangement in which a lender gives money or property to a borrower, and the borrower agrees to return the property or repay the money, usually along with interest, at some point(s) in the future. Usually, there is a predetermined time for repaying a loan, and generally the lender has to bear the risk that the borrower may not repay a loan.

Related Terms for loans are numerous: asset conversion loan, balloon loan, bank term loan, bridge loan, broker loan, callable loan, consolidation loan, day loan, demand loan, discount loan, evergreen loan, floor loan, indexed loan, interest-only loan, non-conforming loan, partially amortised loan, participation loan, piggyback loan, policy loan, purpose loan, recourse loan, securities loan, single-payment loan, unsecured and secured loans, wraparound loan, instalment loan, predatory lending.

No matter the term, the loan must be repaid.

A loan is a contract.

It can be orally delivered (as on a hand-shake) or written in stone. Generally, once formalised on paper by listing terms, conditions, remedies against default, collateral damage and so on, the contract becomes the purview of the law and attorneys. And so it should, since the rights of both parties entering into any contract need to be considered and protected. Legal contracts enable this process, given that memories of terms and conditions become shorter and shorter, the longer that the contract lasts. Where many years ago each and every loan might have been painstakingly constructed by hand and individualised for the parties involved, most loans today (like other contracts, such as leases) are standardised and generated on demand. "Sign here", says the loan officer.

Informal loans between

people particularly relatives (otherwise known as rels in our family) may not contain any binding clauses to keep the agreement from slowly falling apart.

Money issues are always difficult to discuss in families making communication and misunderstandings into classic default cases. These types of arrangements generally end up causing all sorts of family nastiness, disenchantment and adolescent behaviour ranging from freezing out various family members, to good old-fashioned fights in some parts of the world.

In financial planning practice, insistence on arms-lengths transactions between close relatives is a required action for loan implementation.

Everyone in the relationship knows exactly what their responsibilities are!

Loans are not always what

we think, in a conventional sense, such as a car loan, a bike loan, a mortgage, etc. When one pays up front for a service or product, you are temporarily loaning your money until the service or product is delivered. An example is the process to build a house where a significant down payment is expected. You are loaning that contractor money, in return for his/her good faith promise to build the home of your dreams, on time, on budget, and on point - that all building corners are square and the tank doesn't leak. If he/she doesn't make that happen, without a contract of terms and conditions in writing, your recourse against him/her for delivery on the contract may be limited.

A. Pension and old age contributory monies, Life/Health insurance fees withheld from an employee's wages are never loans to a business, even temporarily

If an employer 'borrows' these moneys, this a big problem. Not only must the employee be reimbursed with interest, but a crime has been committed. In the US, stealing payroll taxes and pension contributions from employees is considered a felony. See further details on this important topic in Chapter 3. When Employers (and Employees Steal).

B. Credit cards are debt, actual formalised loans. Credit cards are not free cash. Read your credit card contract - all those tedious pages, however long! In return for the use of the credit card issuers' money (credit) you are promising to pay the balance in full. Credit card abuse is on the rise, often from individuals who know better, and by those who want to scam the lot. The issuer, whether a bank or a credit card company is not going to absorb defaults from slow or no payer card holders. Instead, they will penalise by charging higher interest rates, penalties, sometimes across the board. Wouldn't it be nice if those with impeccable credit had their credit card rates reduced arbitrarily? PS Some credit cards provide for a small life insurance policy, too.

C. IOU's stuffed into a cash register is a total no-no, a dismissal offence!

And they are informal loans even if tucked into an office friend's desk draw. Never let them mount up. Trying to pay back these back appropriately can be a cumbersome and inevitably a prosecutable task.

D. Overdrawing your account – whether unintended or not so, is a loan. When you open the account, be sure to check out the fine print. If and often it is a big if, it is your fault, the bank has the right to charge penalties and interest. You know all too well that the burden of proof is on you to justify why the bank may be wrong.

E. Families and friends' loans. These loans (and their lender/borrowers) tend to be notorious for not communicating. Can you imagine what happens when two friends go into business together, one loaning the money and the other charged with making the business profitable? Suppose the loaner gets restless when he sees the manager having a swell time every night down at the local jive bar, not only spending all the profits but the loaned capital as well. Not a good scenario, but it happens – that's what contracts are intended to prevent. Written formal loan contract documents prepared and executed by a good ethical attorney are worth their weight in gold. Appropriately composed contracts spell out the rights, resources of all concerned parties along with provideing an arbitrator who understands and will remember ten years down the road the original terms and conditions, not what was thought to be happening.

Finally, regardless of the structure of the loan, and even though the intent of the loan initially is business-like, understood and needed, as the years go by and payments are made, emotionally, we may resent making loan payments.

And we tend to transfer that resentment on to the lender. Is it because what we wanted so badly to own, now has lost its lustre!

Whenever you enter into a contract to borrow money, particularly if it is for a very long time, remember to remind yourself every day of just how much you wanted that thing, property, jewellery, vehicle, etc.

In other words, choose carefully. Those massive car payments five years from now become an incredibly heavy burden.

And the only winner is the lender.

OUR respected elder folks believed in cash.

If you want it, find a way to earn, then pay for it – IN FULL.

Idealistic today, realistic back then.

Save your loan paying skills for the one thing you need the most, your home.

 Listen to
The Deceitful
Allure Of Debt

https://tinyurl.com/yj8e7lyc

 Listen to
Debt: Good, Bad,
and Necessary

https://tinyurl.com/yz8s4nje

References
& Resources

Budget Calculators, Spread sheets and 360 Degrees of Financial Literacy - See References Chapter Six and Credit Card calculators

Bankrate Debt payoff calculators - See References Chapter Six

Jamila - See References Chapter Six

Your Loan Review

Know What

You Owe!

The Spirit of Bermuda

Scott Stallard Photography

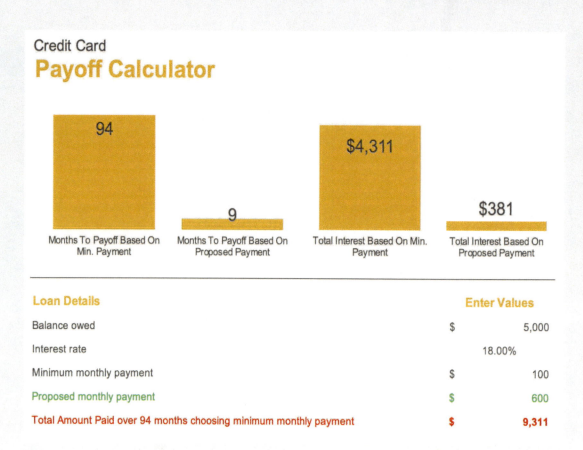

Figure 3 - Credit Card Debt Calculator

Step Eight - Your Loan Review. Know What You Owe

One - Review All your Loan Statements: Debit cards. Credit cards, auto, home mortgage, equity lines, personal loans, etc.

Review your debit, credit card statements, a mortgage statement if you have bought a home, auto loans, equity lines, and don't forget personal debt payments to friends and family.

CONSUMER CAUTION!

The difference between debit and credit cards is huge!

Debit cards deduct the charge immediately from your bank account using your money. Credit cards let you borrow other people's money (banks) and for that privilege, these generous people (well that is what we want to think) are going to charge for the use of their money.

They are never in the business of lending for free!

Yes, debit and credit cards look the same and because of the similarity – it becomes easy to use them both the same way - on all the little insignificant extras, AND the larger "cause-I-need-to feel-good" impulse purchases.

People use cards for convenience – they are so easy, making it doubly hard to keep track of what expenses, where, why, and how you paid for.

So, how much do you owe - in the short term, and the long term?

Hopefully, your answer is a good one:

Very little in short-term debt, but probably a pretty high balance in long-term debt. Why would that answer be just fine?

Two reasons:

- Consider what you have bought (you and the bank that is) by incurring that debt. Generally, this high-cost asset will be your home. However, those little every-day quick stops can add significantly to your overall debt. Your job now is to categorise your purchases into appreciation and depreciating assets. You may be very surprised at the answers.

- Mortgage interest rates are significantly lower (7% say) - more than three-four times lower - than immediate gratification credit card rates of 18%-24%.

- Verify for yourself.

Appreciating versus depreciating assets.

There are very few things in life that can be called appreciating assets; inevitably, the word asset is almost always linked with acquiring, not necessarily appreciating.

Starting with the obvious choices, clothes, fabulous shoes, jewellery, cars, toys and games, residence, computer and other electronics, intellectual capacity, in a no-brainer test, which of these listed here actually appreciate over the years.

Truly - Only one – your intellectual capacity, brainpower! Even a piece of real estate not cared for will depreciate, slowly, to be sure; the rest of the list loses anywhere from 50% to 100% of its value the minute you claim it as yours. I have seldom heard of anyone realising a profit on a fine diamond, have you? Generally, treasures in resale situations only attract 5-10% of their value; maybe that is all they are really worth.

So, does it not follow that the first place to invest is, in yourself by upgrading your education, by upgrading your job skills; never stopping the process of learning and acquiring knowledge?

That is not what we do.

We all – and I among them – fall into the purchase mode of depreciating assets, to feel good, look good, be good "trap."

Not that there is anything wrong with this, but the more defeated we feel, the harder it is to turn down the quick fix.

Appreciating assets generally grow in value over the long-term, keep that "long" in mind given that Bermuda real estate (generally an appreciating asset) lost value during the re-cession of 2008-2016 (from which Bermuda has yet to fully recover). Historically, however, Bermuda real estate has appreciated. Real estate also provides a permanent roof over your head and you own it!

Thus, debt itself is "never good," because you and someone else owns the asset until the debt is liquidated. However, long-term debt in your financial profile is ultimately a good idea, if it is manageable (not crippling). The principal component payments of your monthly mortgage are building equity ownership into your purchased home, an incredibly right financial reason to make that your goal.

This is your challenge!

To save for the long-term appreciating asset, while forgoing racking up debt on "things that make us feel better."

See charts next!

Assets?
Appreciating or Depreciating?

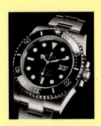

Appreciating or Depreciating Assets?		
	original purchase price	estimated resale market price	asset appreciating / depreciating?
Convertible - luxury	75,000	40,000	(35,000)
Designer handbag	2,100	600	(1,500)
Designer shoes	695	34	(661)
Designer watch - Rolex, etc.	12,000	8,000	(4,000)
Real estate	650,000	715,000	65,000
1 Share of stock in global company - Apple	22	210	188
valuation date	1980	August 2019	

Does not include Apple stock splits in 1987, 2000, 2005, 2014

Estimated numbers stated in US dollars. Second hand prices after 1-3 years of use culled from various websites: eBay, watch shops, auto books. Note that resale prices fluctuate due to many factors: scarcity, popularity, durability, condition, etc.

Photo sources: Amazon.com, autoblog.com, fashionphile.com, ebay.com

Two - Categorise Your Serious Purchases by Future Value.

What are your appreciating / depreciating assets? Examples: Designer bags, watches, antique chest-of-drawers, or taking friends out to lunch, groceries. When you sell these purchases (if you can sell them) – be honest now – will you get more than you paid for them?

No, almost always no, you won't - not even close to your original purchase price.

Truly. How many assets can you name that you want to (or have) purchased that will increase in value, especially if you took on debt to buy them? Answer as above, your real estate, and the Apple share certificate!

Three - Compute Ratio of Appreciating to Depreciating Assets.

Now, look at your ratio of balances between depreciating spending and appreciating assets charged.

How much have your depreciating assets decreased in value since you bought them; do you think that you can sell them at all?

How much have your appreciating assets increased in value since you purchased them?

How are the various debt repayments calculated on your credit card statement? Are you paying late payment penalties as well?

How many of these purchases did you make with a credit card?

Did you consider what the total cost would finally be, and have you figured into that purchase how quickly the asset or the entertainment could depreciate in value.

Entertainment depreciation is immediate, absolutely.

The Dreaded Debt Repayment Situation. Let's review credit cards.

See Figure 3. Credit Card Repayment Calculator chart above.

How long does it take to pay off a credit card balance? It depends upon your monthly payment!

We have a $5,000 credit card balance, built up through purchases for a designer bag, electronics, dining out, entertainment, and the like.

What is the real cost to carry this debt?

18% a year or more! Calculated on the principal balance and any unpaid interest.

- Simple calculation. $5,000 times 18% = $5,900 balance due in first year.

- Not good - an almost 20% more increase than the original amount paid, meanwhile the things you bought are rapidly depreciating in value, Particularly those dinners, wine, and beer out.

- Beware the minimum balance payment trap. Take a look at the FIGURE 3 again.

- A $100 a month minimum repayment will take 8 years plus with a huge amount of interest = total repayment over $9600! You may be paying twice, three times or more than the original cost in carrying charges. Meanwhile, your watch, and designer goodies have depreciated to less than half of the original price. Horrific! Review that depreciation chart again!

- Even with a huge increase in the monthly payment to $600 a month, it will take discipline and nine months to reduce this debt to zero including interest fees of $94 plus.

- When you are mentally persuaded to pay the minimum on your credit card, run your numbers first using any number of credit card payoff sites on the web. Most are free and can be used again and again.

- You will know exactly where you are and can plan accordingly.

There now, don't you feel better when you are in control of your finances?

Review your amortised mortgage fixed payments.

Amortised means that for every payment you make on your mortgage, the principal value owed and the amount of interest owed is reduced. After each payment is made, the new ending principal balance payment is used to recalculate the interest owed. Generally, the loan payment is the same every month, but the amount applied to principal payoff and interest varies as the amortisation process works out.

However, it is vital that you and your family as homeowners keep track of your mortgage payments, each and every month.

Mortgage servicers / banks, etc. can make mistakes.

You do not want to find out at the end of your mortgage repayment term that the payments have not been correctly applied.

A disturbing real example of this occurred when a couple walked into a bank (no personal facts disclosed here) to collect their house deed. They had paid off their mortgage. It took them twenty years, and now they fully owned their home, or so they thought.

Devastatingly, they were told that according to the bank, they had an interest only mortgage and so still owed the whole principal balance.

Of course, it was later found that the bank had made a huge mistake in not transferring the original construction loan (on paper) to an amortised loan, nor had the family ever been notified of the error.

One more hint - be sure that you fully understand the terms of your original mortgage deed, and that you do indeed have an amortised mortgage contract with your lender! And that you can pre-pay your mortgage principal without penalty.

Verify, verify your finances! Call your loan officer if you don't understand. I enclose links to a mortgage amortisation calculator. Consider running your numbers every other month or so against one of these calculators and verifying it against the bank mortgage statement balance.

Illustrative Example of an Amortised Fixed Rate Mortgage.

We assume initially,

- a loan amount of $420,000
- term 30 years, payments monthly
- 7% interest rate
- monthly payment, fixed of $2,794.27

Note the total interest paid over 30 years - more than the original loan!

This is reason enough to pay off your mortgage as soon as you can!

Mortgage Summary	
Loan amount	$420,000.00
Term	30 years
Interest rate	7%
Monthly payment (PI)	$2,794.27
Total principal and interest payments	$1,005,937.70
Total interest	$585,937.70

At the mortgage amortisation start, the beginning principal balance owed is the full amount as stated above. Then, it is multiplied by the interest rate attributable to the current period (MONTH) to find the interest amount due for the period.

The interest due for the period subtracted from the total monthly payment results in the dollar amount of principal paid in the period.

Hard to picture just as it is described.

See example below Chart 1 - for the first-year set months 1-12 of principal and interest payments on a mortgage!

Payment Schedule

Nbr	Payment	Principal	Interest	Ending Principal Balance
				$420,000.00
1	$2,794.27	$344.27	$2,450.00	$419,655.73
2	$2,794.27	$346.28	$2,447.99	$419,309.45
3	$2,794.27	$348.30	$2,445.97	$418,961.15
4	$2,794.27	$350.33	$2,443.94	$418,610.82
5	$2,794.27	$352.37	$2,441.90	$418,258.45
6	$2,794.27	$354.43	$2,439.84	$417,904.02
7	$2,794.27	$356.50	$2,437.77	$417,547.52
8	$2,794.27	$358.58	$2,435.69	$417,188.94
9	$2,794.27	$360.67	$2,433.60	$416,828.27
10	$2,794.27	$362.77	$2,431.50	$416,465.50
11	$2,794.27	$364.89	$2,429.38	$416,100.61
12	$2,794.27	$367.02	$2,427.25	$415,733.59

Mortgage payment chart 1

Notice that the first month, the interest owed - $2,450 - is subtracted from the monthly payment. or $2,794.27. The remaining amount $344.27 - is applied to REDUCE your actual loan - the mortgage principal. Since this is a fixed rate loan, the total monthly payment does not change. Ah, but the amount applied to reduce the principal does. Read and see!

At the beginning of month 2, the interest 7% divided by 12 (a month) - is recalculated on the reduced mortgage principal. The interest amount owed is less than the first month, so there is more cash available to apply to REDUCE your actual loan principle again.

And so on each monthly payment period - the amount of interest owed goes down and the remaining amount applied to reduce the mortgage principal goes up.

See how the amount of principal applied by the 12th payment has increased over $20 and the mortgage principal owed has been reduced by around $4,200.

If not, you need to call your bank immediately, because the entire monthly payment may have been applied to interest. Correcting this mistake is so time sensitive! Individuals who did not monitor their amortised mortgage have found it tedious and difficult to have the payments corrected, long after the fact.

Let's take a look at the payment amortisation in the 11th year - the 121st-132nd monthly payments.

Notice how your principal payment is now significantly higher while your interest payment is lower as well while the monthly payment is still the same. This is because more and more of the fixed monthly payment is being applied to your principal loan reduction.

121	$2,794.27	$691.87	$2,102.40	$359,720.16
122	$2,794.27	$695.90	$2,098.37	$359,024.26
123	$2,794.27	$699.96	$2,094.31	$358,324.30
124	$2,794.27	$704.04	$2,090.23	$357,620.26
125	$2,794.27	$708.15	$2,086.12	$356,912.11
126	$2,794.27	$712.28	$2,081.99	$356,199.83
127	$2,794.27	$716.44	$2,077.83	$355,483.39
128	$2,794.27	$720.62	$2,073.65	$354,762.77
129	$2,794.27	$724.82	$2,069.45	$354,037.95
130	$2,794.27	$729.05	$2,065.22	$353,308.90
131	$2,794.27	$733.30	$2,060.97	$352,575.60
132	$2,794.27	$737.58	$2,056.69	$351,838.02

Mortgage payment chart 2

This schedule carries on, until the very last payment in the 360th month.

I will state again please be sure to verify that your mortgage principal is being reduced - EACH AND EVERY MONTH!

The Strategy Behind Adjustable (Variable) Interest Rate Mortgages.

A variable - adjustable rate mortgage presents a greater tracking challenge, but it can be done.

An adjustable (variable) rate mortgage is a different kettle of fish entirely. Individuals may choose a variable because the initial interest rate offered will be lower than a fixed rate mortgage, while the bank will increase (or possibly decrease) the rate over a set time frame. Five-year adjustable-rate mortgages are popular. The strategy focuses on the calculated bet that five years on, the interest rate will be lower - than the current rate - at which point, the borrower may elect to move to a fixed rate loan.

However, global interest rates are subject to change fairly quickly. Your bank sets their current rate based upon global interest rate markers, say the LIBOR rate plus a local bank base rate.

What can happen is that a family may buy in at a decent lending rate, only to see the rate climb, instead of decrease. With that change in interest rate, two adjustments will happen. Your mortgage officer will lower the amount applied to your principal reduction - because the interest rate is now higher and your monthly payment remains the same; or, the bank will increase your monthly payment to compensate for the higher interest rate - meaning a higher monthly cost to you.

There are literally thousands of mortgage calculators on the Internet - with similar formats. Find one you are comfortable with - or surprise, your local bank will have calculators online as well.

The Accelerated Mortgage Principal Paydown Strategy

Fixed Rate Mortgages Provide Certainty, but what if you want to make principal payments alone (say a bonus, or savings) to reduce your mortgage faster?

Here is where you must be extra vigilant in tracking these extra principal payments each and every single time. You do not want them to be misapplied as another monthly payment - with more interest attached.

Further, you need to be assured that pre-payment is allowed under your mort- gage contract by carefully reviewing your original mortgage contract, or if you are a new home-buyer making sure you understand the conditions of the loan. Communicate with your loan officer.

Anecdotally, at least one Bermuda bank only allows principal pre-payment on mort- gages once a quarter.

I do not agree with that restriction.

Your goal is to eliminate long-term debt as quickly as possible.

There is a calculator for that action, too.

The Accelerated Mortgage Payoff. Try working with this one, to see how much faster you can reduce the time and the interest by making extra PRINCIPAL payments.

See the amazing difference by making $300 a month on the principal ONLY each and every month, or $900 a quarter.

You SAVE! $110,648 in interest!

Mortgage repayment shortened by 5 years and 4 months.

By increasing your mortgage payment $300 per month, you not only shorten your mortgage, but it will also save you $110,648 in interest.

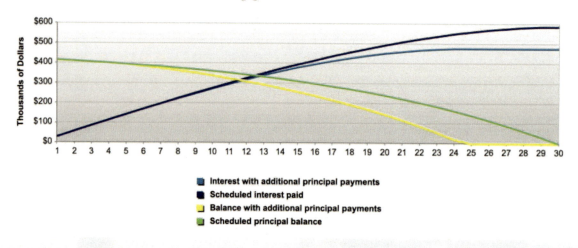

Mortgage Balances and Interest

- Interest with additional principal payments
- Scheduled interest paid
- Balance with additional principal payments
- Scheduled principal balance

Negative Equity.

This negativity related to your home can become an overwhelming issue in a declining economy. All along you've been encouraged to own your home - because over time it appreciates in value, now suddenly, this is not the fact in a declining economy.

Negative equity occurs when the current market value of your property is less than the balance owed on your mortgage. Example:

- you paid $500,000 at closing, borrowing $400,000.
- Your real estate agent says he can sell it for $340,000, but you still owe $372,000, or more on your mortgage.
- If you are forced to sell, not only will you not make a profit, but you will owe the bank $32,000 on the original loan, while you walk away with Nothing!

A property owner's first instinct when realising this problem, which generally, is not due to anything that the owner meeting his/her mortgage payment responsibility, is to try to sell, get out while there is still income value left.

Owners should reconsider that proposition, if they are still current on their mortgage premium payments.

Here is why!

Real Estate Market Values Are Influenced by Economic Conditions!

An economy stalls, or turns negative; real estate values, generally, will correlate with the overall market demand. Good economy= high demand= higher prices.

Conversely, poor economy = lower prices = less demand in a declining economy!

> When Economic positivity returns, real estate values are driven up again.

Negative equity is a function of the determination of the property value at any declining economic point in time. As the demand for property decreases, the supply of property inventory for sale increases; fewer number of buyers are intereste d, so the sale-able value attached to the real property depreciates. Sometimes, the price valuation is lower than the mortgage - because the property was purchased during a strong up- ward economic trend. Your mortgage may have been calculated on this sometimes significantly higher property valuation when the overheated Bermuda real estate market in 2005-2007 drove values to unsustainable levels.

This is most often occurring in a stagnant or declining economy as investment in the town, city, or country decreases. Or, if a large manufacturing or services base relocates, leaving the residents with far, fewer sources of good benefit jobs. The United States is replete with small towns that have lost their major income production industry, e.g. Maytag Appliances - moved to China; textiles, GM, paper companies, Reynolds, steel mills, and so on.

All just devastating to middle class families.

The exact opposite occurs when an economy is overheated;

- investment capital flows in,
- demand for property increases,
- insufficient supply occurs;
- prices are bid up as multiple buyers aggressively seek ownership.

What should you do if you purchased your property say, during the overheated Bermuda economy of 2005-2008, paying a premium for your home?

Nothing! Right away.

Instead, take a wait and see attitude, unless you are having increased difficulty in managing your monthly payments. You still need a roof over your head. And you would be walking away from your home, that you have loved and cared for to make it yours.

Your bank may not implement foreclosure proceedings if you are always current in your payment plan. If you are experiencing cash flow challenges, talk to your mortgage lender to possibly negotiate easier payments terms until you and your family are back on track.

Banks really do not want to be in the real estate marketing business. They just want to protect their investment, that is loaning you cash - with an eventual payback of principal and interest. Non-performing loans may impact their financial statements, in changing their capital reserve ratios.

Real estate values in Bermuda traditionally have increased an average of 3-5% annually.

Eventually, as the real estate tide does turn assuming that more foreign direct investments flow into Bermuda, and while this is not a guaranteed statement, you may see your property value gradually increase once again above the value of your mortgage.

Caution! Do not miss a mortgage payment!

Three – Manage Debt Payments Efficiently for Best Results!

Your goal is to decide how you are going to manage these debt payments better – by saving better and creating a realistic budget for you. Go to the beginning of STEP SIX to start your budget process.

> Malcolm Raynor, a reader of the Monseywise column contributed this so very true comment.
>
> "The key to saving is to track your spending to the penny. Your regular and big expenses items are not the ones that break your budget; it is the small items that are not planned for that can get out of control."
>
> Thank you, Malcolm!

Credit Card Debt Observations. In August of 2014, the Royal Gazette featured two in- depth articles (written by me) relative to credit card debt in Bermuda. They may be helpful to readers starting their financial review process. Link to these articles in references below!

> Uncleared credit card debts can last for years! Your impulse lunch or entertainment night – the final cost could be three to five times more than that great (or just so-so) meal.

The two questions to always ask before you hand off that debit or credit card:

- Is this purchase an appreciating asset – can I sell it for a profit, or will I get some of my money back, or will the thing be close to scrap in less than a year?
- Can I pay the total balance on my card due next month?

The potential permanent damage caused by using credit cards published in the Royal Gazette, August 23, 2014. This article is particularly relevant because it demonstrates how credit card balances increase exponentially when the family does not pay the entire balance due.

Note that you should always check with your local credit card provider to ascertain current terms and conditions. And read your credit card contract. Yes, I know it is tediously long, but…… don't you always want to be financially aware?

Those readers focused on appreciating your home as an asset, try the three-part series on Mortgage Tracking and Payment Calculator articles.

Part I - Why would you want to accelerate the principal payments on your mortgage? July 26 2014

Part 2 - Manage, track your mortgage - Martha's how-to guide, July 19 2014

Part 3 - How to use a mortgage calculator, July 12 2014

 Listen to Mortgage Basics - Part 1

https://tinyurl.com/yf6h4shr

 Listen to Mortgage Basics - Part 2

https://tinyurl.com/yefyt6c5

 Listen to Mortgage Basics - Part 3

https://tinyurl.com/yelouo9o

References
& Resources

Thousands of free finance calculators, encompassing all facets of a financial life cycle to help individuals and their families manage their financial affairs are available on-line. Just search us, Canadian or UK websites.

Bermuda islanders not connected to the United States - simply ignore the sections on US taxation.

You can also connect with your local Bermuda mortgage lender on-line.

Clarien Bank.

Clarien offers the HomeStart Program
– helping you own a piece of the rock in collaboration with Bermuda Housing Corporation (BHC)

Butterfield Bank. Bermuda

Butterfield has a mortgage calculator on its website for estimating your financial mortgage affordability.

HSBC Bermuda. HSBC Bermuda has a mortgage calculator on its website for estimating your financial mortgage affordability.

Employee Benefits

Hypothetical Bermuda Wage Deductions

Gross Pay = $5,000 per month	Deducted From Paycheck	Employer Match
5% Bermuda National Pension Scheme	$250	$250
Old Age Contributory Pension	$130	$130
Health insurance	$400	$400
Payroll Tax (2017-18) percent varies by employee compensation threshold	$287	$88
Subtotal, monthly	$1,067	$868
Total deducted/paid per month	$1,935 per employee	
Total deductions/paid in year	$23,220 per employee	
Total pension accumulation per year	$9,120	
All computations based on estimates or actuals where confirmed		

Figure. 4 Hypothetical Wages and Deductions / Contributions by Employer

Step Nine - Employee Benefits

Tracking Your Employee Benefits in Bermuda

Bermuda Employment Laws, Benefits and Rights

Keeping an eye on your paycheque deductions and employer-employee benefit responsibilities

Your budget process is not just comprised of checking your income and expenses relative to your bank transactions / statements.

You should routinely review your paycheque, the net amount deposited in your bank account, and whether the deductions and benefits that you are entitled to are math correct and have been deposited by your employer on your behalf!

A BIT OF BACKGROUND. To outsiders, Bermuda's legislative and economic infrastructure is amazingly sophisticated for a tiny island. It is not so surprising, though, when one considers that Bermuda has had an actively engaged Parliament for more than 400 hundred years.

The Bermuda Employment Act was legislated into law in the year 2000. The Act encompasses employment applications and contracts, recruitments/advertising, statutory claims, discrimination, references and background investigations, visa/work permits, compensation and benefits, work hours/overtime/leave of absence as vacation, sick and bereavement, leave, public holidays, medical and maternity, workers' compensation, severance allowances, whistle-blower protection, harassment, public access to information, workforce reductions (redundancies), non-compete covenants, occupational safety & health policies, drug testing, privacy concerns relative to personnel records, union activity, and more.

Bermuda Employment Act 2000

http://www.bermudalaws.bm/

Employees are legally entitled to the following benefits from employers, including:

- two weeks holiday (vacation) after one year;
- no unauthorised deductions from wages;
- a written contract must be provided after one week's employment;
- a 40-hour week; time and a half, or time off, after 40 hours, with possible exemptions;
- paid Public Holidays;
- a rest period of at least 24 consecutive hours each week;
- 8 days paid sick leave per year; unlimited time off to attend ante-natal classes for pregnant employees;
- 8 weeks paid and 4 weeks unpaid maternity leave after one year, it appears maternity leave in-creased in September 2019;
- a statutory notice period;

- bereavement leave of 3 days unpaid or 5 days unpaid if traveling abroad;
- a right to a disciplinary procedure;
- time off for public duties such as court duty, voting, meeting of Government Boards, Bermuda Regiment, Reserve Police, Senate or House of Assembly;
- notice of 1 week if weekly paid, 2 weeks if bi-weekly paid, 1 month in any other case;
- probationary periods, generally three months;
- specific actions for termination, misconduct, unfair dismissal, remedies, and enforcement.

Employee Welfare and Benefits:

- Employers are also mandated to provide the following contributions for their employees' well-being:
- health insurance plan for employees (working more than four hours a week) and their uninsured dependents on a "minimum hospital benefit" at a 50% of total plan rate;
- a private pension plan (Bermuda National Pension plan or equivalent) at a 10% rate (5% contributed by employee);
- social insurance (Government Contributory Plan) at a fixed amount split 50% between employer and employee;
- payroll tax (which does not benefit the employee) payable on salaries and benefits by the employer at generally, 14-16% - with 5.25% of this deducted from employees, but check the government website for any changes! The employer is solely responsible for this tax.
- other benefits may be provided on employer discretion, but are not mandatory;
- Most of these items are applicable to self-employed individuals, given that they are their own employers.

What's in my paycheque? Where are my deductions?

See hypothetical illustration of a payroll compensation chart above. These numbers are illustrative only and will not reflect your OWN personal employment compensation statement!

Take a good look at the chart above. Let's assume an individual Gross Salary of $5,000 per month.

Review your basic paycheque deductions and employer contributions on your behalf. Are you surprised at this number of deductions - $1,067? Of course, your individual wage sheet will be different; the above is just an example for discussion points.

Yes, indeed, the total amount deducted from your paycheque each month represents a 21% payroll hit to you.

Now add in the amount required by law that your employer has to match: pensions, payroll tax and health insurance - $1,130 for a total of $2,197, a significant sum each month to keep you insured, saving for retirement and eligible for social services.

Now, check the full year figure of $26,364 per person with more than $9,000 a year destined to contribute to your future.

This is why I constantly harp on monitoring your wage deductions and contributions, every single month.

We cannot even begin to calculate the loss in long-term investment appreciation in your pension assets, if you lose out on yours and your employer's contributions.

*Payroll tax assumes a business with five employees and new rates as at August 2019.

The Employer and Employee Relationship.

Our Bermuda forebears and the futuristic minded leaders of today enacted employment legislation to define employee positions, rights, and future security that far surpass much larger countries – the United States comes to mind first.

The employer / employee relationship is a serious two-way street. Each individual is co- dependent upon the other in a bond of trust in order to succeed personally, and corporately. If either person undermines the business relationship, neither will benefit financially, in the long run.

In an ideal world:

Employees should respect what great employers have accomplished, a successful business and an optimum working environment for you to also succeed. It is your absolute employee duty to show loyalty, good work ethics and contribute your skills unequivocally to this continued success. Your job and your future depend upon it.

Employers should treat all employees – from the lowest position to the highest - with respect, personally, and financially with position-appropriate employee benefits and promotional rewards for increased business. In return, that mutual respect accompanies the right to ask for loyalty to the firm and good work ethics. A large component of business success depends on responsible committed employees, who represent the firm's image in the global marketplace.

When Employers or Employees Steal.

However, in the real world, not every individual operates from a position of integrity. I am talking about employer (and employee) theft.

EMPLOYERS stealing from employees is fraud - robbery, just as if your house was invaded. Payroll fraud can be perpetrated in a number of ways, in a variety of forms, including paying employees in cash, filing false payroll tax returns or simply ignoring the filing process by never depositing the employee withholdings.

What does such a payroll financial loss mean to an employee?

Trust in the employer is destroyed. Financially, it really hurts the individual employee – health care denied, pensions depleted. See the illustrative Figure 3 chart above of a hypothetical single person wage earner and his or her total payroll withholdings and employer match contributions.

This is Your Money. Review just the total pension joint contributions to the Government Old Age Contributory Pension and the Bermuda National Pension Scheme for the private business sector.

The consequences of losing your payroll benefit contributions is significant. Short answer, it is your responsibility to act if you think your benefit tank is close to empty.

However, anonymous reader feedback indicates that employees find it terribly difficult to inform on a disreputable employer. Terrified of losing their jobs, even more concerned that their whistle blowing will prevent them from finding any job again, they elect to remain silent. We all know how word travels, even when considered confidential,

Bermuda is just too small and a close community to keep a secret.

And quite frankly, up until now, the legal punishment for such crimes has been a complete joke.

One composite case (years ago), a local employer stiffed his crew of more than $250,000 in earned benefits. The result a $250 dollar fine. Note that the amount stolen was never repaid to the employee victims because he, the employer, left the country, never to return!

Another dishonest employer tactic is to just quietly close down the existing company with the benefits' arrears, declare bankruptcy, and then, outrageously start up a new company - doing the same thing but without all those annoying benefit liabilities owed to former employees.

Summary:

Not every employer (employee) is dishonest.

- Your employer may not be depositing your employee benefits (to your accounts) as mandated by Bermuda law.

- It is your responsibility to monitor and track these withholdings.

- Save every single paystub - forever, or until you receive the pension you are entitled to.

- You have a right to request a current copy of your Bermuda government social insurance pension accumulation, no matter how far away from retirement you may be.

- Do not wait to notify the appropriate authorities, if you think your employer is stealing your benefits.

Bermuda law currently allows this!

Employee benefit debts and taxes are never discharged in bankruptcy in other countries. Our laws need to be changed.

Flagrantly stealing from not only his/ her loyal employees and our (not his!) government public purse was a means to keep the money. The excuse, he had a lot of bills, was building his own house, and "got a little short." Such conduct should never be tolerated. Legal action - put a lien on owner's house, car, company! Freeze bank accounts. Cancel their credit cards. Garnish their salary. Confiscate their property! Shore up our Bermuda legislation for crimes against Public Trust Funds!

Such malfeasance! Other countries' taxing authorities move quickly to prevent payroll fraud because the collateral damage hits everyone's pockets with increased tax bills as governments are duty bound to reimburse the social service agencies for the missing funds. Further, the longer the wait to collect, the more difficult, impossible it becomes to levy the delinquent employer.

In the United States, Canada and the UK, anyone / company/ etc. that abuses Public Trust funds is punished, quickly, with draconian actions. First, with significant penalties and interest, then by having wages garnished and bank accounts frozen, less than three months after the first delinquency! Then, the defendant's property is attached, often is sold. Declaring bankruptcy will not discharge Public Trust debts – they follow the debtor to his/her grave. The final ignominy is that the defendant may find himself/her wearing those stylish orange jumpsuits. What happens to the disadvantaged employee? In our Bermuda locale, the employee victim is cut off at the knees.

A lax attitude still permeates government in its ability to force collection of delinquent employee benefit contributions. If you are shorted on your benefits, it is your problem. The Bermuda government has no legislated mandate to reimburse your personal accounts. Instead, government has to absorb the payroll tax loss with increased levies on all businesses, meaning that ethical employers ultimately pay more than their fair share!

Ethical Employer Competitive Disadvantage. The delinquent-fraud employer can undercut bids on jobs because his/her overhead is lower, due in part to illegally obtained loans (from employees) that provide a readily available cash float.

It follows that those who short the payroll system also avoid other obligations:

- inadequate or no employee health insurance;
- little or no workers compensation and general liability insurance;
- property tax defaults;
- skimping on materials;
- marking up wholesale materials way above cost;
- poor repair jobs using inferior product components;
- mediocre or poor professional service;
- inadequate or no job safety measures, and so on.

STEALING transcends all economic, social, ethnic or cultural boundaries. Dishearteningly, honest, everyday working people are the real losers. Many may never recoup such losses. Older individuals with employer-shorted retirement assets may quickly exhaust resources only to suffer the humiliation of needing financial assistance.

What to do and where to go to report your missing payroll deductions?

Let's take each section in turn.

Health Insurance Deduction

If you suspect, or were informed by a pharmacy or doctor, that you are not covered by health insurance even though the deductions are being withheld from your wages, take action as follows.

- Immediately,
- Notify the Bermuda Health Council by phone, and a follow up email detailing the missing health insurance payments.
- Alert your insurance health care provider, who may already know that your employer is not current with your health benefits, that you are reporting your employer.

BHEC TEL 1 441 292-6420

BHEC website page. See list of non-compliant employers, www.bhec.bm/

BHEC email address
healthcouncil@bhec.bm

Payroll Tax Deduction

This deduction is your employer's responsibility and is deposited directly with Bermuda government. Your employer is allowed to deduct a portion of this tax from your wages, while the company contributes the rest.

You do not receive any direct benefit from this deduction, although it is assumed that if you need financial assistance or other government benefit, it is funded by this general funds.

Important. Please check the table enclosed to be sure that your employer is deducting your percentage share, not the whole tax. I note this because readers have reported that some employers are deducting the entire payroll tax due from employee wages - this is a huge mistake, or deliberate error!

Since this particular tax does not directly fund your benefits, nor are you actually even able to determine that your tax withheld has been paid to government, reporting is a non-event.

There is some controversy regarding this deduction as Bermuda law clearly states that the entire deduction is the employer's responsibility. One wonders what would happen if an employee challenged this arbitrary deduction taken from his/her wages without the employee's consent?

Social Insurance for Your Old Age Contributory or Non-contributory Pension

You have a right to request your contribution record from the Bermuda Social Insurance Department - at any age.

Always a good idea to track your contributions on a routine basis.

This is a very important feature that you should use immediately if you are uncertain as to whether your employer is depositing your benefit deduction/contributions into the fund!

Bermuda Government Department of Social Insurance.

Request a copy of your contributions by calling (441) 294-9242 ext. 1117 or 1718, or send an e-mail providing your social insurance number and date of birth. Reporting your missing Bermuda Contributory Pension Fund payments

Call (441) 295-5151 or send an Email: https://www.gov.bm/contact/1641/196 through the Government website.

Report suspected violations of the pension plan.

Are your social insurance contributions accurate and up to date?

IF NOT?

Go to the Bermuda government website, find the pension section. Complete the Complaint form if you observe any violations of pension protocol.

Source URL: https://www.gov.bm/

The next step for government may be prosecution of employer if malfeasance is discovered.

Statement excerpts from the Bermuda Government Department below,

"The Tax Commissioner and the Director of Social Insurance will start to forward employer files to the Director of Public Prosecutions for prosecuting employers, companies and individuals, for offences related to delinquent payments pursuant to their respective legislation. As both employers and employees well know, social insurance contributions provide for an employee's pension when they reach the age of 65."

The amount of the (YOUR) pension is directly linked to the amount paid in over the years. It is a serious breach of the law to not pay in the social insurance contributions deducted from the employee. It is equally serious for the employer to not pay his/her statutory obligation.

Employees of companies and other businesses can check with the Department of Social insurance to ensure their contributions are paid up by contacting the Department at 295-5151.

Delinquent companies will be pursued not only in the civil courts but also in the criminal arena, as both the Contributory Pensions Act and the Taxes Management Act allow.

Recouping missed payments is very slow.

The law is not on your side.

The most tragic aspect of this type of theft is that even if the employer accepts responsibility to pay, government allows minuscule monthly payments plans - nowhere near enough to cover a soon-to-be retiree's expected pension income.

Frankly, the retired employee may even pass away before he/she is repaid the entire missing pension balance owed!

What's in your Bermuda National Pension Scheme.

See pension plan statement example under the pension section.

This accounting for all contributions is a bit more complicated because your pension plan provider only issues a monthly, quarterly, or an annual statement that generally, lists

- beginning balance
- contributions made for the time period
- capital market appreciation / or depreciation
- new ending balance.

See Hypothetical chart in the pension review section

It is critical that you track your monthly contributions, including your 5%, and your employer's 5% share plus, any extra voluntary contributions. Always refer to the prior statement to be sure that the balances carried forward are correct!

Keep all Bermuda National Pension statements from your Day One enrolment.

You never know if you will be asked to prove correct balances, plus your statements are proof of your ownership and accumulated pension portfolio assets.

To report any discrepancies, contact your pension administrator and the Pension Commission.

Bermuda Pension Commission: The Occupational Pension Schemes under the National Pension Scheme (Occupational Pensions) Act 1998.

Contact.
info@pensioncommission.bm
Telephone: 441 295-8672

Currently, the Pension Commission does not have a specific section for an employee to report delinquent employers.

However, an employee with pension entitlements can request in a written format "Information from the Plan Administrator to review any documents and information relating to the pension plan and the pension fund."

My opinion.

This is nowhere near adequate when time is of the essence - in the case of employer fraud as by the time the information is received, it may be too late.

Thus, as the beneficiary of these contributions in the future, you need to make persistent queries to the pension office to ascertain the truth - and hope is not too late to enforce a collection proceeding.

When Employees Steal.

And, unfortunately, there is another side to this coin.

Dishonest employees' theft.

Honest, ethical employers who honour their financial commitments to their employees also have to cope with dishonest employees who steal consistently, without a conscious thought to the damage they wreak, while all along receiving on-time, everytime paycheques.

The US Chamber of Commerce estimates that 75% of all employees steal at least once.

One of every three business failures are the direct result of employee theft - my family relatives have experienced this - first hand!

The American Society of Employers report that:

- businesses lose 20% of every dollar to theft;
- 18 months is the average time to catch an employee fraud scheme;
- 55% of perpetrators are managers (in positions of trust);

These statements were reiterated by a Security / Compliance manager of a large Bermuda financial institution, further noting that 30% of employees will think about stealing while 5-10% are actively perpetrating fraud of various kinds.

How do employees steal? Hard core blatant theft, and the much harder to document, soft core, almost unnoticed theft.

Let me count some of the many ways. Why scammer employees can't devote as much energy to career advancement as they do to torpedoing their own positions, I will never understand.

Jobs are so precious these days.

Everyone can be replaced. No employer can afford to keep an unmotivated, unethical, employee.

Hard core theft.

- Cash. The tantalising opportunities here take place within the accounting, sales, cashiering departments where there is ready access to cash, bank accounts, and accounts receivables and payables departments - along with insufficient segregation of, and unsupervised, duties. Phony or duplicate invoices, phantom accounts, check signing authority without counter-signatures, access to electronic transfer mechanisms, etc. In small businesses - far too much trust is placed in one or a small group of employees who can collude to steal.
- Wire transfers. Employees utilising specialised software with the ability to manipulate accounts (transferring cash) within the company's electronic storage systems.
- Trade secrets passed off in return for favours, cash, and other forms of payment.

- Customer lists sold on or removed when an employee leaves the firm.
- Inventory shrinkage - the industry name for stealing company products. Friends, family are the recipients of this largess, or the "lifted" products are sold on. These employees make a practice of walking out the door with "extras."

The justification: my boss is wealthy; he/she can afford it; the company will never miss this stuff.

True story. Many years ago, a house guest presented us with a beautiful set of bed sheets from a high end US department store. We were effusive in our thanks. Her response, not to worry - the gift didn't cost her anything and she could get us lots more!

Her former boyfriend had a whole closet full of these items that he walked out the back door of his employer every week. I'm no paragon of virtue (readers), but this "gift" bothered me so much, I couldn't use them.

They went to Goodwill.

- Back of truck deliveries - works like this. Wholesaler employee (WE) makes a large delivery (deliberately withholding some items) to a retail business. Retail receiving clerk signs for full delivery after only a cursory item check, or if in collusion, ignores the miscount. WE keeps the withheld items, selling them on at discounted prices (or benefiting friends and family).

Soft core theft by employees is so much harder to detect, and can be even more damaging to a company and its business reputation.

Attitude negativity.

Customer impressions of the retail or service business attitude become negative reactions, too.

Customers vote with their feet and their wallets.

Malicious sabotage.

A new owner of a business keeps on employees of the former owner, thinking that they would be great in maintaining goodwill with clients. He inadvertently discovers that said "kept on" employees were telling existing clients that the new owner was not only incompetent, but perhaps, clients should look elsewhere for advice. These employees couldn't understand why they were terminated for cause.

Time Stealers.

Tardiness, every day more than fifteen minutes late; long coffee breaks, lunches, social media cruising, online shopping, false call records for marketing new business, and the like.

Inefficiency.

Why be efficient, churning out delegated tasks in required time frames to the best of ability, when one can take one's time deliberately and still receive a full paycheque every week.

Time wasters are not always solely inefficient.

Sometimes, an entire department is complicit in working at a go-slow mode. Any efficient, forward looking employees focused on career-performing excellence are resented, shunned and sabotaged by their peer group workers.

These are numerous examples of insidious atmospheres that - allowed to perpetuate can destroy a business.

And regrettably, in many cases, employers are not aware until it is too late.

The employer / employee relationship is a serious two-way street where each individual is co-dependent upon the other in a mutual bond of trust.

If either person undermines that relationship, the continued viability of the business involved may be affected.

Listen to
Employee Benefits

https://tinyurl.com/yjhxmw8g

Listen to
Independent
Contractor Benefits

https://tinyurl.com/yzz8yluz

Independent Contractors Are Very Different From Employees

The Bermuda Government Throne Speech 2020 indicated that the Bermuda Employment Act 2000 would be upgraded significantly, the first time in almost twenty years.

On November 28, 2020, government illuminated specific changes to Act for employers and employees, but left focus on clarification of independent contractor classification to "guidance from the labour relations manager."

So, what is an independent contractor(IC)?

We are not privy to the independent contractor guidance, so will approach this universal category, generically.

An IC as this business shall be known is a unique entity. Labelled as a sole trader, or a sole proprietor, generally unincorporated, an individual can enter the business world – needing very little to start up and appearing to have no encumbrances, whatsoever.

The construction industry (where this author had numerous clients) refers to IC's as pickup builders, as in buy or lease a truck, assemble your tools in cargo bed, print up a DBA (doing business as) business card and wow, you are an owner, ready for serious ventures.

In effect as you have hired yourself, you are both your own employee and your employer, since there is only you. This is an important concept for taxes, as we shall see.

Think about it!

Your new business, funded by you, self-employed, responsible you (and no one else), independent decision making, setting your own hours, sink or swim by your own efforts, you are in control.

It is an exciting powerful concept.

And it works.

Millions and millions of tiny one-person independent contractors have initially used the same format, successfully.

You know them, numerous global giant corporations that started their successes as single entrepreneurs in a garage, a studio, kitchen table:

Amazon, Yankee Candle, Harley Davidson, Maglite, Under Armour, etc.

Tax authorities, in defining who, what, when, why and how taxes are assessed, delineate numerous differences between ICs and employees.

The three major categories are:

1. control
2. benefits
3. responsibility, liability

Control, Benefits, and Responsibility/Liability

Who Has Control of Your Actions?

The differences between employee and independent contractor control of their work environment and decision making can be clear cut or ambivalent, depending upon where and what type of industry. Real estate agents, taxi drivers, and now UBER-type drivers operate in a "flexible" environment, so to speak.

Uber has been sued by taxation agencies regarding the driver status. Legal decisions have varied by country.

As an employee, your employer (company, etc) is in control of your time at work: where you report at required hours every day, take set instructions from management, submit completed tasks, participate in required group meetings, are provided a contract, an employee handbook, benefits, a rate-set salary, and so on.

Problems arise when an employee tries to, say publish work independently that was done on, and paid for, on company time, or regrettably, has an accident in a company- owned vehicle. In the first instance, the company owns that manuscript, and the second, the company is liable, generally.

As an INDEPENDENT CONTRACTOR you are solely in control, everything is your decision, you use your own equipment, vehicle, you set your own work hours, you bill your own time, etc. on a job, you contract for a specific project at a pre-determined price. Generally, you have multiple customers.

Who Pays for What Benefits?

See the Wage Benefit Cost Comparison Between Employees and Independent Contractors.

Employees receive numerous benefits; the cost generally split between employee and employer for some, while others are completely covered by the employer.

Independent contractors foot the entire bill for all benefits. Typically, then what will ensue is that the IC carries the most common benefits at 100% of cost, because as stated above the IC is both an employer and an employee.

The more popular fringe benefits such as family vacations, professional development, gym/counselling, and so on are basically ignored – as cost is derived from operating profits. Vacations and leave are almost never taken – because when an IC does not work, no income is received.

Additionally, the benefits paid out of the IC pocket, must be computed as a major factor overhead when pricing projects. Health insurance alone will run $2,500-$3,000 a month for a local family of two parents and two children = $30,000 - $36,000 a year. It is that simple.

EXAMPLE of Benefit total costs paid by the Independent Contractor – see the chart for the rest!

- Health insurance – 100%
- Taxes – 100%
- Social insurance – 100%
- Pension – 100%
- Meals – 100%

- Vehicle/transportation - 100%
- Life insurance – 100%
- Disability insurance – 100%

Who Has Responsibility for Liability Incurred On the Job?

Employee responsibility/liability is generally covered by the employer blanket – but caveat, generally is not everything! Irresponsibility is not tolerated and can be grounds for dismissal. Liability coverage is also generally attached to strict definitions in the governing contract of employee behaviour, financial conduct, and relationships within the company and the employer.

Liability is the Largest Most Concerning Factor Difference for Independent Contractors.

- IC is responsible for everything financial, legal, risk, health, product and service
- Taxation may be higher
- Sole proprietorship is extremely vulnerable to lawsuits
- Personal property and other assets may be attached
- Must have very comprehensive liability insurance

There is a price to pay for success, however, when being a one-person operation becomes unsustainable in its present format.

Many business owners find that they do not, and/or cannot remain sole traders (IC).

These three imposing criteria listed above are probably the BIGGEST REASON IC'S incorporate their businesses.

There are numerous other reasons, some greatly positive, others purely protective:

- Unmanageable growth,
- burnout,
- disability,
- personal cash infusion limits,
- avoiding use of personal assets as collateral,
- inability to secure capital funding without a corporate structure,
- no asset protection,
- additional expertise required for progress implementation,
- personal responsible for debts and lawsuits, including employee lawsuits, yes IC's do hire personnel,
- no automatic business shelf life if owner dies,
- inability to sell out at retirement.

Wage Benefits Cost Comparison Between Employee and Independent Contractor

Benefit Cost	Employee	Employer	Independent Contractor- IC
Health insurance	50%	50%	IC pays 100%
Dental and vision insurance	50%	50%	IC pays 100%
Health savings accounts	varies	varies	IC self funds
Pension	50%	50%	IC pays 100%
Payroll tax	varies	varies	IC pays 100%
Social security, or insurance	50%	50%	IC pays 100%
Company stock at discount	EE pays	ER discounts	None available as unincorporated business
Paid family leave		ER funds	IC self funds
On work environment – meals/snacks		ER funds	IC self funds
Financial planning		ER funds	IC self funds
Work-related liability insurance		ER funds	IC self funds
Flexible work conditions/hours		ER funds	IC self funds
Professional development, e.g. masters, sabbatical leave		ER funds	IC self funds
Assistance with student loan		ER funds	IC self funds
Workers comp, unemployment insurance		ER funds	IC self funds
Group term life insurance		ER funds	IC self funds
Disability insurance		ER funds	IC self funds
Health counselling and gym memberships		ER funds	IC self funds
Stock options		ER funds	None available as unincorporated business
Restricted stock awards		ER funds	None available as unincorporated business
Mortgage subsidy		ER funds	IC self funds
Transportation subsidy		ER funds	IC self funds
Internet, device subsidy home office/ travel		ER funds	IC self funds
Bonuses		ER funds	IC self funds

References
& Resources

Bermuda has additional laws for the protection of employment / employees all found at the Bermuda Laws website

Bermuda Immigration and Protection Act 1956

Bermuda's Human Rights Act 1981

Bermuda's Labour Relations Act 1975 & the Trade Dispute Act 1992

Bermuda Worker's Compensation Act 1965

Bermuda-Labour-and-Employment-Law-Handbook 2017 authored by Juliana Snelling - Canterbury Law Limited

Bermuda Employers at Bermuda- Online.

BERMUDA Government Website links - attention regretfully, these sites are not always guaranteed to work! https://www. gov.bm/payroll-tax/

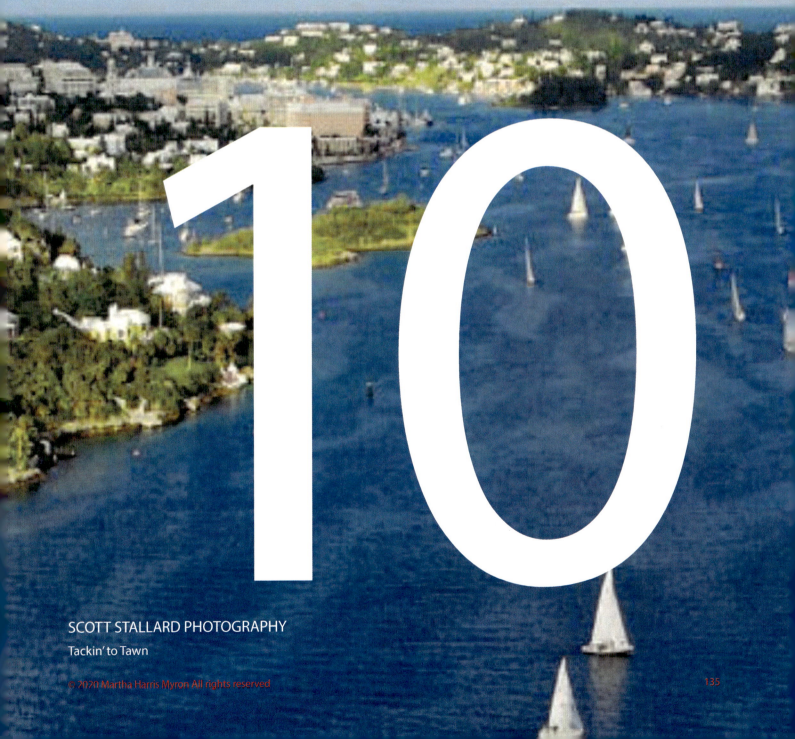

Your Personal Basic Investment Review

A. Cash & Stocks

10

Step Ten (A) - Your Personal Basic Investment Review

Your Personal Investment Review Process

This phase of your financial review may be bit more tedious for some, but it is also the most important, so we will cover it in steps Ten - Thirteen.

We will review

A. Why invest at all in capital markets?

B. Investment basics - just a few (a much more complete review will be featured in Book Two, the First Bermuda Every-Day Investment Primer coming soon;

C. A quick look at a hypothetical small Bermuda business start-up relating to stock ownership (a more complete picture leading to Book Two is featured in the Appendix A);

D. Assess, in general, your personal investment holdings and asset allocations, if you own any;

E. Show the characteristics of a balanced portfolio if you want to own investments outside of your pension.

And in Steps Eleven and Twelve, review your pension plan accumulations and performance, and how it all relates to your future financial planning.

We are reviewing the basic investing concepts as well as relating them to your personal investment planning goals and as you can correlate them with Your Bermuda National Pension Scheme (BNPS). Note: the BNPS section may not be as applicable to civil servants with the Bermuda Government Superannuation Pension Plan.

My simply suggesting a brief review of investments may assume an understanding that many individuals have neither the time, or the energy to initiate.

Over the years, numerous comments from individuals have been similar as the following, "Well, the investment people met us. While they were very professional, they tended to talk too much jargon about markets, risk tolerance, volatility, some things that I really couldn't follow, so I just picked a fund. I have no idea how well it will work for me!"

Plus, the thought of investing and investments can be unnecessarily intimidating!

But, if you are pretty comfortable with investment concepts, you may want to skip to the section on reviewing your personal investments.

But, consider this, whether we like it or not.

We, in Bermuda, are part of the global investment environment.

The simple concepts of local Bermuda shares that were most often (in the good old days) held in paper certificates because there was little access to a local trading platform (BSX), and possibly a bond or two, (you may not remember the municipal bond floated to the Bermuda public to finance Hamilton City Hall) are now fully integrated within the global investment theatre.

Further, capital trading markets are not the same as they used to be as we have learned from the terrible global Coronavirus catastrophe impact.

But what in our life is the same as it used to be?

Change is inevitable.

Over the last century alone, the dominant United States investment industry has experienced monumental change as well as enormous growth from:

- the close-to-obsolescence of physically situated stock markets where original paper transactions, runner trade deliveries with brokers on an exchange floor have gradually been replaced by electronic multi-millisecond high-speed anonymous trades direct between the parties, with no middleman;

- artificial intelligence has overtaken human interaction, but as Market Watch stated, "AI (Artificial Intelligence) will change stock-market trading, but when a trade is complex, there is no substitute for human judgment;"

- computer-generated mathematical algorithms in quantitative analyses trigger thousands of specific set point trades, on a daily basis;

- traditional business day trading hours replaced with after-hours market trading, literally, 24-hours a day interchanges across the globe;

- virtual interaction between world trading markets where significant events can trigger cascading correlated results in different time zone markets;

- investor research via internet search engines generating almost instantaneous results means less obscurity for investment decisions, but greater care must be taken to weed out "fake news/reports" and unscrupulous schemes such as "pump n' dump" type websites before any credence can be given;

- changes in numbers and kinds of investors from all spectrums and classes;

- the corporate insider share buy-back phenomenon that has dominated investment sentiment for a number of years;

- economies other than the US have grown, too, taking examples from and emulating the US investment success story. The power race is on to affect more diversification choices in world-wide trading markets, and foreign exchanges;

- the empirical, possible popularity contest, decision as to who will remain or become the country to dominate the world's reserve currency, given that Russia, China and other European countries (INSTEX founded January 31, 2019) are actively working to sideline the US dollar out of global trade to avoid sanctions, while oil is now traded in other currencies, backed by gold in lieu of US dollars;

- the ever-shifting interplay of oil commodities on capital markets, trade, war, and country economic dominance;

- blockchain and its derivatives of digital currencies, an innovative anonymous force that clearly defines and delivers complete, irrefutable transactions between consenting parties;

- the relentless regulatory enforcement of Know Your Client, economic substance transparency and international tax compliance in cooperation amongst almost all OECD countries participating and those beyond;

- and the tragic, material, virulent COVID pandemic that individuals, families, communities and countries across the globe are still heavily impacted by financially, emotionally and physically.

The number of investment products has grown existentially as well. Where the ordinary stock, bond, mutual fund, or option trade may still be basic staple for many investors, new, or more complex investment products, some more esoteric than others, abound:

- exchange-traded funds, structured notes;
- synthetic (or what I call real versus ethereal) investment products built upon or dependent upon values of other underlying products, debt, or indexes, e.g. leveraged loan funds, CDO's, CMO's, even risk itself is an investment product, e.g. volatility (VIX) funds and related simulators;
- mortgage-backed securities, commodities, indexed-annuities, initial coin offerings, cryptocurrencies, credit default swaps, securities futures;
- alternative investments: hedge funds, reverse convertibles, leveraged inverse ETFs, event-linked securities;
- viatical settlement funds, catastrophe bonds and more.

How did we ever end up with the entire concept of investing in intangible assets that today – for the overwhelming part – cannot be realised fundamentally by touch, sight, or stored on a personal basis?

We are focused here on digital investments, not physical assets such as precious earth-derived elements: land and real estate properties, diamonds, golf, silver, other stones, metals, oil, shale, crops, livestock, the munificent sea (and salt), water, and the like. We know these physical properties; we've been surrounded by them, in one form or another, all of our lives.

The concept of virtue world investing via intangible investments is daunting. Now almost completely processed by modern technology – less hands on, stored electronically (and hopefully, rigorously secured) on remote server custodians, heavily-reliant upon reputationally-compliant financial institutions, with the only real evidence of ownership composed of front-facing numbers on a smart phone, a computer screen or down-loaded paper documents, is overwhelming.

Think about it – owning digital assets in our social media age represents a strong belief in the fiduciary oversight and implied safety of financial institutions because that is where your invested assets are electronically (not physically) held.

Bermuda has not escaped this tremendous amount of complexity, volatility and commerce in global motion. We, in Bermuda, are impacted by everything that occurs within and without our precious island. And the more we understand these influences, the better we can take advantage of them, anticipate opportunities, and protect our financial assets.

A. So yes, investments influence you and Investments surround you.

Indirectly, and directly from cradle to grave - every single day. As an infant at birth, you have no understanding of such an impact, nor are you much more aware on your exit day that consumerism choices made by you, or for you, shape your life, and influence the success - or failure - of thousands of businesses world-wide!

Every Bermuda business is an investment.

Yet, the easy access to these businesses in one format or another - has almost generated indifference to their roles in our lives - because we are so very comfortable having products, services, and ideas right at hand. Imagine if we did not?

Take a look at the list of an ordinary Bermuda islander's stock (company) exposures on an average day in the chart below. Recognise these company stock symbols? Who can you identify? You know them because you contribute every day to their profits!

Most of our Bermuda BSX Listed publicly traded companies are included, along with numerous international names. Since, this is a partial list, you can only imagine how many more could be included.

All of the esoteric descriptions above regarding the changes in global investing do not take away from the basic premise - that the basics of investing are still there, still very relevant, and still can achieve great results – for the small investor, too.

Investing should not be intimidating at all.

Because…. Guess what! You are already invested, indirectly and directly.

You already are consuming and purchasing:

- Real estate
- Savings accounts, particularly foreign term deposits, subject to currency fluctuations
- A pension invested on your behalf
- Other appreciating asset acquisitions, e.g. your personal investment account(s)
- Acquiring education and skill sets. The greatest investment of all, YOU. Are you taking advantage of every opportunity to invest in you: gaining knowledge, increasing skills?

Just Some of The Every Day Stocks That Impact Our Lifestyles

Activity	Company	Symbol	Exchange
morning arrives, lights on	Ascendant	AGL.BH	BSX
special coffee or tea prepared	Starbucks	SBUX	NASDAQ
shower	Watlington Waterworks	WWW.BH	BSX
toothpaste, cleansing lotions	Proctor & Gamble	PG	NYSE
breakfast cereal or toast	Kellog Company	K	NYSE
makeup	Estee Lauder owner of MAC	EL	NYSE
briefcase, purse	Moet Hennessey Louis Vuitton	LVMH	OTC
vehicle	Honda Motors	HMC	NYSE
gas	EXXON	XOM	NYSE
text colleagues, check in at office	ONE Communications	ONE.BH	BSX
charge phone	APPLE	AAPL	NASDAQGS
winding down from work, Internet social media	Facebook	FB	NASDAQGS
park and walk	NIKE	NKE	NYSE
pick up daily newspaper	Bermuda Press Holdings	BPH.BH	BSX
car insurance	Argus Group Holdings	AGH.BH	BSX
ATM withdrawal	Bank of NT Butterfield	NTB.BH	BSX
doctor visit for allergies	BF&M	BFM.BH	BSX
pension review	Coralisle	a private company	
call to investment advisor	LOM Financial	LOM.BH	BSX
end of day, shopping for weekend	Bacardi	a private company	
rebuilding patio	CEMEX	CX	NYSE
airport departure	Bermuda Aviation Services	BAS.BH	BSX

B. Investment Basics -
Just a Few of Them

Some basic reasons to invest:

- liquidity,
- long-term appreciation greater than bank savings rates,
- for achieving goals and time frames,
- global diversification of assets,
- owning hard currency, Bermuda dollar being a soft currency, is not legal tender outside our reefs, thus, worth nothing to the rest of the world,
- outpace inflation, here in Bermuda, personal purchasing erosion never goes away in an island economy,
- building investor confidence,
- unlimited upside potential success, ownership and profit participation in businesses you already financially support as a consumer are all good reasons to broaden your investment outlook,
- there are downsides, too, such as no investing guarantees, volatility, systemic/ unsystematic risk, under performance against savings vehicles and losses in recessionary markets (if you sell at a low).

Nevertheless, we make a few additional points to contrast saving and investing.

Everyone is familiar with checking, savings, and term deposits (or certificates of deposit). You deposit an amount of money and based upon

- the interest rate controlled by your bank,
- the number of compounding periods, e.g. daily, monthly, quarterly,
- the time to maturity, including lock-up periods, and
- the amount saved,

What you receive after one year, two years, five years, etc. is based upon pure mathematics.

Cash in Fixed deposits are Linear.

What you see is what you get - no more, no less. We say that term deposit savings are linear, increasing at the same rate of interest each year - assuming of course, your interest rate is fixed for the term of the deposit.

Of course, you will notice immediately that your term deposits are not earning anywhere near 5%, this chart was created during higher interest rates! But hopefully, you get the picture!

There is no capital market appreciation or depreciation in fixed, term savings deposits as your monies are not invested therein, nor would you ordinarily be subject to investing volatility and market risk. However, there are other not so readily known risks.

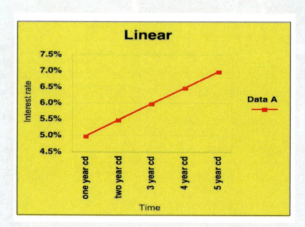

Several term(fixed) deposit factors that come into play:

Your monies are listed as part of the bank's balance sheet as a liability: meaning that cash, savings, term, fixed, accounts (yours) are not held in segregated accounts.

The responsibility to return your capital to you with interest rests upon your bank operating in a healthy financial environment.

If a bank's future is undetermined, your deposits may be subject to the demands of bank creditors.

Bermuda banks offer term deposits in other currencies, sometimes with more appealing interest rates. The value of that currency will fluctuate against the Bermuda dollar (pegged to the US dollar). You may profit or not, depending upon those values (compared against the foreign country currency price at inception) when your term deposit matures.

Deposit insurance offered in Bermuda is minimal. Bermuda banks mutually support a small Bermuda government-sponsored deposit insurance fund. The maximum balance insured is $25,000 per only one individual account, some comfort, but nowhere near enough if you have significant savings.

Bermuda islanders have always diversified by having monies in various currencies and financial institutions, both locally and abroad.

Investments in Capital Markets Fluctuate in Value

Security investments, on the other hand, are launched into capital markets, and are subject to many and varying investment market influences, trends, economic news, pressures of trade wars, company profit forecasts, and so on.

A beginning investor may purchase a security, a stock for instance, at one valuation only to see it fluctuate on a constant basis - in the short term, but over the longer term, the chosen stock of a stable, profitable company generally appreciates far more than having cash in term deposits.

Diversification is accomplished by investing in both savings accounts and capital markets - being sure, of course, that you and the family first set up an emergency fund with no restrictions - that can be accessed if needed.

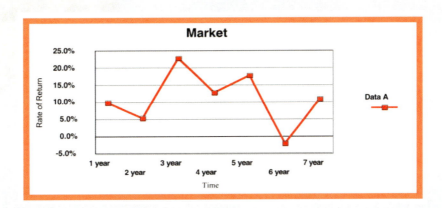

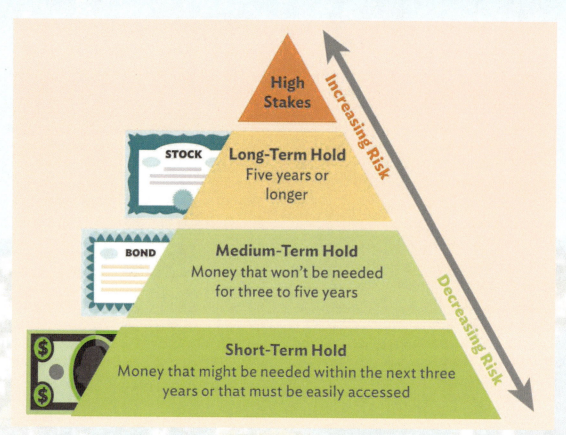

Building Wealth, a Beginner's Guide to Securing Your Financial Future US Federal Reserve of Dallas

Cash is still king.

You never want to have to sell investments in a down market, having regrets when the market recovers. This is the classic example of buying investments at a high value and selling at low values. Full access to liquid cash in uncertain times is always a prudent idea. It can be a financing problem for over-leveraged, and cash short global companies during the uncertain and recessionary conditions .

> Never invest your contingency cash in risky investments; keep it safe and accessible.

Basic Investment Asset Classes.

There are really only four asset classes:

- cash - near cash, money market accounts (not funds), etc. may not always keep pace with your purchasing power;

- stocks can appreciate exponentially in value, and lose the same in a down market, over the long-term stocks in successful companies will appreciate more than cash, and generally bonds;

- bonds and fixed income are a resource of safety (high-grade sovereign debt) and fixed interest income;

- commodities derived from natural resources and agriculture, are far more volatile than the above, but opportunities to capitalise are there.

There are many, many more securities originating from these four underlying classes: derivatives, hedge and mutual funds, futures, options, collateralised mortgage obligations, structured notes, real estate investment trusts, etc., all developed in different combinations.

Digital currency.
It has been stated that digital currency is another asset class, but the point is still debated as cryptocurrency is not yet readily embraced as a mainstream stable alternative currency. Generally, as well, most investors still need cash to purchase the initial digital currency and will also be evident when the investor sells digital cash for use in ordinary transactions. Digital currency markets are evolving to be completely separate from conventional fiat currency but have arrived at the transparency accountability era to be enforced by governmental agencies. The future of digital currency has yet to be fully developed; while it continues to grow in popularity; however, there is little regularity guidelines for the ordinary person as yet. Fiat (regular) currency is issued by governments, but not backed by a physical commodity such as gold; instead, the currency value is backed by reputation and stability of the government issuer.

Cash (near cash) can be held in many formats:
We just discussed holding cash in fixed/term deposits and savings accounts above.

Cash (and near cash) is used extensively in capital markets:

- in the Forex currency markets, where participants can buy, sell, exchange, and speculate on currencies in the largest financial markets in the world, more than $5 trillion in daily transactions. Forex in- vesting carries

substantial risk - as a form of derivatives trading;

- to purchase very short-term maturity sovereign debt securities (stand-alone individual securities, not funds), such as US Treasuries bills, a medium that the world over uses as liquidity, to stash cash between trades, during investment market volatility and when economic uncertainty is high, note the so-called slang term "flight to safety;"
- to fund daily trading activities for primary dealers, brokerage and institutional investment firms.
- for ultra-short-term overnight lending in repo markets, reverse repos and
- utilised by central banks to manage funds flow, interest rates and the like.

Warning of Changes in Money Market Mutual Fund Asset Allocations

Cash can also be held in money-market mutual funds invested in government securities, tax exempt municipal securities, and corporate debt securities. The small investors must be aware of the differences in investment asset allocation issued by fund managers.

Why? The investing world assumed (until the 2007-2008 US/global market crash) that money market funds were safe, in fact, some investors noted that they were guaranteed, which was never the case.

During that financial crises, there were breaking-the-buck events that occurred in some US (and global) money market mutual funds, where the ability to hold the NAV(net asset value) at $1.00 per failed due to liquidation runs on the funds - generating severe losses. Some money market mutual funds were forced to close their doors, including the first money market mutual fund established in 1971, The Reserve Primary Fund.

The result.

After the 2007-2008 financial crisis, the United States Securities and Exchange Commission amended regulations relative to the composition of money market mutual funds to make them more resilient to credit, interest and liquidity risks:

- Funds of government securities would endeavour to maintain the $1.00 net asset value. Such money market mutual funds are comprised solely of say, US federal government treasuries, called Government and Treasury money funds, more than 99% invested in same and fully collateralised.

- So-called prime institutional money market mutual funds (composed of various types of corporate debt securities, such as short-term unsecured commercial paper, less than nine months in maturity.) would now have a floating NAV, no longer maintaining a stable price value. The fund management would be allowed to assess liquidity fees and apply redemption gates - to stall future investor cash-out runs.

If you are purchasing money market funds, be very sure to read the entire prospectus as well as obtaining the most recent financial statements of the fund to ascertain that you are comfortable with the underlying asset allocations. Your financial representative should be able to assist you with this concern. If you are more conservative in nature, stick with US federal government treasury money market mutual funds.

Be careful of the terminology; do not confuse money market mutual funds with money market accounts.

Money market accounts are actually bank deposit accounts, not a collection of debt securities in Money Market Mutual Funds.

US Money market accounts are insured by FDIC in the United States.

Cross border caution. Money market mutual funds will generally, come under SPIC protection, but if you are an offshore investor with assets held in a nominee account, you may not have that protection.

Stocks. When and Where did stocks (shares) originate?

In the early modern 1700's period (after the so-called dark ages), the Dutch developed several financial instruments that helped lay the foundations of our modern financial system. The Dutch East India Company (VOC) became the first company in history to issue bonds and shares of stock to the general public, officially the first publicly-traded company to ever be actually listed on an official stock exchange. Source: Wikipedia: Public Company.

Stock ownership starts with the incorporation of company.

From tiny seedlings to giant oak trees, so it goes with the growth of a publicly traded companies. See our illustrative hypothetical Zina Pizzarina story below.

IPO
Initial Public Offering

Millions of tiny private businesses, often with only one owner, start in someone's garage, home office every day. Once such a business incorporates, grows exponentially successful over time, the limited group of private owners/shareholders will elect to "open the doors" to the general public raising much needed capital for expansion, innovation, and infrastructure.

The upshot, the celebration of a growing industry is to "take the business public" in an IPO - Initial Public Offering - where shares held by a few private shareholders are expanded in numbers and offered for sale

to the public. And from that initial public launch, companies continue to grow!

Most of us know that a stock (share) is a percentage ownership (equity) of a company. Internationally, think company stocks like Toyota or Apple; domestically, we know Argus, BF&M, NTB, Ascendant (Belco), etc.

Yes, I know it is Ascendant (and recently sold), but we'll always remember the Bermuda Electric Light Company. 200 hundred shares of Toyota (out of more than 1.5 billion shares in circulation) means you have a tiny, tiny equity position; 200 equity shares of Ascendant, while still small, represents a larger ownership percentage out of 21+ million shares outstanding.

Stock ownership gives every shareholder common stock equity and certain company rights.

Stocks present in two formats:

- common stock having unlimited upside growth potential, while
- preference shares trade in a narrow value band and act more like bonds.

Stocks are classified by category / sector / country / industry / capitalisation and market valuation, growth, value, defensive, income producing, large cap, mid cap, small cap, penny and more.

Company Life Cycle Line

Small cap companies $300M- 2 billion
Mid cap companies $2- 10 billion
Large cap companies $10 B + above

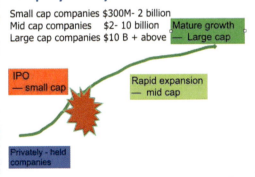

Stock Ownership
Equity Slice of the Pizza Pie

Companies issue stocks for varying reasons.

First and foremost.

Stock ownership (in a micro company start-up) is aligned in proportions of original capital contributed by the first shareholders who decide to incorporate an unincorporated sole proprietorship or partnership business. An unincorporated business is not a stand-alone legal entity, completely detached from an owner, meaning that personal assets and responsibilities for liabilities can be claimed against the unincorporated owners. Additionally, if an unincorporated business owner dies, the company has to be wound up or sold to a new owner, difficult when the original owner has passed. Incorporation offers liability coverage, protection from creditors, and continued existence detached from primary or other shareholders.

Second and more: Companies issue stock in public offerings to

- Enhance cash liquidity at certain times
- Reduce outstanding debt
- Launch new products
- Expand into new markets, and countries
- Manage and grow infrastructure for future demand

Investing in stocks in a massive, voluminous global market is heavily dependent on investors and the companies' issuing stock, both large and small, participation. The largest players (owners) are financial institutions, retirement pension plan portfolio managers, hedge funds, mutual funds, and activist investors according to Zacks Stock Research.

Additional help - See also Individual Stock Selection Criteria Checklist in STEP TEN references section below.

Example of a paper stock certificate issued on December 30, 1903 to Goldsmith, Wolf Inc. for 10 shares @ $100 per share. The Baltimore and Ohio Railroad Company was the first common carrier and the oldest operating railway in the United States (1828-1987).
It merged with the CSX Transportation network that is still in operation today.

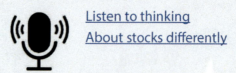

Listen to thinking
About stocks differently

https://tinyurl.com/yjg2oofe

Step Ten (B) - Your Personal Investment Review Bonds & Commodities

Bonds Are Debt, Not Equities

Bonds are debt, a much more sophisticated form of a loan legalised into a security that can be publicly traded.

Par value.

A bond, issued generally in $1,000 increments, is a promise at maturity to pay back the principal (and interest) as listed on the offering certificate (namely, 100% - in this case ($1,000 bond) regardless of the purchase price or trading prices thereafter. You, as a creditor, with your purchase, have loaned cash to a company, a state, a municipality, or a country in return for the interest consideration and repayment of principal.

Bond investors (you) have no ownership stake, no long-term appreciation, but generally, purchasing a high-grade credit rated bond of a country, say United States (or any G7 country: Canada, France, Germany, Italy, Japan, the United Kingdom), means safety and assurance that your principal invested will be returned to you.

Purchase price and non-correlation with par value

of a bond at issue may be exactly $1,000 (100%), but generally, is determined by market interest rates, fiscal strength and credit rating of the country or company issuing the bond. Note: Regardless of the purchase price, at bond maturity, you will receive the par value stated on the bond ($1,000) back - if, the country is considered a safe haven, high grade credit rating, and low investment risk.

A United States Treasury 30-year bond, or an Austrian government bond or an Argentinian government bond, regardless of the original issuance value or coupon interest rate listed, will command very different prices in secondary trading markets.

At February 2020, for instance, a US 30-year bond or the Austrian bond price (the premium) will be significantly higher than par value due to very high credit ratings and country fiscal strength. The Argentinian government bond on the other hand is selling at an enormous discount to the par value of 100% as there is significant doubt that any investor will receive their entire principal, if any, returned to them.

See Chart comparison between Austrian (high grade) and Argentinian bonds (almost junk) below.

Bond Coupon Rate

is the annual rate of interest to be paid, generally, in two semi-annual payments. The coupon rate does not change, but the yield on the bond will. See the example of a US 30-year Treasury bond below.

Bond Credit Ratings

Bonds are given credit ratings by rating agencies - actually, the issuer of the bond receives the rating. Great sovereign debt and fiscally sound companies will receive "investment grade" ratings from Triple AAA to Triple BBB, anything below that is considered higher risk downward to CCC to D - default. See chart below.

Bonds have An Inverse Relationship of Price to Yield

Bonds prices have an inverse relationship to capital market interest rates. When overall market interest rates climb, current bond prices decrease while yield increases. Conversely, when interest market rates decrease, bond prices climb, and existing bond yields drop.

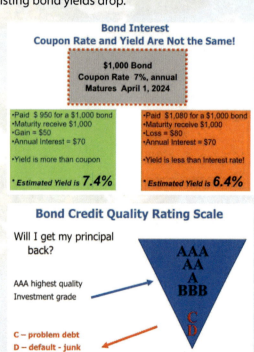

Bond Interest
Coupon Rate and Yield Are Not the Same!

$1,000 Bond
Coupon Rate 7%, annual
Matures April 1, 2024

•Paid $ 950 for a $1,000 bond •Maturity receive $1,000 •Gain = $50 •Annual Interest = $70 •Yield is more than coupon * **Estimated Yield is 7.4%**	•Paid $1,080 for a $1,000 bond •Maturity receive $1,000 •Loss = $80 •Annual Interest = $70 •Yield is less than Interest rate! * **Estimated Yield is 6.4%**

Bond Credit Quality Rating Scale

Will I get my principal back?

AAA highest quality
Investment grade

AAA
AA
A
BBB
C
D

C – problem debt
D – default - junk

In times of severe market stress as during the first and second quarter of 2020, safety and liquidity were the highest concerns. Triple AAA bond prices climbed astronomically in investor flight to safety while those below Triple BBB did not fare well, losing credit quality - some reclassified to CCC and D- junk.

Bond investors (you) never own any part of a company - you are just a creditor. You have no ownership stake, no long-term appreciation, but if you hold a high-grade bond to maturity, while not guaranteed, you will receive the principal back.

Ex above: United States 30-year bond certificate issued November 16, 1981 at 14% coupon interest rate and $1000 Face Value with a maturity date of November 15, 2011.

Imagine! this interest rate of 14% covered the total cost of the bond in 5.14 years using the Rule of 72 - a terrific investment during a time of high inflation in the US.

Today's environment - 30 year - bond interest rates are in the 2.5%-3% range with even lower yield!

Ah, the good old days....

Bonds have a definitive redemption date and may be called before maturity.

- Bonds may offer a convertible-to-stock feature, as well as a built-in put strategy. These are more complex strategies to be explored fully in The Bermuda Islander New Investment Primer - Book Two.

- High-grade bonds are considered less risky than stocks and are considered a portfolio diversification with a smoothing effect as bonds values, generally, are non-correlated with equity prices. When equities across the board tank, bond prices (high grade) generally, rise.

- High Credit Grade bonds (AAA) are considered a safety net in tumultuous market conditions, political uncertainty, defensive investing, and so on. Then, investors sell out of more risky assets and buy high grade (US Treasuries considered the safest) driving up the prices (way up at times) - the bond yields drop in this case, too. Interest rates have little influence in frothy investment markets; it becomes a flight to safety - where in the most basic sense, the investor knows that he/she will reduce risk and get all (or most) of his investment back.

- Low Credit Grade bonds (CCC) trend exactly the opposite. The more concern investors have about the ability of a country (or other entity) to repay the bond principal, the lower the asking price of the bond and the higher the yield.

Comparing High-Grade Bond versus Low-Grade Bond High-Yield pricing.

Let's look at the example of the price differences between a 100-year bond of the Austrian government and the Argentina government as trading in secondary bond markets.

The Austrian bond is selling at more than 50% above its issuance price est. 150%, while the Argentina bond could not command close to 100% at original issuance and is now selling (if anyone will buy it) at a discount of around 60% of original value.

By the way, the Argentina bond has a much higher interest rate, than the Austrian bond, but the price is significantly below par, and is worth far less.

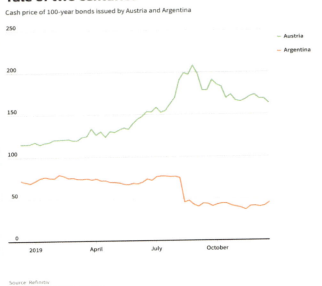

Tale of two centuries

Cash price of 100-year bonds issued by Austria and Argentina

Source Refinitiv
Ritvik Carvalho | REUTERS GRAPHICS

This chart is a perfect example of why investors flee to low risk, low interest rates, high grade bonds - for safety and the assurance that they will get their interest and principal back.

Argentina has defaulted on their government debt more than eight times in the last 100 years - not a good track record especially for beginning investors. And yet, investors will continue to purchase such bonds because of the lure of high interest rates.

See also Bond Characteristics Checklist in STEP 10 references section below.

Bermuda Government Bond Offerings (one example)

Our Bermuda government has issued numerous bonds listed in capital market exchanges (including the Bermuda Stock Exchange). We, the people resident in Bermuda, through our taxes are responsible to pay the interest on these bonds and at maturity (or before) return the original principal to the foreign investor creditors.

One Bermuda Government bond offering listed on the Bermuda Stock Exchange, and the Luxembourg SE is shown below. The listing notes that a US$665million long 10-year bond offering was oversubscribed - with the proceeds reducing higher bond interest offerings and a 200million guarantee to Butterfield Bank. Net debt was increased by USD189Million. http://cbonds.com/emissions/issue/268017

Government of Bermuda - 3.717% Senior Notes - Due 25 January 2027 - RegS

Listed Since: 2016/10/19.

Currency: BMD

CUSIP: G10367AD5.

ISIN: USG10367AD52

Offered in $200,000 increments

The net proceeds will be used by the Government of Bermuda ("the Government") to

i. fund the deficit for the current fiscal year (assumes 2016-2017),

ii. to repay US$200,000,000 of obligations under the credit facility with Bank of N.T. Butterfield & Son Limited and

iii. to pay the purchase price to holders of 5.603% Notes due 2020 and 4.138% Notes due 2023 that are validly tendered and accepted to be purchased by the Government pursuant to the terms of a partial cash tender offer being conducted by the Government concurrently herewith.

The notes will mature on January 25, 2027, unless earlier redeemed. The Government may redeem the notes, in whole or in part, at any time by paying the greater of the outstanding principal amount of the notes and a "makewhole" amount calculated by the Government. In addition, the Government may redeem the notes, in whole or in part, at any time on or after October 25, 2026 (three months prior to the maturity date of the notes) at a redemption price equal to 100% of the principal amount of notes to be redeemed, plus accrued and unpaid interest.

The notes have not been registered under the U.S. Securities Act of 1933, as amended (the "Securities Act"), or the securities laws of any other jurisdiction.

The notes will be offered only to qualified institutional buyers in the United States under Rule 144A of the Securities Act and to persons out-side

the United States under Regulation S of the Securities Act.

The Notes will also be listed on the Luxembourg Stock Exchange for trading on the Euro MTF Market.

Commodities.: Economic Soft and Hard Goods

Commodities (gold, silver, crops, metals, livestock, oil, property, land, etc.) available on futures market trading platforms are more complicated, more volatile, often hedged or leveraged, and not as easy to understand, manage and obtain.

Interestingly, commodities were routinely traded thousands of years (witness the gold present in ancient civilisations) before stock and bonds markets - a fact that makes sense when you consider the types of commodities and their essential functions in everyday life: energy, food, metals, and so on.

Commodities can be found supplied by companies, e.g. Exxon, DeBeers, and are also traded heavily with the use of futures and options contracts, ETFs, mutual funds (mining companies) and index funds. Commodities are usually considered a hedge against inflation, volatility, currency devaluation and the like. However, commodities themselves can be volatile: oil production down due to geographical conflicts and trade wars (currently in March 2020), agriculture products affected by natural calamities and unpredictable weather patterns and so on.

A beginning investor may wish to avoid these products until the individual is comfortable with investing concepts, including the many investment risks.

That, of course, does not translate when one has the ultimate goal of owning property, one's own home! A personal investment, to be sure, rather than a capital market choice, but very, very important to an individual and family's wellbeing.

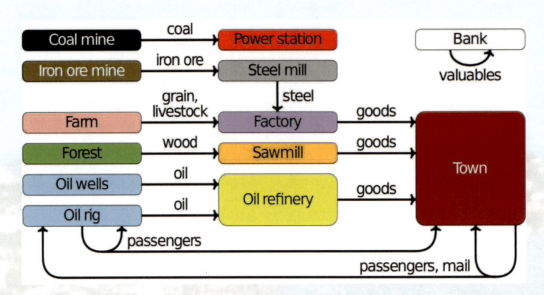

Simple Commodities Flowchart commons.wikimedia.org

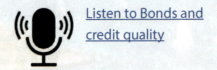

Listen to Bonds and
credit quality

https://tinyurl.com/yhjljjor

The Balance: Why Are Commodities More Volatile Than Other Assets? Andrew Hecht, Updated December 12, 2019

Commodities: Basics, Research, Metals, Energy, Grains, and Others

How Commodities Trading Affect Food Prices

All articles available at www.thebalance.com

Step Ten (C) - A look at a home-grown company Your personal investment review

C. Overview Introduction to the First Bermuda Investment Primer - Book Three

The Hypothetical Zina's Pizzarina™ (ZZEE) Bermuda Business Venture.

Let's focus on the most familiar basics – stocks in private and publicly traded companies, by tracking the raw beginnings of a start-up Bermuda business using our very own illustrative hypothetical Bermudian family - the Smiths and their matriarch -

A Bermuda Islander Start-up Business - in Their Home Kitchen

Why Invest?

And in what?

How does an investment arise?

Our Hypothetical Bermuda Island family story will illustrate how they home-grew a business creation, that ultimately was formalised legally as a private corporation with each family member owning a percentage of the stock issued.

Their ultimate long-term goal is to take their Bermuda company "public," offering shares for sale to all Bermuda Islanders - a chance to own a "Piece of De Rock!"

Their full story and Introduction to Book Three of the Bermuda Islander Fundamental Financial Planning Primer - The New Bermuda Investment Primer, published date estimates late summer 2022.

Read on.

We introduce the one and only famous Zinnia and her Pizzarina Business Plan. We will tie in her financial planning with textbook investments concepts because as we know from much experience, the more we can personalise difficult topics, the easier they become to understand.

As we progress through the New Bermuda Investing Primer Book Three, the family will be featured in further parallel articles, loaded with information that look at finances in Bermuda, our economy, investing for the future, money, credit, and relationships, risk management, retirement, estate planning and related items.

All these financial topics (that are integral to financial planning) are intertwined with, and influence everyone's lifestyle, whether we realise it or not.

It is in our very DNA to work, become successful, enjoy our lives, love our families, and build relationships with our community. You may not think so, but dear readers, it is ordained in the stars.

THE ORIGINAL IDEA TO START A BUSINESS.

The Illustrative Zina Pizzarina Business Venture. Meet the Smith Family.

Rose Zinnia (known mostly as Zina) and her husband, George, have three adult children: Sonny (George Jr.), Julie and Calvin – all employed in various segments of Bermuda's economy. Zinnia met George years ago when she came to Bermuda as a work permit employee in the Italian restaurant businesses.

The Smiths are an exuberant, energetic family who love to have a good time with friends, relatives, and grandchildren. Gatherings on holidays or just for fun are routine events at the family household. The large kitchen that Zinnia insisted on, when George and she built their home themselves, is constantly in motion. Everyone pitches in to produce traditional family favourites: mac n' cheese, cassava pie, peas n' rice, chorizo soup, bread & rice pudding, cheese biscuits, paw-paw montespan, papaya chutney, hot ginger / loquat jam, homemade pizza, you name it.

Zinnia and her family are fabulous cooks. So good, everyone says they should open a business. So, recently, and restless, the family quite dissatisfied with the rate of savings for retirement, heed the challenging advice provided in a recent Bermuda Back-to-Basics Financial Review plan to increase their income.

They have decided to start up a take-out / home-produced pizza business. They will put this plan into action, working at night after their day jobs!

They come up with a name. ZINA'S PIZZA- RINA™ (ZZEE).

Then, the five family members pool their cash to start up. And just like that, they are in business!

Five individuals working as partners;

- no corporate papers,
- no trademark,
- no advertising,
- no forward planning,
- nothing, except the minimum licenses required to prepare and market pizza and the determined drive to succeed!

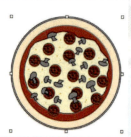

What is a Stock?

Your Equity piece of the pie
Unlimited life (almost)
Grants certain rights of ownership
- voting
- dividend
- management say
- proportionate share

Word spreads rapidly; popularity is immediate, gratifying, and quickly moves them toward financially stability. But, the whole family is working non-stop at day-jobs, night time with the home business. Exhaustion is setting in; a coherent, coordinated business plan going forward needs to be implemented.

The Business Momentum has to be managed.

The informal highlights of the Famous Zina's Pizzarina's business plan is put together by Zinnia, who is ambitious, shrewd, calculating and instinctively very good at marketing, visibility and selling products — any product.

She has had a serious long-term plan for years and has been waiting for this opportunity forever, it seems.

Now is the time for implementation.

The Zina Pizzarina Business Plan.

1. Start up a business by investing in herself and family first. George has not been in the best of health for a long time. She worries constantly about what will happen to her and the family if he passes prematurely. Their current savings are simply not going to carry them through their old age. They need another income source.

2. Make it profitable, so she can leave her day job.

3. Become completely legitimate by incorporating, then issuing company stock to all family members involved.

4. Borrow additional financing for the business, but paydown as soon as possible.

5. Grow the business to a self-sustaining, enviable production level.

6. When business viability reaches maximum saturation with just the family ownership,
    a. take it public or
    b. sell the business off — but she will not sell it to her children unless they obtain bank financing.

7. Celebrate all the way to the bank.

8. Use the profits along the way to set up retirement plans for herself and her children.

9. Learn about other companies, invest in them and develop an investment portfolio.

10. Fund the family's life insurance.

11. Pay off the family home mortgage, to protect all their assets for their grand-children.

12. Acquire other Bermuda assets to help her children with their future personal lifestyles.

13. Become a business mentor and guiding light for younger family members and other interested upwardly mobile employees.

14. Retire on her dividends, rents and savings. You know, the familiar Bermudian financial story.

D. What Is in Your Personal Investment Portfolio?

An Introductory Investment Review Encompasses the Following:

Overall, what are your investment goals, e.g. suggestions:

- Short-term, appreciation better than savings accounts
- Medium term, home ownership, university and other large goals
- Long term, retirement, eldercare

What type of investor do you think you are?

- Aggressive, moderate, conservative, completely out of capital market investing?
- What age category are you in?
- In what industry are you employed?
- Is your job and company position economically strong?

Do You Understand Risk, Particularly Capital Market Risks?

There is lots of risk in this world, oh Bermuda. Take your pick of examples:

Plane trips, automobile excursions, bathtubs, boats, politics, hurricanes, pandemics, electrical shorts, fear of losing a job, being embarrassed, relationships, public speaking, pandemics, and so on.

Revealing your true feelings even to a cherished friend is a risk some just will never allow themselves.

Trying to make it through the funnel at Crow Lane in one piece at the end of each workday is a risk to those who don't want to end up in a limestone and metal sandwich.

Crossing borders can be a very risky business, as many have discovered through lack of appropriate documentation, rights to residence, expired passports, unknown taxation hurdles, and the wrong kind of associates. See Pondstraddlers Crossing Borders Step Eighteen below.

What is the risk of working with relatives? You hire your brother-in-law's friend to sub-contract with you on a renovation project. Sometimes, he shows up, sometimes not. Adding insult to injury you've given him an advance for equipment. In the way of human nature, i.e. for every really responsible person there seems to be another individual just as irresponsible; he abdicates the job. You think that relationship will ever be the same? He has placed your business investment at risk and demolished your trust.

Investment risk is in a different category altogether. There are so many moving parts to investment risk, so many types of securities, currencies, markets, capital, shareholders, debt, custody, layering and leveraging, advisory, credit, stability, business, managerial, electronic, behavioural risk, emotional risk, and many more.

Yet, without fail, whenever investments are mentioned in the context of planning, advising, and determining investment choices, the emphasis is focused on risk.

This is as it should be. Investing is not an exact science.

Nothing is guaranteed, but is there anything truly guaranteed in life? The much difficult piece of the equation is to understand what investment risk means to each individual investor.

Over the years, the feedback from beginner (and even more savvy) small investors is that they don't really understand the whole risk equation, as spelled out in the following statement: "Every investor needs to determine what kinds of investment strategies are appropriate given their risk tolerance level."

An all too common refrain is "I've taken those risk profile tests, said one individual, and I still don't know what I'm supposed to be doing, or what I ended up with for investments. I hope they will be ok. "

Do we honestly think okay is ok? The risk tolerance mantra is repeated endlessly in the investment world, with almost parrot-like insistency. If you don't understand the real investment risk in a stable environment, your level of comfort certainly won't increase when capital markets become volatile.

So, the basic question will be explored. Should you be invested in capital markets? And how will you know the answer?

- Have you calculated the temporary probability (you hope) of what is the risk of loss (on paper) is to your overall finances? See below as we proceed.
- And can you recoup those losses?
- Do you have the employment time in the workforce and good earnings capacity to withstand investing long-term cycles? Generally, younger individuals fully employed can better withstand a market downturn than individuals retired living on a fixed income can. This is an important assessment, especially for beginner investors.
- Do you have an emergency fund and other savings to draw from, if your investments do hit a bad patch? You never want to be forced to sell out in a short downturn if ordinarily,

your investments are considered good risks in the longer-term.

- What securities are you currently invested in:
  o single security stocks, both local and global?
  o sovereign bonds, corporate, or high- yield bond debt?
  o currency trades? Hedge funds? Mutual funds?
  o Exchange traded funds, aka ETFs?

Single positions or a few stocks or bonds may represent a higher concentration of risk as these positions are not as diversified as a mutual fund. Exchange Traded-Funds ETFs can also be concentrated in one sector.

How Much Time Do You Have to Monitor Your Investments?

- How often do you review their performance?
- Do you perform your own research, or rely upon an internet investment guru?
- Are you a buy and hold, conservative investor?
- Are you a frequent trader, but, do you find yourself missing crucial trades?

Emotions and Investment Market Volatility

See the Dalbar Quantitative Analysis of Investor Behaviour December 2020 CHART below. from the 2021 QAIB Report

How much do your emotions play on seeing market volatility in your investment account? The recent coronavirus global severe disruption of global market rapid downturns after so many years of market up-trends can affect personal psyches. You may start to lose confidence in your investment choices, at some point capitulating and selling good investments at losses.

The chart below - Dalbar Quantitative Analysis of Investor Behaviour has tracked the investment returns of average investors in the United States versus the equity S&P 500 and Barclays Aggregate Bond Index for 30 years.

You can see the difference in the average investor's performance versus the comparable indexes where consistently the average investor has underperformed the market as much of this difference may be attributed to emotional decisions.

Much of this difference may be attributed to emotional decisions.

	Average Equity Fund Investor (%)	Average Fixed Income Fund Investor (%)	Average Asset Allocation Fund Investor (%)	S&P 500 (%)	Bloomberg-Barclays Aggregate Bond Index (%)	Inflation (%)
30 Year	6.24	0.45	2.62 →	10.70	5.86	2.25
20 Year	5.96	0.57	2.89	7.47	4.83	2.05
10 Year	10.23	0.73	4.90 →	13.88	3.84	1.77
5 Year	12.31	1.40	6.12	15.22	4.44	1.95
3 Year	10.37	1.61	4.48 →	14.18	5.34	1.86
12 Month	17.09	3.09	6.13	18.40	7.51	1.36

© 2021   Past performance is no quarantee of future results.   7

Emotions in Uncertainty are Hard to Control

The Fives States of (an Investment) Bubble is a telling picture of average investors' range of emotions in times of market volatility and uncertain, giving meaning again to the observation, "chasing performance, buying at the high valuation and selling at the low."

In 2008, Rodrigue achieved notability with his model of economic bubbles, charting four "phases of a bubble". While the "smart money" has purchased during the earlier "stealth phase", institutional investors begin to buy during "take off". Following media coverage, the general public begins to invest leading to steep rise in prices as "enthusiasm" and then "greed" kick in.

"Delusion" precedes the peak."

The chart was widely syndicated during the late-2000s financial crisis.
Jean-Paul Rodrigue (born July 20, 1967) is a Canadian scholar of transportation geography. He has a PhD in transport geography from the Université de Montréal (1994) and has been part of the Department of Global Studies and Geography[1] at Hofstra University in Hempstead, New York, since 1999

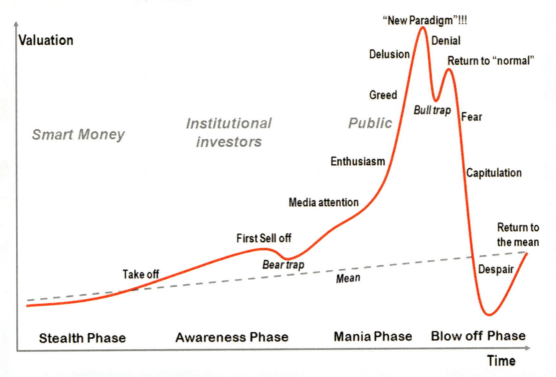

2008 Jean-Paul Rodrigue   permission at Wikimedia Commons

This is a classic average investor emotional reaction in following herd mentality.

Chasing the market rather than going back to reason you invested in the first place - to participate in the growth of good companies, with long track records of stability, profitability and consistent dividend distributions.

Your decision to invest boils down to How Much Risk You Are most comfortable Taking.

There is no right or wrong answer, but thinking about these questions may help you define the volatility tolerance and total rate of return that you are most comfortable accepting - compared to the risk-free rate of return, while helping you with waiting out extreme market volatility.

Which of these statements below do you think reflects your investment attitude?

- I can tolerate short term volatile markets.
- I find longer term uncertainty, especially from outside influences, very unsettling.
- In extreme markets, I have to hold down the panic button that just wants to end the stress, by selling out of all capital market positions.
- I feel that I have picked good investments, good companies, and can wait out market upheavals.
- Good companies just don't go out of business, suddenly, and for no reason.

Market Swings and Attitude/ Anxiety Examples.

Know how much you can afford to lose - on paper if the market drops precipitously and unexpectedly - not that it won't go up again and end up recovering nicely.

We saw this example again in 2020 as global markets recovered from the initial COVID pandemic reactional sell-off.

How do you feel emotionally when market valuations are all over the place in a downturn?

1. Plus/minus 5-10% swing. Market volatility seems to be an everyday thing, so I take the wait and see attitude;

2. Plus/minus 10-15% swing. Not happy, but ok - have other savings;

3. Plus/minus 15-20% swing. Will hurt quite a bit, on paper, but not enough to make me sell off;

4. Plus/minus 20-30% swing. Absolutely devastating, all my spare cash is in the market.

 # 4 - is NOT a good market strategy

Comparing Your Investment Returns to The Risk-free Rate.

What exactly does the risk-free rate of return mean? In business valuation the long-term yield on the US Treasury coupon bonds is generally accepted as the risk-free rate of return. Generally, the current risk-free yield on US 10-year Treasury is around 1.5%. Thus, depending upon your risk tolerance and remaining finances, anything above the risk-free rate will provide higher returns, but at a higher risk of loss of investment.

Risk Return reward chart by Martha Harris Myron.

Stocks return averages means that some years will be good, very good, or just plain awful. But, in general, an average stock return is around 7-9%, assuming you are invested for the longer-term. Simply using that as an illustrative benchmark, you can assume that some stocks will be below average and others far higher.

According to the chart here and investment history, very large, capitalised companies tend to have smaller returns on investments than small companies.

Why?

Because smaller new companies tend to be far more volatile, grow quickly, show higher returns, but can almost as quickly, 'die on the vine.' Conservative or emerging market bonds also have different degrees of risk and return.

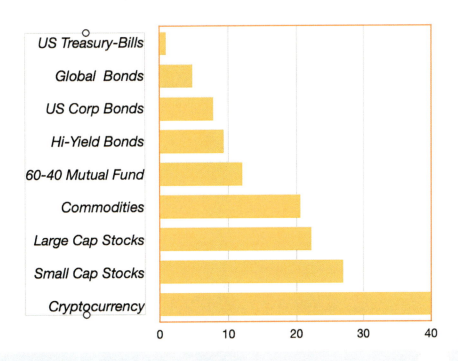

■ Illustrative Average Securities Risk Rating - Compared to Risk-Free

Mutual Fund Structures and Choices

What do you do if you want to invest, but don't have confidence in picking individual securities? Not a problem, consider purchasing a mutual fund. While another popular choice are exchange-traded funds (ETFs) they should not be an initial choice for a beginning investor as they are structured quite differently.

A beginning investor may feel more confident purchasing a fully diversified mutual fund, either actively managed or a passive index fund. There are many choices at local financial institutions. A balanced mutual fund option may be a good first choice.

Hedge funds are also not appropriate for beginning investors as hedge funds employ the use of loan leverage - that can exaggerate losses - as well, hedge funds may not actually own any of the underlying securities.

Currency trading, options, futures, foreign exchange/ digital currency trading, private equity, volatility indexes, short and margin positions are generally not recommended for beginner investors.

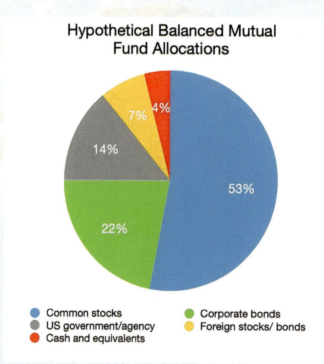

Hypothetical Balanced Mutual Fund Allocations

- 53% Common stocks
- 22% Corporate bonds
- 14% US government/agency
- 7% Foreign stocks/ bonds
- 4% Cash and equivalents

● Common stocks
● US government/agency
● Cash and equivalents
● Corporate bonds
● Foreign stocks/ bonds

E. Characteristics of a Mutual Fund.

If you, as a small investor are more comfortable with the broad asset allocation provided by mutual funds, THE ABOVE CHART is a simple example diagram of a typical balanced mutual fund asset allocation, ASSEMBLED by the author, for illustrative purposes only.

Keep in mind that each mutual fund is a separated incorporated entity with all of the requisites that come into a corporate structure, including a portfolio management team, a board of directors and an Investment Policy Prospectus that details the actual operation and guidelines of the management of the fund. This is an incredibly important document running to more than one hundred pages. Every investor purchasing any mutual fund should read this document from cover to cover.

Balanced mutual funds (actually a pool of investor monies) tend to be just that with relatively equal weightings between stocks and bonds. These funds appeal to the middle of the road investor who would like a decent return on cash invested, but not at the risk of extreme volatility.

Individuals closer to retirement, who have previously invested more aggressively will often opt for a scale down to the more comfortable balanced fund approach.

Average return on a 50%-50% balanced portfolio over the very long term is around 5%-8%%, but keep in mind that average - is not median - and will include high return years and loss return years.

References
& Resources

Investor.gov US Securities and Exchange Commission: Introduction to Investing; Financial Tools & Calculators, Protect Your Investments, and more. One of the absolute unbiased best informational investment websites!!

Starting up a business: The Pizza Delivery Business Plan

http://www.bplans.com/

Investing 101: http://finance.yahoo.com/

Real Investment Advice Survival Guides

See more on FinancialSamurai historical returns of different stock and bond portfolio weightings.

Learn to Earn: A Beginner's Guide to the Basics of Investing and Business by legendary Peter Lynch Published: January 25, 1996 Pages: 272 ISBN: 0684811634

One of the most famous investors of all time, Peter Lynch (still active at age 77) explains in a style accessible to anyone who is high-school age or older how to read a stock table in the daily newspaper (now on-line), how to understand a company annual report, etc.

He explains not only how to invest, but also how to think like an investor. This is an old book, but well worth your time.

The Lightbulb Press Guides and Booklets

Courtesy of NEFE National Endowment for Financial Education

Investing: How It Works

Determine Your Risk Tolerance

Investopedia: How to Achieve Optimal Asset Allocation By Shauna Carther Heyford, Updated Oct 9, 2019 An absolutely excellent article describing how asset allocation compositions based on risk, age, time factor and so on actually work

Kiplinger: The Psychology Behind Your Worst Investment Decisions by: Katherine Reynolds Lewis July 22, 2021

 Listen to your personal investment review

https://tinyurl.com/yh394ehz

The Investing Educator

Focused on improving your investment knowledge

Excellent website to learn about investments

FINANCIALSAMURAI.COM

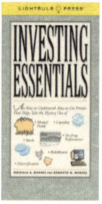

Investing Essentials
$6.95

Why Read Financial Samurai?
Financial Samurai delves deeper into investing, real estate, retirement planning, career strategies, and more, so we can all achieve financial independence sooner, rather than later.

Financial Samurai has been highlighted in major publications such as Forbes, The Wall Street Journal Online, The Consumerist, The Sydney Herald, The Chicago Tribune and The Los Angeles Times. interviews with AARP, Newstalk Radio 910AM (KKSF San Francisco) and Bloomberg.

INDIVIDUAL STOCK SELECTION CHECKLIST

CRITERIA	WHAT TO LOOK FOR
☐ Revenue	Has revenue steadily increased or decreased each year? Positive trend - increased business indicator
☐ Net Profit (Loss)	Revenue is great, but net profit after all expenses, taxes, and adjustments is far more important.
☐ EPS - Earnings per share	Amount of profit per share showing steady growth through each reporting quarter is a good sign
☐ Stock Sector Group Performance	Just how well did this company's stock perform against its peers in its sectors such as auto, media, utilities, finance institutions, etc.
☐ Debt-equity ratio	Company total liability by shareholder equity from reviewing balance sheet. Ideal ratio is less than .1 meaning more equity than debt carry.
☐ Size in market capitalisation	Market cap size means a lot. Very large cap companies with long organisation history are generally more stable, less volatile than
☐ Beta rating	This indicator is a measure of the stock's risk volatility where the market risk beta is 1(one). A stock with lower beta than 1 is less risky, but may also generate lower returns. The converse is true for high-beta stocks.
☐ Dividend yield	How many years consistent dividend payments?
☐ Dividend payout ratio	Percentage of annual profits paid out of retained earnings. 35%-55% considered acceptable with retention of remainder internally for future growth. Very high dividend payout percentages, while great for the stockholder are considered unsustainable
☐ Corporate governance rating	Very important. A well-managed responsible company implies stability and reliability.
☐ Analyst recommendations	Periodic in-depth reports from various investment analysts rating the stock and financial performances.
☐ Forward Guidance	Indicates future expectations for growth and profit, often disclosed in company outlook releases.
☐ Do you know the company or use its products?	If you are familiar with the company and use their products or services, do the research to ascertain its investable qualities!

You don't need a specific website for these answers, just type the name the stock and question into a SEARCH ENGINE for numerous informational websites.

INDIVIDUAL BOND SELECTION CHECKLIST

CRITERIA	WHAT TO LOOK FOR
☐ Entity Issuing Bond	Identify as country sovereign, municipality, state, agency, or company, etc.
☐ Size of entity issuer	Large country, multinational company, small state, small business. Size, stability, and financial success matter.
☐ Size of bond offering	Millions, billions. Amount of offering once placed in secondary bond market can mean difference between instant buy/sell, or significantly wait for securities that are thinly traded.
☐ Entity's other balance sheet debt	This discovery necessitates additional research. Multiple bond offerings, and debts on an entity's balance liability sheet are meaningful to balance sheet ratios.
☐ Entity (and underlying bond) credit rating	How is this entity rated? Risk, liquidity, and performance indicators that demonstrate a stable, successful, cash positive entity. Country ratings focus on sovereign credit worthiness, economic, financial and tax management, political risk influences, debt service ratio, compliance with international tax and fiscal policies.
☐ Original issuance, or secondary market	Bonds purchased at inception launch are at full maturity, then can trade on demand in secondary markets where, e.g. a ten-year note for sale or purchase may have only five years to maturity.
☐ Bond terms, prospectus (offering statement) disclosures	Review additional bond terms for agreement terms, underlying entity qualities, maturity dating, the issuer's other conditions, e.g. callable, or call protection provisions, puttable, convertible-to-stock, bond insurance, detailed plans to raise capital to repay bond holders, etc.
☐ Coupon interest rate and market price	Check the predetermined coupon interest rate, generally, payable in two tranches - semi-annually. Market price at time of research will provide the bond yield.
☐ Entity governance	Very important. A well-managed, responsible government/agency/entity implies stability, reliability, and positive earnings trends.
☐ How is bond repayment financed?	Companies from business and other earning profits. Countries from tax assessments, fees, and business investments. Municipalities and states from individual and business taxations and fees.
☐ Analyst recommendations	Periodic in-depth reports from various investment analysts rating the bond security and entity financial performances.
☐ Forward Guidance	Indicates entity future expectations for growth and profit, often disclosed in company outlook releases.
☐ Do you know the company or use its products?	If you are familiar with the company and use their products or services, do the research to ascertain its investable bond and/or stock qualities!

You don't need a specific website for these answers, just type the name of then bond and questions into a SEARCH ENGINE for numerous informational websites.

MUTUAL FUND CRITERIA CHECKLIST

Fund Name	legal registered name, not say generic "aggressive fund"
Security identifier ISIN	absolutely necessary for identification across the globe
Country of Origin and Registration	important information for international tax purposes
Prospectus provided	mutual funds are legal entities. The prospectus spells out all terms, conditions, investment policy, leverage, debt, directors, portfolio managers, tax implications, fees, purchase and redemption terms, auditor, custodian, risks of investing, and much more
Annual audited financial statement provided	financial statement presents the financial condition of the company and the composition of every asset acquired, held, sold. A must to understand what the fund's asset allocation is, and whether it represents your risk factors - or not.
Fund composition	basic asset allocation percentages: e.g. 40% stocks, 30% high grade corporate bonds, 15% real estate, 10% emerging market debt, 5% cash
Open or closed-end fund	quite a difference between: open-end and closed end funds where open end funds are offered for sale to the public by a mutual fund company. Closed-funds have a fixed number of shares, place for sale in an initial public offering (IPO) and trade on a securities exchange through a brokerage, among other characteristic differences.
Style category	declaration of style, say 90% US large cap stocks means portfolio manager legally must stick to that allocation, otherwise owning a group of mutual that the buyer thought were diversified may instead be almost the same.
Style drift	when the fund does not adhere to its investment policy statement - pumping up returns by picking high flying securities outside the asset allocation mandate
- individual securities	denotes kind of assets held in the fund but all individual security positions, stocks, bonds. etc.
- fund of underlying funds	a mutual fund holding mutual funds. these have more layered fees, but also represent huge diversification for the small investor
- proprietary or brand name	denotes funds sold by a financial institution under their own label, as compared to a mutual fund company with a global brand name, e.g. Blackrock, Vanguard
Number of security holdings	funds may hold as little as twenty positions, hundreds, or thousands (in a fund of funds)
Total shares outstanding	numbers of shares held by owners, generally this is stated as total shares and their total cumulative market value
Portfolio Turnover Rate, annually	amount of buying and selling of positions, high turnover rate often means higher fees and more volatility
Asset Allocation	Denotes the specific risk allocation with the composition of various securities, e.g. capital appreciation might be 80% stocks, 10% bonds, 10% cash.
Currency	self-explanatory, but know the same fund can be carried in different currencies, while some funds purchase foreign assets and convert with FX to home currency. currency values can be hedged to protect against FX market fluctuations
Fund Manager Tenure	Turnover in fund manager is not recommended for stable consistent return on investments. Fund management long tenure very often denotes a highly successful fund.
Performance	What is the NET rate of return AFTER FEES? How does it compare to its peers (say large cap stock funds) and to its index in the market?
Current year	Return On Investment - current year
Annualized Return since inception	Self-explanatory, see your MF fact sheet
Cumulative return since launch	Self-explanatory, see your MF fact sheet
Return calculated gross or net of fees	Return on investment shown at gross values without the deduction of all fees, can be misleading. Return on investment, net of fees is true indicator of performance.
-performance, gross or net of fees	These numbers are shown for many reasons, high fees can affect performance
-three years	Look for consistency in returns
-five years	You don't want a one hit wonder where it only had one good year, the rest poor
-ten years	return one year, and 9 years of losses - remember how average return math works!

Page 1

Fund Launch date	Important. Moneywise does not like young funds. Three years is the minimum time of operation for an investor to consider investing in. Why? Well, three years might be fabulous, but the next few years could be mediocre or worse. Historical performance is important.
Fund Size	Size, liquidity, cashing out, gates and bars - all very important. Small funds may not achieve cost efficiency or large runs on cashing out, and lower ability to withstand withdrawal runs.
Performance against benchmark	How does your fund choice compare to the performance of the benchmark it is rated against. This information is provided on MF fact sheets.
Fees	Fees add up, you want to know exactly what the fund (and underlying funds) is charging.
Front end load (commissions)	This is a mutual fund sales commission charged upfront at purchase - fee ranges anywhere from 1% to 5% of more of cost to purchase.
Back end loads (commissions)	This commission is deducted over time. The full cost of the fund is invested at purchase, and each year, say for five years, 1% is commission deduction.
Management fee, annual	The portfolio management fee charged by active mutual fund management, generally on a quarterly basis, e.g. annual/four
Custody fee, annual	The fee charged by the custodian who actually holds the mutual fund assets. US securities law dictates that the custodian must be independent of the mutual fund company. Think Madoff - who custodied in-house all assets for his clients, thereby escaping the scrutiny of securities' compliance.
Underlying fund fees, annual	Fees for auditors, board of directors, and the like who run, monitor the mutual fund company.
Trailers paid to salespersons	Self-explanatory. Some MF's pay trailers, others do not.
Redemption fees	Mutual fund company management have a right to charge redemption fees (as well as placing gates and bars on redeeming during volatile periods) under the stated mandate of the fund prospectus. Be sure you understand your rights to withdraw from the fund. Read the prospectus from beginning to end.
Risk statistics	Generally, stated alongside beta, standard deviation, and compared to other like-type funds.
Consistency of performance	How stable the performance over time, somewhat in line with peers, or volatility high - when fund is stated as conservative, for instance
Volatility	Fund fact sheet should list volatility - Beta - compared to the market.
Rebalancing frequency	How often does portfolio manager rebalance securities in line with the investment policy, e.g. conservative, balanced, etc.
Leverage used	Some funds employ leverage by borrowing against the security values to enhance performance. High leverage increases losses in a down market.
Top Ten Holdings	This is a very important component. Review these allocations and be sure to compare them against other mutual funds you own. You may find that many or all of the top ten securities are held in all your mutual funds. This is not diversification. Each mutual fund that you own, should demonstrate different securities and investment risk profiles.
1-	The top ten holdings are used in various ways:
2-	- see the percentages of each position relative to concentration of risk
3-	- compare to investment policy to ascertain any style drift
4-	- compare against other mutual funds - if the same or different holdings
5-	- positions are ranked by their market value to the rest of the fund
6-	- top ten can be equities, other funds, ETFs, bonds, etc.
7-	- heavily concentrated top ten holdings can outperform in a up-market
8-	but may show greater losses in a down-volatile capital market
9-	
10-	

Tracking Your Pension

11

SCOTT STALLARD PHOTOGRAPHY

Modern day classic Bermuda dinghy race. When the wind is too light, crew are tossed overboard to lighten the load, and increase speed

Step Eleven - Tracking Your Pension

It May Possibly be Your Largest Investment Asset

You have been courageous in attempting this "long" review of your finances. Now, you are more than halfway through. This is the hardest bit, though – thinking about investments and what they mean to your successful financial future.

Here is a little factoid.

Your Bermuda National Pension Plan (formal name Occupational Pensions Act 1998) is probably going to be your biggest asset, besides your home. Spectacularly, a 25 -year old in the Bermuda private business workforce today could see values at retirement even higher than the value of his/her home. Further, I can assure you that if you understand what is in your pension plan, you will feel more comfortable about other investments you might want to make on your own. This assumes that you make it a personal consistent goal to monitor your pension plan on a quarterly basis.

THIS is your money!

What is in your pension?

Generally, your pension investments are managed as mini-portfolios, that is a mixture of various kinds of stocks, bonds, money market funds, cash, an assortment of exchange-traded funds, real estate investment trust funds, and other smaller asset allocation percentages such as commodities, such as food, oil, precious metals are put together in a fund, then invested in capital markets.

All investments have risk, some are far more, risky than others. The degree of risk drives the percentage of the allocations to various single security positions within the portfolio.

The return on your investments over the long term is generally determined by the amount of risk you feel comfortable accepting and the performance of investments and the underlying companies.

Our Bermuda Government is heavily weighted down by debt, foreign dollars mostly loaned to us by foreigners - as we all know. Institutional investment firms buy debt such as Bermuda's for positions in their portfolios. Wouldn't it be ironic if our Bermuda pension investments held bond positions in our own government debt?

Your Bermuda National Pension Scheme (BNPS) is within your control.

Yes, the control is limited, but you can make a choice of investment allocations based upon a number of personal criterias, talk to a Bermuda pension administrator retirement specialist and keep track of this very important financial piece of your future!

See the following in STEP Twelve. Don't forget your BNPS is managed by qualified licensed investment portfolio professionals who are highly experienced in portfolio management with a global focus.

Why?

Because, generally, your Bermuda National Pension accumulations are invested in capital markets, unless you have chosen a guaranteed investment component (GIC), a choice that is managed by your pension provider. It, too, will be wholly or partially invested capital markets in conservative fixed income (bonds) of varying investment grades, including high-grade, but hopefully not high-yield bonds - a far riskier vehicle - obtainable in capital markets.

The guaranteed investment choice means that you have transferred the direct risk from capital market investments to your pension administrator to manage for you.

What's in Your Bermuda National Pension Scheme?

We will review a number of items:

What is it?

A Defined Contribution Plan under Bermuda Pension law, see the Act under www. bermudalaws.bm is a "defined contribution benefit" that is determined solely with reference to, and is provided by, accumulated contributions made by, or for the credit of a member together with the investment yield of such accumulated contributions and that is determined on an individual account basis; and

"Defined contribution pension plan" means a pension plan providing a defined contribution benefit;

Vesting — is immediate at employment with funds locked after one year.

Contributions during your employment life are made by you (currently at 5 per cent of your gross salary, monthly) and your employer matches 5% directly to your pension plan company administrator

who hires professional investment managers to invest your portfolio, based upon your investment choices, your risk profile and investment allocations that are suitable for you, e.g. for example, if you are conservative by nature, a conservative portfolio allocation is recommended.

During the life of your pension, a hardship premature withdrawal application may be made with Pension Commission approval, along with extenuating emergency circumstances during the COVID pandemic. At your planned retirement age (55-60-65), the market value of your account is what you see is what you get.

You will have a choice of:

- A 25 per cent withdrawal of your lump sum, converting the remainder to either an annuity (with various term choices) or a drawdown account where your remaining pension continues to be invested in capital markets with a drawdown calculated for each year, until account is depleted. The drawdown account allows you to capitalise on continued appreciation (depreciation) in capital markets.

- Converting to an annuity (with various term and payment choices). Your return is fixed for the life of the payments. An annuity is a contract that once signed, cannot be cancelled.

- Converting to a drawdown account in whole or in part. See above description.

- Smaller pension sums can be withdrawn in a lump sum, now increased to approximately $50,000 in total.

- An additional temporary amendment allows the employer (with consent of the employee) to reduce matching contributions to 2% instead of 5% each. This change will be effected through December 2021.

- An addition, that may not yet be in place is a change to a uniform fee structure for all pension providers along with detailed disclosure, according to the Bermuda Pension Commission.
- COVID pension legislation has authorised an additional individual $12,000 withdrawal due to the pandemic lockdown and further drawdowns.

Where is it?

Your plan is a legal contract established by your employer and administered with one of four Bermuda insurance firms offering pension plan products. Yours and your employer contributions are distributed by your employer to the pension administrator who then deposits your funds - converted into US dollars - into your pension investment account - to be managed by qualified portfolio managers

Your pension investments are not held in Bermuda custody, but rather at one of many large custodian clearing financial institutions hired by your pension administration, possibly US / UK / Canadian custodian banks. This separation of duties between administrator and portfolio manager is required by securities law.

You have a choice at retirement or other circumstances, such as moving to another employer to use one of the four pension administrators, or the investment products provided by four additional Bermuda investment firms. This assumes that you elect a drawdown account and elect to move to an Individual Retirement Account, rather than purchasing an annuity.

See List under reference section.

Where can I find resources to track my pension investments?

Each pension administrator and financial services firm should be providing quarterly or semi-annual statements listing names of the funds invested on your behalf, contributions, capital market appreciation - depreciation, and fees.

Generally, the current fund fact sheets should be visibly available on each pension provider's website. Research your pension provider, then download the fund fact sheets for review each month or quarter to track how your pension portfolio is performing.

If such is not easily obtainable, give your pension advisor a call.

Is my pension investment choice right for me?

Review STEP 10 above for starters, then, please keep in mind that the Coronavirus pandemic of 2020 Market affected volatility significantly, but generally temporarily, depressed some market valuations, as all recessions historically have done. However, your pension portfolio managers are professionals experienced in investing in good companies with consistent results. Eventually, just as in the 2008-2009 recession, capital markets did (and will again) rebound eventually to previous normal valuations or above.

So, you should take a deep breath, and not change your allocations impetuously. Otherwise, you will be selling out at a possibly large loss.

If you still have a significant time in the workforce, seriously consider just keeping your current portfolio allocations in place. Every single market downturn since 1929 has rebounded with further investment appreciation going forward.

Also take a look at the Individual Asset Allocation Suggested Guidelines for a pension in STEP Twelve for more guidance on your investment asset allocations by age, working stages and rate of return.

Take a look at the Capital Market Recovery Chart shown in Step 13 for verification of the above statement!

If you are close to retirement, now is the time to discuss your time horizon with your pension provider's financial advisors to plan a strategy - for a possible gradual change in your pension portfolio to more conservative investment approach.

Are all my contributions accounted for?

Hypothetical Bermuda National Pension Scheme Semi-Annual Statement

STATUS	Active	SOC INS NO	99999	DOB	1985
STRATEGY	Balanced fund			HIRE DATE	January 2005
				ENROLMENT DATE	January 2005
ANNUAL SALARY AT HIRE	$60,000			RETIREMENT DATES	55 - 60 - 65

	beginning balance JUL 01-2019	Contributions/ ER/EE 5% match	transfers / withdrawals	fees	investment gain / (loss)	closing balance Dec 31- 2019
EMPLOYER /EE contributions and investment gain/loss	128,000	6,000	0	0	6,968	140,968
MEMBER (EE) voluntary	9,000	none	0	0	572	11,565
TOTAL	$137,000	6000	0	0	7,540	$152,533

Hypothetical assumptions	1. Salary assumes no raises - just to keep math clear and computational = total of $90,000 plus gain on balanced fund for 15 years
	2. Very conservative average cumulative return on investment of a pension balanced fund for 2005 through year end 2019 = 4.5%
	3. Member contributed and additional 1-2% over 15 year time frame, plus investment gain
	4. Your pension statement will NOT look exactly the same. This is an illustration.

- Seems like the total is less than last year? This may be a direct impact from the most recent COVID-19 market crash, again that is predicted to be temporary.
- How is it doing - is my money growing?
- Will there be enough when I retire, is timeline important?
- Should I be aggressive or conservative?
- Should I be in these investments? I have a US green card / US passport.

Open your statement. What is there (or not) on your quarterly statement? Note: other firms may issue monthly, or semi-annually, so use the most current one instead.

Our hypothetical employee has kept a constant $60,000 for the past 15 years. Yes, this is not realistic, but we are keeping the math simple in order to explain the statement itself.

You should see the following: The opening balance (from last report) contributions, withdrawals, fees, investment gains or losses and closing balance – with a line for employer and employee 5 % of your salary, separated.

Your Contributions should total $128,000. This represents a total of $90,000 plus the capital market appreciation for the same fifteen years. The contribution column should reflect the current year con-ribution $3,000 X 2 = $6,000, representing 5% from you, 5% from your employer. There have been no transfers or withdrawals for hardship, and no fees are listed as that information may differ . The transfers, withdrawals and fees are subtracted from your total, then investment gains for the year are added - for the final total of $140, 968. If no fees disclosed, it is your responsibility to ascertain the total deducted fees from your pension advisor.

Notice that your extra voluntary contribution is stated separately. You may know that the reason is because voluntary contributions and appreciation are returned to you at retirement, not locked into a drawdown or annuity account.

First question - are all your contributions there? This is extremely important! You should check your pension - online every month, or at least quarterly, to be sure that all monies are distributed by your employer and deposited in your pension account.

Contributions Don't Match Your Pay Stubs

Lower than calculated contributions amounts that should have been deposited is pure cause for alarm. Contact your pension provider and the Bermuda Pension Commission. See List in references for con- tact information.

How do I pay for my pension management? What are the Fees?

Looking at the fee column, there may or may not be a column or amount for fee deduction, depending on the pension provider. If no fee is listed, contact your pension administrator for the information. Fees affect the final rate of return. You need to know what that fee is, and whether it is embedded in the other numbers, or not stated at all. You may also be able to locate the management fee if your pension uses mutual funds - by reviewing the mutual fund fact sheet.

However, the fact sheet will not generally state your pension administration fee, or other fees.

Generally, several fees are deducted from your pension account plan. The fees for pension administrator, the underlying mutual funds fees, if used, the portfolio manager fee, a custody fee may be charged separately, a foreign exchange fee to translate Bermuda dollars into US dollars, and finally, there may be upfront or backend sales commissions fees charged if certain mutual funds are used.

Consult with your pension administeator advisor for their fee policy.

Fees for portfolio management are incorporated in the mutual fund fee - appropriately disclosed on the mutual fund fact sheet as return - gross of fees, or net of all fees. If gross of fees is reported, you must subtract total fees charged to arrive at the important number - the Total Return Net of Fees number.

In early 2020, the Pension Commission announced mandated changes. Fees charged for pension administration and management by pension providers will adhere to a uniform fee structure, that will be displayed prominently in pension disclosures and investment brochure.

This was welcome news. No more trying to figure out the real net rate of return.

How are Management fees Impacting Performance?

Fees reduce your total return on pension, or any invested, assets, so reviewing those costs is prudent. The thing is, fees are not a big issue when investment market performances are solidly high, but one's attitude may change when market value of your investments decrease, even temporarily.

What is your pension's real net growth after fee deduction? We will explore the effect of fees on investment performance indepth in Step Thirteen

How am I doing – is my money growing? Review the investment gains or losses column on your pension statement. What you chose and how it should be performing should be listed below your pension account transaction details for the reporting period; it will be titled as your investment profile or similar language.

To review those pension investment values, use the closing balance of your statement compared to the opening balance. Your ending pension value, if the market is up, should increase by the amount of your additional contributions plus an appreciation number that is predicated on the asset allocation you chose.

Try an even better indicator – the closing balance of last year 2019, and if you really want to be on top of things, pull out your closing statements for 2018, 2017, 2016, 2015 – hoping you kept these records! If you have not, start now to keep track of them all – very important when you are ready to retire.

Is your pension steadily appreciating (above and beyond your total annual contributions) over the total time frame, even if there have been intermittent losses - on paper? Remember, there have been several temporary market downturns in the last 15 years, but markets and security valuations have recovered each time.

Doing well? Then you should continue on with that investment profile.

If not, then you need to find out, why not.

Lower performance, which is not necessarily a bad thing, and could be attributed to a number of factors, such as the severe market downturn during COVID-19, or your choice to change to a more conservative approach.

This is why it is so important to keep every single one of your pension statements. It may be difficult to track your contributions when market valuations drop, making your total pension number drop - unless you have those statements.

Too conservative?

An investment choice, if your workforce longevity is more than ten years from retirement. You, as younger careerist, need to allow time horizon and longevity in investment choices to do their job - appreciate. Don't take my word for it - there are millions of websites that discuss this very thought - just looking at the S&P 500 Index in a passive mutual fund performance over the last twenty years to see the significant appreciation, by simply leaving your money intact, allowing it to grow.

$10,000 invested, just once in the S&P 500 Index over the last ten years could have grown to $29,793 plus/minus as at April 30, 2020 - far more than a savings account, See chart - according to Vanguard.

Recurring contributions from a pension plan of say $800 per month ($9,600 per year) will have grown significantly more.

Hypothetical growth of $10,000
as of 04/30/2020

500 Index Fund Inv

Too aggressive?

an investment choice, particularly, if you are close to retirement – you may not have the workforce time, income, (or stamina) to make back temporary investment market losses. Further, the continued market volatility and risk always associated with aggressive security choices may begin to wear on your psyche, causing needless anxiety. Timing of selling market securities or moving to more conservative choice is critical. Need cash or want to lock in appreciation, the market may surprise with an abrupt downturn, leaving the contemplation retirement either on the back burner, or facing a smaller retirement fund.

Reacting Emotionally to Investment Volatility?

Succumbing to your investor emotions by moving your pension (and other) investment choices every time you are concerned there is market volatility, is not an issue if market is high, unless your reaction means that you are selling at a loss thereby perpetuating the common mantra of small investors – see in red below. It is important to think about investment allocations, especially during turbulent investment environments. If you are comfortable with the investment management of your pension, you should not change allocations.

Go back to STEP 10 and review Investment thinking and the DALBAR chart that demonstrates average investor returns versus the indexes. The Do-It-Yourself individual returns are significantly lower!

Sell at the Low, Buy at the High!

Never a Good Move! Note that re-allocating your pension portfolio is selling security positions!

Happy with Your Investment Choices?

Reviewing your investment choices. What are they? It depends upon which pension provider your employer uses and what your pension advisor recommended – based upon how you feel about investing.

Where are you in your career, and how should you consider allocating your pension portfolio? Are you aggressive, balanced, moderate, very conservative?

What do your investment choices mean in rates of return (appreciation) by reviewing the benchmark guidelines that portfolio managers base for their investment performances.

Read on to STEP TWELVE!

Cross border caution regarding Bermuda National Pension Scheme!

United States citizens, green card holders and dual citizens should not be in the Bermuda National Pension due to US tax and reporting complications. Having said that, if you meet these nationality criteria, you may have been placed in the National Pension anyway, if you were/are the spouse of a Bermudian.

Please consult with a US tax practitioner, preferably a US CPA fiduciary professional for assistance with the tax implications of this pension investment each year and withdrawal/distribution tax implications.

You may be able going forward, or if you are just starting within the Bermuda workforce, to elect to be invested in a United States qualified pension plan.

DO IT early on - waiting years to correct tax misinformation is never a good idea.

Two Bermudian firms offer United States qualified plans that also meet the Bermuda Pension Act guidelines:

- Freisenbruch Meyer (for more than 15 years) and
- since 2016, Argus Group Holdings.

Listen to
Tracking your
Bermuda Pension - Part 1

https://tinyurl.com/ygbh4qmz

References
& Resources

Bermuda Pension Administrators

Argus Group Holdings Limited - Pension Department

BF&M Insurance Company

Colonial Group Insurance International

Freisenbruch Meyer Group

The Bermuda National Pension Scheme (Occupational Act) 1998 Consolidated

The Bermuda National Pension Scheme (General Regulations) 1999

www.bermudalaws.bm › laws › Consolidated Laws

The Bermuda Pension Commission.

Pension Lifestage
Choices

12

SCOTT STALLARD PHOTOGRAPHY
Serene Safe Harbours

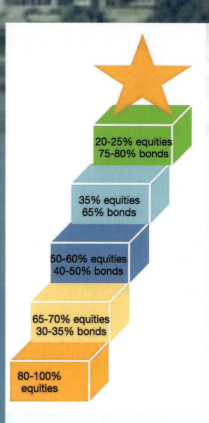

20-25% equities
75-80% bonds

35% equities
65% bonds

50-60% equities
40-50% bonds

65-70% equities
30-35% bonds

80-100% equities

INVESTMENT ALLOCATIONS PLANNING
STEPS TO RETIREMENT

YEARS to RETIREMENT

RETIREMENT pending! Revisit all allocations in your portfolio.

- 2-4 years of living expenses in cash or low risk, safe money market funds

- Mortgage must be paid off

- Line up part-time work

- Redo retirement calculator with new information

- Gradually reduce equity, and more risky exposures – you can always reinvest later when retirement financial picture is clear

- Assess capital market conditions at least a year before retiring - to be sure when you cash out that you are not selling at a low valuation point!

05-10 YEARS to go

Take position for preservation of capital (shorter-term bonds, money market funds, term deposits), along with building a cash cushion and focus on financial independence, e.g. pay down mortgage, but you still need a percentage in appreciating equities. This time may also be your very best earnings years, allowing significant additional savings/investments. You will need the extra capital as you may be in retirement a very long time, in some cases longer than your entire career.

10-20 YEARS to go

Time to lighten up a bit on more risky investments. Pay real attention to your work environment. You are now approaching your best earnings years, but also vulnerable to industry changes and repositioning. Upgrade skills. Initiate proactive healthy lifestyles. Capitalise on your expertise and experience.
Save, invest in appreciating assets.

20-30 YEARS to go

Your proportional investment position can carry more equities if you have been able to reduce long-term debt to manageable levels. These years are also heavy in family responsibilities, elder-care issues,

30-40 YEARS to go

You can be more heavily invested in equities. This is your opportunity to grow your career and accumulate a significant portion of your life savings. **Go for it.**

Step Twelve - Pension Lifestage Choices

Pension Monitoring, LifeStage Choices, Annuity/Drawdown & Calculators

We are now at the process to review the performance of a illustrative selected pension account:

A. Monitoring the performance of a balanced pension fund;

B. Discuss Lifestage differences in allocations and rates of return for conservative, balanced and aggressive portfolio relative to your age and years of employment in the workforce;

C. Comparing your investment drawdown account versus the annuity pension choice;

D. Walk-through a couple of different retirement calculators to project some possible estimated amounts to expect for retirement.

Everyone, who invests, yes, even in one's pension, wants their investment to be the one where values only go one way – upward.

In other words, investments guaranteed to succeed that never, ever show losses. We cannot help wishfully thinking that such an investment utopia is really true, but this is not how capital markets and investment valuations work.

Investments in capital markets are subject to many oscillating variances and trends: interest rates, consumer drift (away from once-in-demand products), global currency fluctuations, political instability, consumer inflation, employment statistics, governmental firm hands – or not, credibility of security valuations, and so on. These often- unexpected variables can increase or decrease volatility on a short-term basis to affect the value of investments.

Pension fund management, generally, is geared toward much longer timeline environments. And, statistically, long-term stable investments and their indexes, for example, tend to appreciate upwards, albeit with short-term losses (on paper) along the way.

Feedback received over the years on pension investment activity goes like this: "Why do I, as an ordinary person, have to cope with all of these crazy terms, try to pick what I think is best for me when investments are so hard to understand, and then have to watch their performance run up, go down, and vice versa? Sometimes, I feel so helpless with so little control."

Then, some individuals may go on to say that they would rather have all of their cash in savings accounts – cause at least they know where it is.

Why does anyone invest in capital markets and its underlying securities, of all types?

- Cash in term deposits just may not accomplish the savings goals for many people, heavily dependent on prevailing market interest rates, and no excess appreciation - yet investments have done the job.

- Appreciation opportunity is significantly better, sometimes astronomically so, rather than placing pension funds into cash accounts, then eroded by inflation. Additionally, the universe of securities is full of diverse choices, allowing a portfolio manager to pick hundreds, sometimes thousands of small security positions over a very broad range thereby minimising the risk of loss.

- Stretching your purchasing power and beating inflation is critical for a satisfactory lifestyle. Your money needs to earn something (interest, dividends, capital gains) to outpace inflation in Bermuda, particularly, with the incessant increase in cost of living – and what you actually receive for each dollar you spend.

- Broad diversification (otherwise known as asset allocation) to spread out the concentration of risk with currencies, country-specific securities, businesses, and industries. Remember that local Bermuda investors concentrated in domestic investments experienced higher losses in security values than those in more diversified global investments during the ill-fated SUBPRIME capital market downturn of 2007-2008.

Your pension asset allocation is an integral part of your entire portfolio strategy.

Yet so many of us do not make the time to give these long-term accumulations the attention and the respect that they deserve.

Perhaps, it is because the money is unreachable, untouchable until retirement that we tend to be a 'tiny bit' **indifferent**.

As employees get closer to the golden handshake, pension accumulations should be scrutinised very closely indeed. If you haven't been paying much attention, and your final lump sum appears to be significantly less than expected, emotional behaviour patterns can override logic.

Sometimes too much so, with magical thinking, "if I just increase my asset allocation to more aggressive for the next couple of years, I will have the amount that I am counting on for the big day."

It does not always work that way.

If you are lucky and the investment gods are with you, you may cash out a huge winner; but in the short term, you have a random chance that the market could stall out just around that happy lifestyle change. Even if the investment market is kind, you could have a lovely sum to retire on, only to realise that in a low interest rate environment, your annuitisation distribution formula for the rest of your life will be nowhere what you thought it would be.

An appropriate asset allocation for you is truly critical for a well-balanced portfolio.

Regrettably, we have had the truly tragic, recent COVID-19 Global Market Crash March 2020 where investors allocated strictly to stocks, and other more risky assets: emerging market and high-yield bonds, mortgage-backed REITS, ex-change-traded funds, any leveraged products, commercial paper liquidity problems, hedge fund issues, and many more, saw significant asset devaluations on paper and actual realised losses, if they cashed out.

Sovereign debt, particularly US Treasury issues performed at the top of the heap with unbelievably high price values and very, very unprecedented low yields.

And we cannot forget the tragic loss of lives due to this pandemic - the worst human and economic debacle of this century.

If you are completely turned off investment markets, your pension should be invested only in a cash product.

This means that you will have to save significantly more cash due to the low com- pounding interest rate environment – that seems to be staying for another significant period of time while economies begin to grow again - if experienced market pundit opinions and market watchers of the US Federal Reserve are to be believed.

And as I have stated before, investing in a GIC or like retirement product means that you have turned your pension monies over to the insurance pension administrator to manage for you. It also means that in order to return a decent interest rate, said pension administrator will have to invest in capital markets, generally high-grade bonds to achieve the savings rate. So, even though you personally are not in the market, your insurance company probably is. Please be sure to ask exactly what your GIC account contains in invested assets.

What is a pension fund generally comprised of?

Let's stick to a simple formula for now:

- stocks of large and small publicly traded companies (think Apple (APPL) and say Netflix (NFLX),
- bonds of sovereign governments, large and small corporations, etc. (think US Treasuries, UK gilts, Bank of America bonds, Deutsche Bank bonds),
- cash (generally, money market funds that can be converted into real cash).
- far smaller percentages may be invested in more aggressive securities (funds) such as real estate, commodities, hedge funds, and private equity. See balanced fund chart courtesy of About Money. http:// www. about.com/money/

A. Monitoring the performance of a balanced pension fund

How is my pension portfolio doing (and constructed)? It depends upon the pension administrator firm and its investment managers.

A balanced fund is very popular and is offered by Bermuda pension providers, along with conservative, capital growth, aggressive choices, etc.

Balanced fund risk is relative in that it is not too conservative, not too aggressive.

Composition of the balanced portfolio security holdings is focused generally around 50-60% stock and 40-50% bond positions.

See the pie chart example on PAGE 163

General Average Returns

Balanced mutual fund returns average 6.0%-7.5%. These numbers are based upon US mutual fund reports from various mutual fund firms, here displayed at beginning of STEP TWELVE are asset allocations from Vanguard.

Your pension returns may be more or less than the average, due to different fee structures and investment management style.

Conservative allocations will be lower than balanced.

Capital and aggressive portfolio allocations, generally, a higher concentration in equities will have a higher return (and a larger loss in a downturn) - remember: the higher the return, the greater the risk.

Your reward (rate of return) is based upon the amount of risk you are willing to accept.

More risk, more return.

- stock returns, generally, beat bonds
- bond returns beat cash
- cash is there for liquidity and expediency sake, possibly earning a little interest.

See average risk rating chart on page 165!

For a good idea on the differences in asset allocations, local balanced and other asset allocated mutual funds' fact sheets are provided by all eight investment firms in Bermuda. You can simply download the fact sheets and begin your comparisons.

However, it is worth noting that these average returns will now also reflect the coronavirus global capital market crises in March 2020 where returns overall were significantly lower until capital markets fully recovered - and they will if history lessons are true. Note, they have!

The Proper Asset Allocation Of Stocks & Bonds By Age
Conventional Model

Age	Stocks	Bonds
0 - 25	100%	0%
30	70%	30%
35	65%	35%
40	60%	40%
45	55%	45%
50	50%	50%
55	45%	55%
60	40%	60%
65	35%	65%
70	30%	70%
75+	25%	75%

Source: FinancialSamurai.com

B. Lifestage Changes in Pension and Personal Assets' Allocations

Your Quick Personal Financial Life Plan to Help with Your Asset Allocations

No matter your age, whether 22 or 62, develop a simple financial plan for yourself by using the following steps.

One – in monetary and emotional terms, define your goals, five, ten, fifteen, twenty, and further out if you can really stretch your imagination.

Two - consider your entire financial picture including items that could torpedo your financial success, such as helping your extended family with nursing home care, for instance. Remember that every financial decision you make, or ignore making, affects the rest of your finances. Maybe not now, but ultimately it will.

Three - Count your assets: what do you have, what have you saved, what do you owe, what do you think your earnings potential will be?

Four – assume only good debt, responsible debt, debt that will allow you to become financially independent. For good debt reading go to STEP Seven. Credit card debt may buy you what you want to make you feel good momentarily, but it will never make you rich.

Five – review your job and employee benefits. Look for opportunities to increase your skills and your compensation, then track your progress, year by year. Some sage advice: the moment you acquire a new job, you should be planning for the next one. Complacency cannot exist in this totally wired New World.

Six – start tracking what you are spending, then lay out a consistent savings plan for your outside cash, keeping in mind how much risk you want to take on to make this cash grow. Should you be invested in the same manner as your pension, it depends? You will need to make that determination after some serious investment research, but what an opportunity to learn!

Seven – review and learn to understand your pension asset allocations.

Eight - Review your individual investment outlook every five years or so as your career progresses, always with a view as you arrive closer to retirement to consider reallocating investments for capital preservation.

Individual Life Stage Asset Allocation Suggested Guidelines:

As individuals, each working age group has different needs, is in different life stages, has different conflicts and stresses getting along in this world.

Starting with young careerists (22-35), the demands of everyday life are diametrically devoted to the present. Middle to old age might as well be a remote wilderness when one is young. Young careerists can afford to be more aggressive with their portfolio; older workers who have scrimped and saved have to think about preserving their capital.

How should you allocate your pension dollars? Not sure? This is a hint to encourage you to learn all you can about investments. Try www.financial-samuai.com a real common sense approach to investing and finance and www.investpedia.com, a bit more sophisticated, but excellent teaching website for the beginning investor.

Why should you invest at all?

Why not just put your money in a Guaranteed Investment Certificate (GIC) choice?

Nothing wrong there if you are extremely conservative. But consider this. If you cannot access your pension for 40 years wouldn't you like to see it grow faster than the rate of inflation over that time frame? Cash and near cash for the most part will not outperform inflation and keep pace with your purchasing power.

Keep in mind also that even your GIC is invested in capital markets - completely managed by your pension administrator/ provider.

C. What Will Your Distribution Choice Be? Drawdown account vs annuity pension choice

What is an annuity?

One of the options upon retirement and the retrieval of your accumulated Bermuda National Pension invested capital is a plain vanilla annuity; that is a series of immediate payments for a set number of periods or for life, guaranteed by the annuity issuer, usually an insurance company.

How is it constructed?

From a layman's perspective (the math equation is more complicated), it is actually fairly simple, and it looks like this. We will use the example of a then 45- year old individual who started with the Bermuda National Pension plan in the year 2000, and will fully retire in 2020 with an estimated $100,000 pension benefit.

This number was arrived at as follows.

- Salary $50,000 per year.
- Her employer started with a 1% contribution and a 1% employee match that was raised each year until the contribution and the match hit 5% for both participants.

- Thereafter, pension contributions continued at 10% of salary every year.
- We also assume that the salary remained the same over the demonstrated time frame, even though it is a given fact that generally employees receive salary raises, possible bonuses, etc.
- There is some luck involved, as in this current pandemic environment, this individual still has full employment. Certainly, the numbers would be different in a job change, been made redundant, or had other contributing factors that lessened the total contributions over time.

Readers will note that while this pension is invested in the Balanced Asset Allocation, we have not counted that investment growth percentage over the time frame into the equation – just to keep the computation simple. Capital markets are uncertain. Different pension portfolio managers may achieve different results over the same time frame even with a similar asset allocation mandate.

The Next Step in Choosing the Pension Pay-out Option

We know what the total pension accumulation is and must now make a decision on how to receive this monthly pension.

Currently, there are two options to choose from.

- The first is the traditional annuity. Her total accumulation, possibly less a 25% lump sum cash pay-out will be converted to an annuity (monthly payments for a certain time frame) along with a current interest rate amount attached, and a fee charged from the preferred pension provider for guaranteeing/managing the payments for the time prescribed.

- The second is a drawdown account (pension portfolio remains fully invested in capital markets) where the percentage payment (generally around 4%, annually) is mathematically calculated based upon general mortality tables and other criteria.

While the choices may seem easy, in order to truly choose the right options for her retirement, however, it is extremely important to understand the individual's complete personal financial profile and how these monthly payments fit in the picture.

Illustration of a Generic example of an immediate annuity.

Our illustrative person may receive more of $100,000. 20 years monthly 2% interest

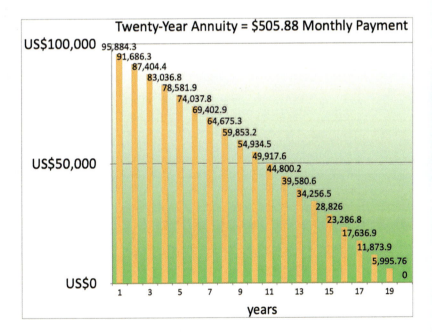

Your Pension May Represent a Quarter of Your Total Financial Retirement

Will it become one quarter of the retirement quadrant along with a home owned debt-free, a steady income, and other capital asset appreciation to control inflation for the future.

- Are the recurring payments needed immediately, or can they be deferred?

- What time frame should be chosen for annuity payments: five years, ten years, 20 years, a monthly payment for the rest of natural life? What will the differences mean for this individual's annual budget?

- Should the entire sum convert to an annuity, withdraw 25% lump sum, or be left in the investment portfolio (a drawdown account) where it will continue to appreciate, or possibly depreciate at times?

- Taking the annuity solution passes the risk of continued payment to the insurance company.

- Leaving the investment component intact under your asset allocation choice generates a continued exposure to capital market risk.

- How does insurance annuity issuer who now has your full pension accumulation invest the money to fund the annuity?

- What kind of fees do they charge?

- Are the annuity interest rates locked in, or are they adjusted according to market interest rate fluctuations?

- The annuity is guaranteed to arrive, month after month, year after year, but who will guarantee the financial strength of the annuity issuer if the company has financial problems?

- What happens if our person lives longer than the total accumulation?

- Who is working with our person to construct the drawdown investment product and what is their experience and background?

It is important to also note that under the amendments to the Bermuda Investment Act that every pension representative in the pension provider product chain has a fiduciary responsibility to be sure that the recommendations for you are appropriate, and suitable for your personal financial profile.

What Are the Differences in Our Illustrative Pension Pay- out Choices?

The Annuity Set-up Factors

- the accumulation amount
- current market interest rate, can be high or low
- term choices: 5yr, 10yr, 20yr, for life
- administration fees
- foreign currency purchase tax conversion from USD back to Bermuda dollars, appears to be exempt for government, but there may be a fee by the local pension / bank administrator
- an annuity is a legal contract – once signed, there is no reversal

The Drawdown Set-up Factors

- the accumulation amount
- investment asset allocation choice
- investment account
- drawdown percentage per year, may generally be around 4%, annually, divided into twelve monthly payments
- investment values subject to capital market activity
- may be converted to an annuity later on

Which Pension Distribution Choice Is Better?

There is no correct answer. The final choice will depend upon various investment and personal criteria. In other words, assessing this soon-to-be retiree's complete financial picture.

*Current interest rate applied to the initial annuity conversion value – if very low, by the time administrative fees, etc. are calculated, the additional interest income generated will be depleted by the fees. An annuity is generally not recommended in this circumstance, but other factors such as the immediate need for a distribution, or fear of losing value in capital markets may override low interest rate consideration.

*Capital markets are subject to risk and volatility. The pension may continue to appreciate in value, even with the annual drawdowns, or lose such value that it never recovers.

*Serious thought and comparison between the two choices must be taken. The soon-to- be retiree should evaluate the choices based upon what-if situations and her remaining financial assets and liabilities; it is recommended to work with your pension administrator who can calculate your pen- sion payouts based upon your accumulated pension value, a more accurate solution.

- Another Explanation of Annuity Structures: Financial Consumer Agency of Canada
- Mycalculators.com
- Retirement Withdrawal Calculator

D. Walking-through a couple of What-If retirement calculators to project possible estimated amounts to expect for retirement.

The BallPark Estimator. The Ballpark E$timate is an easy-to-use, interactive tool that helps you quickly identify approximately how much you need to save to fund a comfortable retirement. The Ballpark E$timate takes complicated issues like projected Social Security benefits and earnings assumptions on savings and turns them into language and mathematics that are easy to understand. This is a US-based web- site, you can ignore the tax inputs at zero. https://www.choosetosave.org/ballpark/

Financial Independence Retire Early. FIRE- Calc®: How long will your money last? The big question:

"With what you have today, and what it costs you to live, can you retire and maintain the same life-style?

Ball park estimator -ASEC

RISE Retirement Income Security Evaluation Score™ by non profit Alliance for Life-time Income - take the retirement readiness test. https:// www.protectedincome.org/retirement-tools/rise-calculator/

See also STEP EIGHTEEN Pondstraddler International financial planning for US citizens working and residing in Bermuda, Bermudians with dual citizenship with the United States, green card holders and foreign nationals who are US residents for income purposes. Conversion to purchasing foreign annuities or attempting to roll foreign pensions into US pension / annuity type plans (won't happen) are decisions that may be saturated with current and future United States tax implications and complications, as well as other countries.

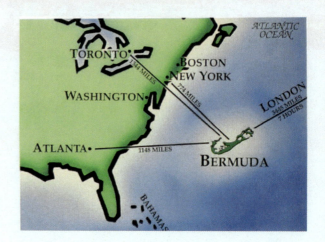

In this viral US Internal Revenue Service, and US Treasury global compliance environment, every financial strategy has significant tax outcomes.

Do not even consider making this decision without consulting US tax practitioners / financial planners with international investment, tax and pension experience. This is a minefield that could have you caught in compliance reporting loops, with significant tax liabilities long after your local pension decision was implemented.

Who can you seek recourse from then?

Multinationals with burdensome tax compliance with other countries need to feel comfortable with the level of sales representative expertise in tax, investments, and pension portability challenges.

Exhibit Examples of annuity payments, drawdown calculations and retirement calculator models are hypothetical - for illustrative purposes only. These hypothetical illustrations cannot, nor should not, be used for your own personal financial retirement situation.

Listen to
Part 1 - Pension
Life Stages

https://tinyurl.com/yztg66mh

Listen to Part 2 -
Pension Annuity -
Drawdown Comparison

https://tinyurl.com/ye4be76q

References
& Resources

Investopedia

360 Degrees of Financial Literacy. American Institute of CPAs

My calculators.com Home of Many Financial Calculators

Financial Samurai. The Proper Asset Allocation of Stocks And Bonds By Age

Don't panic over your pension fund Martha Myron, Moneywise April 11, 2020 The Royal Gazette

Market Recovery
Do-It-Yourself
Rule Of 72

13

GIBBS HILL LIGHTHOUSE.

Since 1846, casting a beacon
of safety into safe harbours
for sailors offshore Bermuda
in treacherous, stormy seas

DALBAR QAIB (Quantitative Analysis of Investor Behaviour) 2013 & 2018

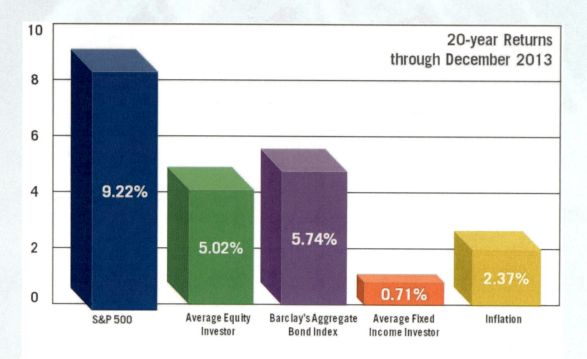

20-year Returns through December 2013

- S&P 500: 9.22%
- Average Equity Investor: 5.02%
- Barclay's Aggregate Bond Index: 5.74%
- Average Fixed Income Investor: 0.71%
- Inflation: 2.37%

ANNUALIZED RETURNS

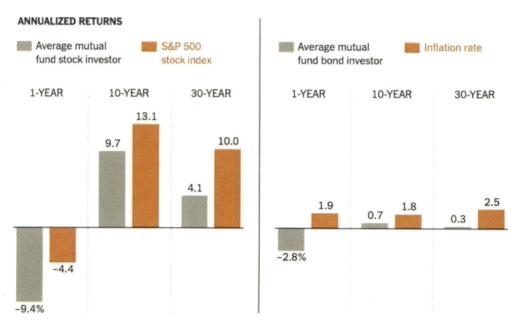

Average mutual fund stock investor | S&P 500 stock index

	1-YEAR	10-YEAR	30-YEAR
Average mutual fund stock investor	−9.4%	9.7	4.1
S&P 500 stock index	−4.4	13.1	10.0

Average mutual fund bond investor | Inflation rate

	1-YEAR	10-YEAR	30-YEAR
Average mutual fund bond investor	−2.8%	0.7	0.3
Inflation rate	1.9	1.8	2.5

By The New York Times | Source: Dalbar 2018

Step Thirteen - Rule of 72, Market Recovery, Do-It-Yourself Investing

Your review plan is almost finished - don't give up now.

What average returns should you be looking for in long-term appreciation of your pension and your personal investing?

The charts above demonstrate on a statistical basis the average return for stocks, bonds over thirty years through year end 2018. Source courtesy of Dalbar Inc.'s QAIB report (Quantitative Analysis of Investor Behaviour) and the New York Times. We see that the S&P index (made up of the weighted values of the 500 largest publicly traded US companies by market capitalisation) returned 9.22%, the Barclays Aggregate Bond Index (representing most US traded investment grade bonds) returned 5.74%.

These indexes are not adjusted for fees.

Yes, there is another set of numbers in that chart. We will discuss them later in the article. For now, take a guess what they represent.

Thus, using simple math assumptions for a pension balanced fund of 60% stocks and 40% bonds, the average return - without taking into consideration any fees for management, administration, sales commissions, custody fees, etc. - would be somewhere around an estimated 7%.

Using ordinary assumptions, then, a more conservative portfolio (more bonds than stocks) would generally have a lower return than the balanced fund, and a more aggressive fund weighted toward stocks will be closer the stock index. Keep in mind, that these are average returns - meaning that on the proverbial bell curve, some securities under-performed while others will reach higher than the average.

Fee-adjusted rates of return.

Now comes the more difficult section because different pension firms, different portfolio managers may calculate fees in different ways.

What does this mean to you? Fees affect the growth of your pension portfolio (or any portfolio) over time. You want your pension portfolio to have competitive fees with the real fee-adjusted rate of return reported on your statement so that you know where you stand.

Mutual fund fact sheets, generally, disclose all fees as well as reporting the Total rate of return - NET of fees.

I was unable to determine – based upon website information currently available – what the total fees are charged by the local Bermuda pension administrators / managers by reviewing their websites. Fees may be disclosed to you individually, as a holder of a pension account - so, it is up to you when meeting with your pension advisor to obtain fee clarity.

Calculating an illustrative fee-adjusted rate of return. Let's assume that the total fees are estimated 2.%. Taking our assumed average rate of return for the illustrative balanced fund of 7. % minus all fees of 2. % = estimated real adjusted rate of return (RoR) of 5%.

How Am I Doing - Investment Wise?

A very simple calculator to track how your investments are accumulating is The Rule of 72. Take an illustrative accumulated pension example: Individual worked for ten years and accumulated 70,000 in a pension. Divide 72 by RoR 5% = 14.4. The answer means that the accumulation of $70,000 MAY double in 14.4 years without any additional pension contributions at all.

But, this is a big point, remember that investment returns will fluctuate. Your pension investments will not compound on a straight-line basis, because they are invested in capital market assets. However, over the longer term, the average return can possibly be around 5%-7% for a balanced portfolio.

The Rule of 72

The Rule of 72 works fairly well for the range from six to 10. Outside that range, there are additional calculations needed; it can be more efficient to use an online calculator.

Rate of Return (%)	Divide into	Approximate Number of Years to Double Investment
6	72	12 years
7	72	10.3 years
8	72	9 years
9	72	8 years
10	72	7.2 years

US MARKET CRASH DATES	RECOVERY TIMES
1987	456 trading days
1997	46 trading days
2000	1015 trading days, including the tech bubble blow up and the terrible tragedy of September 911
2008	230 trading days
2011	116 trading days
2015	30 trading days

Critics will say this is not realistic, but the long-term appreciation bears this out. Imagine adding in additional contributions as well. Most important, this number also assumes that you do not move your pension in and out of various allocations, selling at the low values, and taking losses.

See complete article. "Thirty years of stock market crashes – and the signs they were coming," by Kyle Caldwell, The Telegraph, October 17, 2015. http://goo.gl/6UrslT

If Time is On Your Side, Think Long-Term

Do yourself a favour.

Think long-term, always with the exception of the close-to-retirement individuals.

Be willing to be a little more investment aggressive when you are younger, then, tapering off as you age, accumulate other savings and investments, your first home, an individual investment account.

Why? Because time is on your side.

Do not focus on short term investing results. Further, there have been numerous market volatility episodes as well as capital market crashes. Each and every time, markets have recovered from loss positions, and moved forward into positive territory.

The above chart that records only the major disruptions since 1987 demonstrate that truism. Even the great depression of 1929-1933 in the United States saw the US securities market recapture the loss valuations.

It is reassuring to understand that even though the entire global economy is in severe disruption due to COVID-19, eventually, capital markets will again (and have) returned to normal.

Postscript - and they did recover quickly!

Should You Be A Do-It-Yourself Investor?

Can you translate understanding your pension investments to taking tentative steps as an individual investor? Consider do-it-yourself investing, or taking the passive investor approach with high quality, low cost mutual or ETF funds?

We, along with millions of individuals the world over, have been depleted emotionally, physically, mentally and financially during this tragic, catastrophic COVID-19 pandemic. Thousands of families have lost loved ones forever, had their work and home life disrupted, and have seen their financial security well into the future almost destroyed.

The social-distancing quarantine has been exhausting, as we have coped with the most daunting event of our lifetimes. Most of us would rather not, for a while at least, reflect on our roles or goals moving forward.

But we have to move forward.

Life will not stand still. We are all one-step closer to retirement, whether that day is next year, five, ten, or thirty years away.

We have much to achieve in the interim.

We, as people, are intuitive, incredibly smart survivalist-attitude individuals with highly developed reasoning processes.

We can, and must vote for survival back to normalcy, to begin to plan ahead again:

- to continue to take charge of our finances;
- to keep up disciplined savings and maintain less exuberant spending:
- to become more financially savvy with our goals to financial success

Pluses. Should you think about just buying individual stocks or bonds, since you have more control, and can possibly save fees? The process requires much investment educational reading, opening an individual investing account here in Bermuda or online, keeping your emotions in check when markets are crazy and monitoring of your security positions.

Minuses. Don't feel you can be a successful DIY individual investor? There are valid reasons: Individuals cannot afford to buy sufficient securities to diversify investment risk; they react emotionally, making poor decisions during market downturns; having barely enough energy to focus on family, working and living, DIY just becomes another life stressor.

Investment Mistakes.

You will make them.

According various industry sources, the biggest errors that investors make are these:

- too aggressive a portfolio for your comfort level, especially at a close to retirement age
- young investors who are far too conservative based upon their own career longevity
- the worst of all, reactionary pension (and individual) portfolio moves in and out of aggressive to conservative allocations when markets crash, thereby locking in losses, reducing your portfolio capital, sometimes never to fully recover.

And, that is what the second set of numbers represent on the Dalbar charts, listed above, The average equity (stocks) and fixed income (bonds) by D I Y investors do not come close to index and inflation returns - one of the largest influencing factors is investor behaviour.

You guessed it!

Investors sell out at market low values and pile into investments when markets are at high prices.

Even, if after understanding what investing is about, you decide not to participate, you will have enhanced your investment knowledge and have a better comfort level relative to your personal finances, along with your future pension investment management.

But, taking on this task means that you have to commit to understanding investments and what choices are right for you!

How should you start DIY?

- Basically, with one – to a few stocks of companies that are familiar
- Invest small amounts of cash
- Use the twelve research principles below and other research sites when researching a stock and the underlying company
- No investing until you have your emergency cash cushion fully funded
- Be comfortable and prepared to possibly lose the money you invest

The securities themselves – review the company balance sheet – you can quickly find this information in Yahoo Finance by typing the stock name or ticker into Google.

The company balance sheet is an integral part of the company financial statements.

A. lots of free cash

B. low debt ratio

C. consistent dividends for at least ten years

D. low dividend pay-out ratio

E. decent profits year on year

F. company revenue increasing along with market share

G. little or no company share buybacks

H. more company insider buys than sells

I. stable-type industry, products or services that everyone needs on a consistent basis

J. monitor the industry for changes

K. set a profit margin at which to sell the stock

L. be very careful of young companies operating on venture capital and loans with no consistent revenue and profits

Refer to the Stock Criteria Selection Checklist featured in Step 10 for further help.

Your discovery process needs to be two-fold:

- learning about securities and
- understanding how they work.

So, your work is cut out for you, but you will find it illuminating and so very interesting.

Beginner investment websites for three of our large North Atlantic neighbours that are easy to digest are listed below in References and are good places to start.

Bermuda is a cosmopolitan finance jurisdiction. Bermuda residents themselves often invest overseas, while work permit holders from other countries can utilise this starter information as well.

Once familiar with basic investment concepts, take your curiosity further to explore websites that are strictly fact-based and educational, rather than financial sites that ultimately want sell you something.

Research websites online trading services also listed below also allow you to practice simulated trading, giving you an almost real experience of how capital markets work.

But be forewarned, of the following:

Watch your financial emotions and reactive investing decisions.

You should also know that overall, individual investors have not always fared well – investing on their own behalf. We individuals tend to react emotionally when dealing with issues of money. The educational term is researched under Behavioural Finance (and see the Dalbar Quantitative Analysis of Investor Behaviour) – the Internet is loaded with sites addressing this very topic that boils down to the following:

The emotional herd mentality.

Buying securities at the high valuation and selling at the low, thereby setting yourself up for realised losses.

I highly recommend that you, as a beginning DIY investor start the process with these basic thoughts:

Understand that you may develop an emotional attachment to stocks, bonds, etc., but remember stocks are not people, nor should you love them because they will not love you back.

Develop your own risk assessment and a trading plan to adhere to, so that you do not react emotionally to severe market volatility. The COVID-19 market crash is the absolute emotional test, possibly of this century. Ask yourself, would you be more than tempted, maybe even frantic, to sell everything when seeing a more than 30% drop in value of your investments **– on paper.**

Know this as well.

Capital markets today are not the markets of old. Your small investor trade choices will be up against the rapid activity (micro-seconds) of thousands of remote computer-trading models, short-sellers, high-frequency traders, robo-advisory service firms, and extraordinarily nimble massive global financial institutions with immediate access to investment information that you won't have, along with the trading power to overwhelm the system.

CAVEAT: Bermuda residents may have difficulty opening trading accounts in other jurisdictions due to FATCA, AML/KYC and other international and domestic tax/anti-money laundering compliance.

Know What market conditions are on a current basis always understanding that those conditions can change without notice.

For instance, Capital market security valuations during the COVID-19, on average, fell incrementally well below the euphoric conditions for the prior several years and below the 2008 global market crashes.

There are more than 15 million websites for the do-it-yourself investor – some generic, some complicated, some cumbersome. Moneywise cannot recommend any specific website, but here are some common sense (and experience culled from many years of working with clients) does and don'ts to get you going. There are also some suggested websites to start your DIY in the reference section below.

You can track small investor trading patterns (like yourself) by utilising the TDAmeritrade monthly Investor Movement Index® (IMXSM).

The Investor Movement Index, or the IMX, is a proprietary, behaviour-based index created by TDAmeritrade designed to indicate the sentiment of individual investors' portfolios. It measures what investors are actually doing, and how they are actually positioned in the markets.

Sign up for their monthly email.

The IMX does this by using data including holdings/positions, trading activity, and other data from a sample of their 11 million funded client accounts. Type IMX TDAmeritrade into Google and sign up. It's free, monthly and very, very interesting.

Use Yahoo Finance or a like-kind website for easy access to current markets (and your stocks condition).

Yahoo Finance is featured in numerous country-specific websites, e.g. US, UK, Canada, Japan, Australia, Germany, and more.

The process

1. You will need to open an investment account at a brokerage and/or a mutual fund firm.

   Be careful about this process.

   You may be handed a lengthy contract - read it carefully. A basic brokerage account may also include a request to open a margin account where you can purchase investments on margin (leverage).

   The use of margins or leverage to accelerate your profits – and your losses – is never a good idea for a beginning investor. Essentially, you are contracting for a loan with the brokerage firm; this loan is secured by the value of your underlying stock positions, for instance. If the stock value heads south, you will be subject to a margin call and will be expected to remit any difference in cash to the firm. If you are unable to equalise your position, the brokerage firm will move to sell your positions, and attach lien to other assets you own, if you cannot replenish your account.

2. Set a profit, loss and time limit on each position. Some investors decide on a timeline based upon the 200-day S&P moving average. For instance, if your security position is net after costs 20% above that recent line in three months –you can sell! After all, that is an annualised return of 80% per year.

3. Do not give in to greed by coveting huge gains. Just because one stock is doing well, this does not mean you should buy more of the same – suddenly you may find all your cash tied up in four stocks. **Now that's an emotional roller coaster.**

4. Do not start loving any stock, mutual, hedge, or any other security. If it rises in value and it's time to sell according to your formula, say a 25% gain in a year, sell it. If it drops in value, do not hold on, hoping and hoping. Sell it and move on.

5. Buy small positions, say $1,000 per. If one stock performs really well, and you do like it, sell off all the profit, back to your original position, invest in another gem.

6. Do enough research on each position to understand how it reacts in volatile markets. www.smartmoney.com has a great tool called Map of the Market, which shows hues from dark green to red, with bright red indicating more volatility and price swings in a stock. You can also use Yahoo finance and set up a five-year chart for any stock that will demonstrate quite vividly historical price swings.

7. Buy equities of companies you know and whose products you use consistently, Learn to Earn, as Peter Lynch says. Chasing unknown penny-stocks and other short-term plays is not for the timid, the beginner, or the budget minded.

8. Read Bloomberg every day. Research commentary you don't understand. You will down the road!

9. Do not be tempted by website and media ads to trade currency, options, and other 'get rich quick' enticements.

10. Do not be tempted by the super slick salespersons. They will promise anything to make a sell. Take your time reviewing and thinking about your buys. Research never hurt anyone.

11. Pay attention – at least once a week or more. Consider joining an alert type service (or uploading it yourself) that will notify you if your positions are changing.

11. Compute your real rate of return and watch your fees. Broker commissions, turnover costs, mutual fund fees, back end loads all take a chunk out of your actual profit. Do not delude yourself, do the maths and get the real net rate of return. If you live in a tax regime country be aware of the tax impact on your rate of return, e.g. capital gains, dividend tax, etc.

12. Beware of implementing trades during your workday – this type of activity is not condoned and is considered a redundancy offence in today's heavily-remotely monitored employment arena.

13. It is always wise to remember that investing is a Zero-sum game. For every gainer, someone is a loser. You won't win all the time, but you want to land on the winning side on a consistent basis.

14. Never believe your friends, or anyone else about how spectacularly successful they have been. No one wants to admit to a loss – and if they do, you know it was a zinger.

Now, after reading this, if you feel exhausted or that you'd rather garden or plan your next trip, you know that your homework has a different tilt.

Rather than researching good stocks to buy, consider a focus on establishing a relationship with an objective licensed experienced investment professional.

See STEP Seventeen: The Alphabet Soup of Financial Advisors

Not all of us can or want to do it ourselves.

I urge you to continue to learn about your investments. They are so important for your future financial security.

Time after time.

Finally, A buyer-beware investment anecdote (true).

An individual met with a broker at an investment firm - requesting something that would return a good fifteen percent (15%), then plunking down $25,000 on shares of one single company hot stock.

What a great rate, 15%, but one always has to consider the risk and safety of the security as compared to the US risk-free rate of return, generally, the United States ten-year treasury note. At that time, the US T-Note was paying around 4% rate of interest.

The beginner investor's stock had almost 4 times the level of risk.

A few hours later, after a particularly volatile market day, the customer was over- heard - on the phone, yelling at the broker! "You told me this was a good investment! Look at what is happening, the value is dropping like a stone. This is all the savings that I have."

The customer was devastated - but there are two things that did not happen.

The customer never told the broker this was his entire savings.

And the broker never asked. Who was at fault?

Both of them.

True story.

References
& Resources

Here is a sampling of a few websites for DIY, but there are hundreds more. Use your own discovery process to find investment educational websites that you are comfortable with.

Bermuda Stock Exchange. www.bsx.com Investing Tutorial

Importance of DALBAR QAIB (Quantitative Analysis of Investor Behaviour)

The best financial professionals double as behavioural finance coaches of their clients. When markets are down or even volatile, questions will arise from concerned clients and perspective will be needed. The QAIB report and materials give advisors the tools to tell a story, put things into perspective, and deliver the calming messages that are needed to mitigate return-destroying behaviour. Such messages include:

- The prudence of a long-term, buy and hold approach
- The folly of measuring investment success against statistical benchmarks
- Awareness of common behavioural influences
- Lessons from past markets
- The importance of investing assets as early as possible

Investors Are Usually Wrong. I'm One of Them. By Jeff Sommer July 26, 2019,

The Investing Educator: Focused on improving your investment knowledge

https://investingeducator.com/

For Canadian investments and investors

StockChase.com- 7 Essential Tips and Tools to Succeed as a Canadian DIY Investor

Simon B. March 25, 2019

Investing Sites
Schwab Trading Services
StashInvest.com

Research

The Globe and Mail
Yahoo Finance Canada
Canadian Securities Institute

US Investments and Investors

TheBalance.com. Best Investment Apps of 2020.
Financial Samurai. Slicing Through Money's Mysteries
SoFI Investing 101 Center: Investment Education For Beginners

- TD Ameritrade. New to Investing Research
- Investopedia. Investment Education and Stock Trading Simulator
  Yahoo Finance US
  Seeking Alpha – for the more sophisticated
  US Securities & Exchange Commission

- United Kingdom Investments and Investors
- MoneytotheMasses. Best Investing Apps in the UK for Smart phones Nutmeg, Plum

- Regular investing websites
- Vanguard – funds only The Share Center Research

- This Is Money UK DIY Investing
  Yahoo Finance UK
  UK FCA Financial Conduct Authority/ Consumers

Listen to
Market Recovery1

https://tinyurl.com/yj9qkotj

Listen to
Do It Yourself
Investing

https://tinyurl.com/yhdysfkk

Listen to
Rule of 72

https://tinyurl.com/yg6t5wga

Managing the Risk in Life

14

Scott Stallard Photography

Tourist boats sightseeing at a sunken shipwreck, another victim of Bermuda's treacherous reefs

Step Fourteen - Managing Risk

Managing Risk, Consequences and Resolution

Everyone faces risks and anxieties at some point in their lives, from job security to relationships, health issues, natural disasters, financial uncertainty and the like. Knowing how these all can occur and managing them is important to a having a secure handling of your finances.

The risk of living.

If you asked anyone, your friends, your family, the person on the street "what did they fear / worry about the most" besides Halloween ghosts, that is, the most common answers would probably fall into just a few categories: fear of losing a job, losing money and a relationship, losing good health, and losing one's life.

We live with fear, worry, and risk every day. We don't think we do, but risk of losing some component of our being is there as a completely random event or within our control to manage and prevent.

Risk of job loss.

You cannot control whether the company you work for changes direction to another jurisdiction, or undergoes belt-tightening. You can, however, continually prepare yourself for changes in working environment with continuing education while monitoring your current status. Never allow yourself complacency.

Risk of losing money.

We all make choices in life. We can choose to do nothing; then, inevitably spend just as much if not more time and money reacting to problem situations. Or, we can choose to be proactive by staying on top of our financial situation (and the reason I wrote this series) so that we will always know where we stand – and can weigh the risks before we invest in future opportunities.

Risk of losing a relationship.

Fact: Money is the biggest factor in relationship disasters: how you handle it; how he/she manages it; how your parents dealt with money issues; how you can change money dynamics for the betterment of the family.

Risk of debilitating illness.

Everyone worries about health events, retirees most of all. A Physical health review is no different than a financial review. We can control how we improve our physical well-being with discipline, work, commitment and consistency. The end result – we increase the odds of staying healthy, creative and happy.

There are numerous health quizzes on Google. Take One - how healthy are you?

Risk of Increasing Taxes and Non-Compliance with Global Tax Authorities

Taxation, both increases and decreases, has a direct and indirect effect on an economy.

Increased taxation, both new taxes and current tax increases, reduce the direct net income received by ordinary Bermuda resident households while indirect tax is passed through to them affecting their purchasing decisions for food, clothing, retail products, utilities, health needs, services, and entertainment.

- Household faced with shrinking purchasing power will instinctively cut back consumption, trim other costs, or go without.
- Renters, both commercial and single tenant-type homeowners, will raise leases.
- Retailers and service providers will increase fees to compensate for increased cost of over-head.
- Exempt companies are always cited as getting a "free ride" with their legislated corporate zero tax. However, they too will experience higher costs across the board for personnel, benefits, commercial space, administration, etc. Public companies have an overriding responsibility to their shareholders and investors. They will never hesitate to trim expenses.

Increasing taxes is never an economic accelerator, history tells us that time and time again.

Tax costs are always passed on, because no one is going to absorb (immediately, or indefinitely) arbitrary tax expenses by accepting smaller profits or no profit at all.

Redundancies follow that whenever companies announce corporate language such as, restructuring, better customer service, cost containement, shareholder responsibility, etc.

Tax cuts on the other hand increase house-hold demand by increasing workers' take-home pay, boost businesses demand by increasing their after-tax cashflow, which can be used to pay dividends and expand activity, and by making hiring and investing more attractive. Can any community stand the pain of tax increases? Answer, not really.

The supposedly well-heeled will seek alternative methods, offshoring and moves to more comfortable jurisdictions to generate income, completely nullifying their local tax contributions. Those who do not have such choices, Bermuda's middle class, will have to tighten their belts further while limiting their consumption again, too perhaps nothing but the necessities.

Tell me, then. How does such an initiative help rejuvenate an economy?

Further, Bermuda is a polyglot of residents, citizens and nationalities with international tax compliance obligations to other country tax agendas.

See detailed discussion regarding cross border complexes and taxation for multinational individuals and their families under the PondStraddler Section Cross Border Cautions and Compliance.

Risk of death.

Some consider this a needless concern. Inevitably, we came into this world with nothing, and we will leave the same way. No matter how much we worry, every single one of us will take the final journey, hopefully after a happy, healthy and successful life.

But what about those left to mourn us? From the onset of birth - for most people - our lives become enhanced with broad, purposeful, contacts and community while surrounded by people we care about.

These are the relationships we want to protect against risk of loss.

This is why we insure ourselves, our health, and our property - to protect ourselves, and those we are responsible for and care about.

This is why we provide for our spouses, partners, children, family members, businesses we own and much more - by putting our estate plan in order: wills, wishes, medical care directives, naming and recording beneficiaries, guardianships if needed, trusts, life interests, password access, conveyancing, and any other planning deemed necessary and appropriate.

Insurance - Risk Management Ramp Up

You buy insurance when you don't need it.

Contingency planning is a fancy word for setting up a fallback position in case your world falls apart.

No one that I know can summon any real enthusiasm for the subject of insurance. Well, maybe the insurance experts get a little excited. When the subject comes up, the discussion centres around the cost. Why do we need it, and 'those insurance companies are just raking it in,' and other comments.

The truth is, we do need it.

The real true cost in times of disaster is minuscule compared to the emotional, physical, mental and financial toll that natural disasters, illnesses, and injuries inflict on the best of us **(in the worst of times for us).**

The Insurer Role.

The responsibility to insure for people's health, property and their lives is incredibly long tailed.

What other service proposition do you know of where you can purchase something and expect to cash in on it many years later?

Not many.

Yet, an insurance contract is implicit in its nature that for your prepayment (premium), you will be covered for a certain period of time.

This contract with you and all policy holders demands a rigorous ongoing investment management discipline from the insurance company. Premiums must be managed for eventual probability of a claims expense along with enough of a profit generation for the company to remain economically viable.

Brief History: Health, Marine, Property & Life Insurance

According to Rod Johnson, Director of marine risk management at RSA Global Risk, a major UK underwriter, "financial history has most often been taken to be the history of money, banking and lending, and stock markets. It is a widely held belief by insurance professionals and several researchers that marine insurance — hull and cargo specifically — are the oldest forms of insurance, with the first formal marine insurance policy recognised today as such dated from 1350."

Aptly fitting that to know marine insurance operated before Bermuda island life and its very survival even existed, yet today, the Bermuda risk re/insurance market is one of the largest in the world.

Centuries ago, wise and wealthy merchants insured (and had the assets to do so); the rest of our fore-bears just relied upon hope (nothing bad would happen) to get them through life.

The first property insurance company known as The Insurance Office (TIO) came into being after the Great Fire of London in 1667. TIO did not itself survive history - the first lasting insurance company dates to 1710 and today is known as the Royal & SunAlliance, Britain's largest insurance company. source: International Risk Management Institute.

Health insurance evolved in the United States (the first commercial plan was organised in 1847) from its original purpose, technically that of a pure disability policy, to offset income losses resulting from accidents on the job, probably influenced by the compelling (and gruesome) true book by Upton Sinclair, "The Jungle", of the horrendously short, accident ridden lives of Polish and Lithuanian immigrantes in the 1900's working in the meat slaughter-houses in Chicago. One false misstep during 120-hour work-weeks with a trimming knife, in bacteria laden surroundings near vats of boiling oil, and a young man or woman was maimed or worse forever.

No work, no fallback, no food, no home, no choice in the matter, no future. Sinclair's works lead the US Congress during the Wilson administration to change laws for food processing while attempting to prevent the abuse of these largely migrant workers.

More than one hundred years later, it would seem that they were only partially successful. In our current new century, millions of Americans still cannot afford health insurance.

Regrettably, Bermuda as tiny as we are, has an estimated several thousand inhabitants who cannot afford health insurance.

Insurance companies try to save us from ourselves, particularly in the health insurance area, but should they? Witness how most of us (me included) take health insurance for granted with our less than stellar eating habits, our lack of discipline in exercising, our indulgence in substances that really aren't good for us, but sure make us feel great for about five minutes, our indifference to causative environmental pressures.

We, as individuals, are all in this community health pool together and ultimately, we all bear the cost for each other, in one form or another. In general, how does this health insurance scenario work? This is the analogy, Sherman Folland uses in his book, The Economics of Health and Health Care.

Insurance is like a club. Consider a club with 100 members. The members are about the same age and they have the same lifestyle. It seems that about once a year one of the 100 members gets sick and incurs health care costs of $2,000. The incidence of illness seems to be random, not necessarily striking men, women, the elderly or the young in any systematic fashion.

The club members, worried about potential losses due to illness, decide to collect $20 from each member and put the $2,000 in the bank for safe keeping and to earn a little interest. If a member becomes ill, the fund is used to pay for the treatment. This, in a nutshell, is insurance. The members have paid $20 to avoid the risk or uncertainty, however small, of having to pay $2,000.00. The 'firm' collects the money, tries to maintain, and/or increase its value through investment and pays claims when asked. But what happens if too many get sick in one year? Or the investment account values head south? The informal healthy-coverage club goes insolvent for a number of reasons:

- pool of members too small to spread the risk
- insufficient premiums
- large losses with inadequate reserves.

Health insurance coverage in Bermuda has evolved as a sophisticated mechanism for containing costs of illness and for providing routine preventative health care. We are so fortunate for such a tiny island.

More than seventy years ago in Bermuda, health insurance existed, but not for everyone. Our father, God bless him, like many Bermuda families back then, could never afford health premiums for his large family. This situation was the source of great stress and fear of catastrophe over their entire lifetime. It also promoted the almost total avoidance of doctors to the detriment of his and our mother's health. Good and bad, you might say.

Health insurance is expensive. Utilising the law of large numbers, it is easy to understand that it is extremely difficult to have the cost competitiveness of larger jurisdictions with much larger pools of individuals to draw from. Yet, the insurance companies

here manage to pretty high expectations very well. With insurance benefits mandatory if you are employed here in Bermuda, is there ever much scrutiny as to what those benefits really are?

What your benefits?

Do what you can to control this cost. Work on staying healthy by setting up guidelines in the same manner as your financial review. You can do it.

Go through your policy very carefully, line by line. Know clearly what you are responsible for and what the insurance company will pay. Check with your employer regarding less expensive alternatives.

Poor health, poor relationships, poor financial decisions, poor working habits all cost you (and your family) more money in the end.

Use this financial review to turn your life around.

Addendum. In 2020, with the current Bermuda government initiative mandated move to a single payer health plan, controlled and administered by government, there is little detailed information provided by the Minister of Health or other government authoritative bodies to illuminate this discourse.

The Bermuda public is still, literally, in the dark - even concerning the basic services and resources to be utilised under this Bermuda Government Health Plan Initiate.

So, I am unable to comment fully given massive changes expected and little concrete information for family financial planning purposes. Instead, we provide a brief summary of current health coverage from the Bermuda Government health website as at May 29, 2020.

CURRENT SHB	(DRAFT) BHP	HIP	FUTURECARE
			Allied Health Care
			Prescription Medication ($2000 limit)
Prescription Medication Coverage ($400)		Select Medical and Dental Charges Order	Select Medical and Dental Charges Order Coverage
Chronic Disease Management		Select Medical and Dental Charges Order	Ophthalmic Surgery
Total Maternity Care		Ophthalmic Surgery	Local Radiation Treatments for Cancer Care
Local Radiation Treatments for Cancer Care		Local Radiation Treatments for Cancer Care	Wellness Benefit (max 6 visits)
Limited Outpatient Mental Health Care		Additional Wellness Benfit (max 6 visits)	Outpatient Mental Health Care
Physician Home Visits		Limited Outpatient Mental Health Care	Physician Home Visits
Personal Home Care Services (Caregiving)		Physician Home Visits	Personal Home Care Services (Caregiving)
Basic Vision		Personal Home Care Services (Caregiving)	Vision Care
Basic Dental		Basic Dental	Basic Dental
Overseas Treatment (medically necessary)		Overseas Treatment (60% in network, 50% outside)	Overseas Treatment (75% in network, 65% outside)
Specialist Care Visits (2 visits)		Specialist Care Visits (max 5 visits)	Specialist Care Visits (max 5 visits)
GP Office Visits		GP Office Visits (max 4 visits + co-pay)	GP Office Visits (Unlimited + co-pay)
Hospitalization, Kidney care, Imaging, Home medical	Hospitalization, Kidney care, Imaging, Home medical	Hospitalization, Kidney care, Imaging, Home medical	Hospitalization, Kidney care, Imaging, Home medical

Mock Plan for discussion and consultation purposes

BERMUDA HEALTH PLAN 2020

Current SHB vs Draft BHP

Current SHB vs HIP

Current SHB vs FutureCare

GRAPHIC AT-A-GLANCE COMPARISON OF BENEFIT PLANS

V2.0 updated 190908

GOVERNMENT OF BERMUDA
Ministry of Health

Bermuda Health Council

BHP
Bermuda Health Plan

Caution: it is up to you to verify current health insurance benefits after this date.
Bermuda Health Plan 2020 Package Design. https://www.gov.bm/health-plan-package-design
Launch Video https://drive.google.com/file/d/14QuWEWR4c-ddibo8lEig0k-zXIfQkykK/preview

Reviewing your insurance policies:

Caution: Many of these references are US or Canadian based and provided for general information awareness. Pricing, coverage, and some terms may be different than policies provided by insurers in Bermuda.

Most people will generally purchase some insurance: vehicle - required for a license, property, life, health, but disability, not so much as local disability policies are extremely expensive.

When budgets are tight, pull back will take place. Some families will go "bare" hoping that illness or other natural disaster will not affect them. They may have no choice, financially, but having no contingency plan can create stress as well.

Property Homeowner Insurance Policy

Property Home ownership (and Bermuda investment property) is an absolute sacred trust for most Bermudians. In the decades before the cessation of Bermuda government currency exchange controls, everyone worked to invest their savings into purchasing a home property. The old way to self-sufficiency became savings accounts, dividends from local company shares, and a rental unit, sometimes attached to the main house, or purchasing a second property for rental income.

Property acquisition became even more desirable and achievable due to the entrepreneurial vision of Sir John Swan, KBE, former Premier of Bermuda. His firm built hundreds of affordable houses, offered complete with financing thereby giving possibly thousands of Bermudian residents the opportunity to finally have a home of their own.

Bermuda Home ownership is expensive for numerous reasons, the largest reasons, limited land mass and prohibitive cost of imported building materials. Natural weather patterns in the North Atlantic produce hurricanes every year. Some will track a direct path to Bermuda before racing north- ward in dissipation. Thus, protecting one's property in Bermuda is paramount.

It follows that property insurance is also expensive and cannot be literally compared to say a comparative home in the United States or Canada.

Homeowners - Property insurance.

Families often feel that carrying insurance on a house - is inordinately expensive - higher in Bermuda than some other areas - and will bring up the complaint that they pay this policy fee every year - for nothing.

Year after year of payments can be quite expensive for any budget, but trust me, many Bermuda Island families have experienced hurricane strikes and severe damage. No one wants (or can afford) to pay for the hurricane destruction alone.

Yes, we can justify cutting back or dropping property insurance, hoping that the next random hurricane won't take out the roof, and

Tiny old Bermuda cottage with limestone roof - to catch water in the separate raised water tank below the house.

sidewalls. But it is a gamble, further exacerbated if such event does occur, the longer time and cost to repair damage - all out of pocket. Significant hurricanes, like disastrous Fabian 2003, when so many homes had roof damage, those blue tarps were evident for months. No one really wants to try and cope with a months-long repair schedule - self-financed (if no insurance coverage), so for most, property insurance in Bermuda is important.

We need that insurance.

How to read a property policy.

People tend to think that an insurance policy is a complex piece of paper that no one wants to look at, or begin to contemplate reading through it.

We're going to look at a homeowner's property policy and break it down into some manageable bites. You should make plans, even so, to review your personal home-owner property policy with your insurance agent.

It's really quite simple; what the insurance policy will do is layout your basic information in an outline format:

- Policy number
- Name of the insured, you (and your spouse, partner, other) who own the property.
- The ensured location property; where is it, street address, county, state, country, etc.
- A full description of the property: date built, construction type, grade and protection class, kind of roof, automatic sprinklers, and so on.
- Other items that may be relevant as identifiers, such as a copy of your ownership deed, where your deed is recorded, and mortgage information, bank, etc. This is so that the insurance company knows that the bank has a claim on your property - until the mortgage is completely paid off.

Property Coverages, Additional Coverages, and Limits to Coverages

as well as Exclusions are stated with the total dollar coverages. The policy specifically spells out for you the items they will insure and the dollar limits they will reimburse to you in a casualty event.

Property Coverages are detailed in this illustrative example:

- Dwelling
- Other structures
- Personal Property
- Loss of Use and Additional coverages
- Personal liability
- Medical Payments to others
- Exclusions and perils - not covered.
- Deductibles to the policies. Additional coverage available for purchase.

Your Dwelling and Other Structure e.g. detached garage, storage shed

Generally, a dollar limit called the replacement cost is assigned to your property.

This cost is not the same as the current sales value of your home on an open real estate market.

Let's say that you paid $400,000 for your property; you've owned it for 10 years and the retail sales price of the property might have increased, considerably.

However, this value may not be what your property insurance policy lists as a replacement cost.

They may be completely different. Your insurer is only interested in what it would cost to rebuild your home (after a fire, hurricane, etc.) on the same footprint with basically the same style. Insurance companies rely on enormous numbers of statistics that can estimate pretty accurately the construction cost for your area.

Replacement Cost Caution.

Your responsibility is to assure that your home is inspected on a regular basis (or at least, check with your insurance agent) every few years - to be sure that the replacement cost to rebuild your home accurately reflects the current cost of reconstruction at the time. Some homeowners will obtain a policy that has a low estimated replacement cost, and of course, a low premium - BUT, in the event of a disaster, if you are underinsured, the policy will not cover the entire cost of rebuilding.

Personal Property

Furniture, clothing and other reasonable items are covered. What may not be covered are high value items, such as boats, jewellery, watches, silverware, antiques, etc.

Loss of Use covers temporary lodging and costs of food, etc residing elsewhere while your home is repaired.

Personal Liability and Medical Payments to Others.

Coverage for bodily injury or property damage you or any of your household insured under the policy at, or away from your home. It may include general liability as well.

This is an important component of your policy and should be carefully reviewed with your insurance agent. If your home has certain considered hazards, a dog, pool, large trees near a neighbouring property, etc. you may want to consider an umbrella policy with broader liability coverage and higher limits for additional personal liability coverage.

Deductibles

The second part of the policy will stipulate what your deductibles are that are attached to your coverage. Deductibles can range from $500 - $5000, or more, depending upon additional coverage. Generally the higher the deduction the lower the annual premium.

Remember, in the event of a property disaster event, you will be responsible for the deductible portion of the policy. This can be particularly problematic in the event of a vehicle accident. Your insurance company will only cover the amounts - after the deductible. You will have to furnish the cash - for say the first $500 upfront for the repairs.

Another reason to have a contingency cash cushion for contingencies and unexpected events.

Bottom Line

Review your policy carefully and get assistance from your agent if there is any confusion about coverage and exclusions. Be very sure that your policy premiums are enough to cover the 100% replacement value of your real estate(s). Otherwise, you will not receive full reimbursement for repairs. Check with your local provider, to be certain.

Be sure you understand - what is not covered and make arrangements to increase coverage, if necessary. A basic policy may not cover hurricane damage, wind-storm, hail, ground collapse, vandalism, mold, severe flooding. etc. Three days before a hurricane arrives is not the time to increase your coverage to protect your home and your family.

Vehicle Insurance policy

We dare not drop vehicle insurance, given that the chances when driving on our narrow roads and reckless driving for an accident are rather high.

How To Read a Vehicle Policy

The basic vehicle insurance information required of you and any other family drivers is very similar to what is required for home-owner insurance.

Liability coverage dollar limits for each person bodily injury and each accident are stipulated.

There is one big difference. Generally, a minimum vehicle insurance coverage is legally required.

- Names of drivers. It assumes that drivers have current licenses.
- Addresses
- VIN numbers of cars owned in household
- Estimate number of annual miles driven per vehicle
- Coverage Types and Limits of Cash Liabilities

Liability

- bodily injury - for each person and each accident
- property damage - each accident
- Medical Payments
  - each person
- Uninsured Motorists
  - bodily injury - for each person
  - each accident
- Physical Damage Coverage
  - comprehensive loss
  - collision loss

Life insurance Policy Choices

Life insurance is a different kettle of fish, AMAZINGLY, it has been in existence since the time of the Roman Empire.

Whole life insurance is popular in Bermuda, those with a possible familial tendency to say, kidney or diabetes problems in later years should consider purchasing a policy early in their working years.

Why? Because you may be considered uninsurable in later years, unable to purchase any coverage and typically, in general, whole life insurance premiums do not increase as you age.

However, when budgets are really stretched, those monthly whole life insurance payments may be a real hurdle. More than a few readers, clients, etc. have told me they stopped paying, simply could not afford the premiums.

The policy lapsed. This is so regrettable, but understandable in hard times. Do what you can to restructure your policy.

You buy insurance when you don't need it, because life happens! Often unexpectedly....

If your family is in this situation, call your insurance broker immediately.

You may have the alternative to have the cash value pay the premium (for the short term anyway), or you may be able to convert to a term policy for a few years, or work out another solution.

See what you can do to rescue all the work that went into qualifying you for a life policy, initially.

The better question – is are you adequately insured?

The thing is, we buy insurance against the day that something disastrous does happen. I can easily bet that if you added all the premiums you currently pay to an insurance company against the cost of self-financing the repairs on your hurricane damaged residence, paying off the mortgage, or saving every quarter for a college fund, and additional financial safety for your spouse at retirement, you could not do it.

Insurance gives you, at a minimum, the financial resources to rebuild your life after losing a spouse, partner, to rebuild your home, and to cover catastrophic illness medical fees.

You and your family need life insurance. If you are single, perhaps, not so much. Your employer may provide a basic term life policy in addition to your mandatory health insurance. Be grateful. It is great benefit that you don't have to incur cost.

Reviewing your life policies.

What are they?

Where are they?

Are they enough to get your family through losing you? General reckoning is that your current annual salary times ten times is adequate to see your family along, but what if your family is young when you depart unexpectedly.

Let's just take a page and a half to walk through the most popular life insurance policy structures.

Note: this is a generic overview, not specific Bermuda life insurance product offerings. The purpose is to provide you with discussion points when you meet with a life insurance agent.

Life Insurance Comparisons

Kinds	term	whole of life	universal life	variable life
Premium Term	1- year - must be re-newed each year	permanent for life of policy	permanent for life of policy	permanent for life of policy
Amount	premium may stay same for a set period, i.e. ten years, or in-crease annually or periodically	same premium every year, but will lapse if unpaid	premium may vary	same premium every year, but will lapse if unpaid
Protection	year-to-year	life, as long as pre-mium is paid	life, as long as pre-mium is paid	life, as long as pre-mium is paid
Death benefit, guaranteed?	generally	yes	yes	yes
Cash value	NONE, premium is for coverage only, no cash build-up over time or payments of dividends	yes, cash in placed in a guaranteed mini-mum rate savings ac-count	yes, cash in placed in savings account, but interest rate may vary	no cash savings ac-count, value is gained(lost) through capital market invest-ments
Cash value growth determi-nation	N/A	interest paid on ac-crued cash over time	variable rates de-pending upon insurer	Insurer invests cash in its pool of sub ac-counts in capital mar-kets, subject to risk of loss

Important to keep in mind that policy costs and conditions will vary from insurer to insurer as well.

Some Differences in Policy Structures

Term Life.

- Policies are cheaper initially due to just paying for death benefit, but costs will rise over time.
- Coverage may run year-to-year, or longer, say ten years at same premium, then increase in steps as insured ages.
- Cost effective for young families on tight budgets.
- NOT recommended for individuals who may have tendency to health problems later, or possibly, inherit family health issues and may not be able to pass health exams.
- May be convertible to whole of life, although additional health screening exams may be required over time.

Whole of Life

Premiums are significantly higher than term insurance but remain the same for the entire duration of the policy. Literally, the individual is prepaying as a young person for the increases in cost later in life.

Generally, also, the individual insured is not required to have an additional health screening after policy is in effect.

The difference between the actual cost-to-insure and the premium paid is considered additional paid-in-cash. The accumulating cash earns interest over time, increasing the cash value.

Cash value build-up is a form of forced savings for those who have difficulty in adhering to a general savings plan.

Cash value can be borrowed back by the insured.

Dividends may be paid if the whole life insurance is a participating policy.

Best for individuals who can afford whole of life, who like the continuity of the same premium for life, and who may feel they will incur health issues later in life, where when obtaining a life policy may be unaffordable or denied due to pre-existing health conditions.

Universal Life

- Generally, similar to whole of life.
- Differences:
  - Insured policy holder can adjust both the premium and the death benefit
  - Cash values can also be used to pay premiums during, say periods of unemployment. The death benefit may or may not be reduced depending upon the accumulated cash.
  - Can also skip payments, using cash interest accrued, if sufficient, instead.
  - No dividend payments.
- Variable Life
- Generally, similar to whole of life.
- Differences:
  - Cash value is invested in capital markets subject.
  - Insurer uses only their sub account mutual fund-type investments, thus a limited choice
  - Fees may be higher due to fund management.
  - No dividend payments.
  - Product is not for the risk averse. Any investment in capital markets can appreciate or lose money.
  - Ultimately with this product, in a down market, the insured could be paying a

higher price for the same death benefit only - as term insurance due to loss of most, if not all, cash value.

Group Term Life Insurance offered by employer.

- This is a type of free premium insurance offered as a benefit to a pool of employees.
- It is similar to term insurance.
- Generally, coverage death benefits amounts are limited to one-to two years of a salary.
- It is contingent upon continued employment at the firm, ceasing if employee leaves.
- Some group life policies allow the employee to take on the premium as an individual, thereby leaving with the policy.
- It is a great benefit, particularly for those employees who cannot afford personal individual life insurance.
- The death benefit is usually not adequate for a family; However, some insurance is better than nothing.
- Moneywise recommends that the employee takes out a personally owned life insurance policy as well, if it can be affordable!
- Be sure to keep track of the policy filed with your personal documents.
- Life happens!

How do you know which type of insurance is best for you?

Visit the website WWW.policygenius.com for an impartial review of basic life insurance topics.

Visit our Bermuda's local life insurance providers' websites and talk their agents:

Argus Group Holdings

BF&M

Colonial

Freisenbruch Meyer

Life Insurance policy owners.

Are all your beneficiaries correct?

- When was the last time you reviewed your policies?
- Who are the named beneficiaries?
- Are they the ones you want?
- Have you married, divorced, or changed relationships?

Be very sure that your group policy has your beneficiary(s) names on it, not the company - as beneficiary. In the US, certain large corporations did just that, naming themselves as the beneficiary. When the employees died, the death benefit went to the company and not to the deceased employees' next of kin.

It appears that this practice was discontinued after numerous lawsuits - even to the US Supreme Court - around the end of 2010.

Note: I do not think this type of issue will arise in Bermuda, but one should always assume responsibility for every single aspect of your financial life. It is up to you to review your life policy(s) and get clarification from your broker if you do not understand all the terms.

So many times, individuals forget these very important steps. Then, life happens.

Guess who may not receive your death benefit? Your spouse and young children because you opened the policy when you were single and named your mother. She has passed and now everyone in the family except the ones who need it the most, will be fighting over their share.

Keep your records up to date!

Bottom Line. Buy cheap term life insurance if you can't afford anything else.

Any amount is better than none. When you are more successful financially, and generally, a bit older and more established, then consider a whole life policy structure with a cash value included.

Try the Foresters Life Insurance Need calculator. This insurance company was chosen to eliminate any bias toward local providers.

https://www.foresters.com/en-ca/tools-and-guides/life-insurance-calculator

Tenant Renter's insurance.

Not everyone owns a real estate property or even wants to. Renting a domestic space for yourself and your family has always been a choice, sometimes it is the first home for young adults, singles, couples, families and guest workers. We all tend to make a house or apartment our home with our things, our comfort factors, our valuable possessions, and our family documents - many of which may be irreplaceable.

Life happens. Things get destroyed, unexpectedly.

Originals of all precious documents should be kept offsite of home: safety deposit box, digital copies uploaded to the cloud or independent hard drive as well.

Don't forget to list access/your passwords!

We live in the most cosmopolitan era ever - many of us came from somewhere else, have more than one passport, relatives in Bermuda and abroad, investments held in custody offshore, passwords, account numbers, etc. are kept in a paper hardcover book that is now ineligible - and useless and so on.

Your other possessions and possible exposure to liabilities can be insured through tenant insurance: the upstairs apartment bath leaks onto your electronic equipment, your apartment is burglarised and vandalised, someone trips on your fluffy rug, and hurricane Umberto basically ruined your brand new couch.

Google - Renters Insurance 101 to understand how it works.

Should you buy insurance or self-insure?

Over my 35 years of practice, people have often complained to me in confidential financial meetings that they feel they are paying far too much in property insurance premiums in Bermuda. "Year after year said one person, and "I have never had a claim. They (meaning the insurers) are making all this money."

Why not take this little reality check exercise, since Bermuda has taken numerous poundings from some horrific hurricanes. It is always a good idea to think about

- what it would cost you personally to cover extensive damage / without insurance, and

- compare that total amount to what you have paid in property insurance premiums over the years, keeping in mind the very high construction costs in Bermuda.

The final thought is - that if you go "bare" meaning no property insurance coverage, do you have $100,000-$150,000 or more in savings to cover the cost of rebuilding?

What would you do if you cannot raise the cash or borrow it, and your roof is gone entirely, blown away by a hurricane?

Insurance allows you to be prepared at a minimum cost of the personal stress, and financial insecurity.

Caution!

Pondstraddler Life™ Financial Planning Alert

Multi-jurisdictional citizens (US and green card holders particularly) may not be able to satisfactorily make use of Bermuda Life insurance products as they may be subject to taxation and other regulations in other domiciles.

Never assume that what works in Bermuda will be acceptable based upon multi-national tax regimes, upon return to your home country, or relocation from Bermuda. Always consult with an international tax, legal, and finance professional before you purchase a product that cannot be redomiciled!

References
& Resources

How to read a Homeowner's property policy
https://www.insure.com/home-insurance/
homeowners-insurance-policy.html

How to read (and actually understand) your Auto
insurance policy https://www.insure. com/car-in-
surance/how-to-read-your- insurance-policy.html

A guide to understanding your health insurance
policy

https://www.insure.com/health-insurance/ under-
standing-health-insurance.html

How to read a Life insurance policy

https://www.insure.com/life-insurance/life- insur-
ance-policy.html

A brief history of Life Insurance Corey Dahl

Google - Bermuda Laws Online

Bermuda Health Insurance Regulations

Bermuda Hospitals Board Act 1970

Motor Vehicle Act 1951 Consolidated

Life Insurance Act 1978 - Bermuda Laws Online

Insurance (Property) Act 1978 - Bermuda Laws
Online

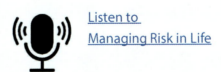

Listen to
Managing Risk in Life

https://tinyurl.com/yhu9rknk

The Dimming of the Day

Estate Planning for your family and legacy

15

Step Fifteen - The Dimming of the Day Estate Planning

The Dimming of the Day Estate planning for your family and legacy

Have we put our affairs in order?

Managing the finances of a single individual is a challenge any day of the week. Imagine how complex it can be when a nuclear family or several generations come into play. Some of the stressors that occur within family circles are the very ones that could be avoided by putting simple, easily understood estate planning into place, early.

We all know the classic example. We may have even experienced it. One family member no longer communicates with another because he "got more than I did when Mom passed on" - because she always liked him best.

We are all creatures of habit. Many of us find it extremely difficult at the end of the day to take care of financial tasks, so we don't; they just get put off, sometime inevitably.

The Pitfalls and Pain from 'Forgetting' to Plan.

Consider the composite scenarios described below drawn from actual case histories (names, places and circumstances have been altered) from thirty years as a financial planning practitioner, but let me politely point out, they are heavily anonymous.

Case 1. XYZ Company is a good stock, the lady says, "my father and I owned the shares together, but he let me have all the dividends. They paid consistently and I used the money to buy our kids things." She is now elderly herself and wants to sell the shares now to take advantage of a three year high in market value. However, the shares are still in paper certificate form, still registered in his name. Her father has been deceased for twenty-five years and today, the XYZ share value is dropping like a stone. It takes weeks to obtain a certified death certificate and reregister the shares in her name alone. Needless to say, XYZ stock does not sell for the value she had hoped.

Case 2. We are in an appliance repair shop. The dear couple running the place have worked all their lives, managing to compile an extremely modest savings account and a few investments. The husband looks terrible. When his wife is out of the room, he leans over and whispers to me: "I know you work with finances. I can't find our stock certificates and I think I burned them by mistake with the trash in the woodstove. I am just sick about it, I can't sleep, and I can't tell my wife. What am I going to do? It is all of our savings!"

Case 3. The client comes into our office seeking tax advice on a lump sum distribution from a pension account. She is 56 years old; has scarce resources and has recently been made redundant. The reality is in today's marketplace that her future employment prospects are bleak.

'She chatters on about divine intervention, "getting' this unexpected money. It seems that her ex-husband – from whom she has been divorced for more than eight years – has just died.

He never removed her name as beneficiary of his pension. Thus, under contract law, she inherits and his current spouse (with two young children to support) is left almost penniless!

Case 4. She is 55; he is 58. Their home is owned jointly, so the husband said. They have put 35 years of sweat equity into the place with the understanding that they will inherit other assets when the matriarch of the family goes to glory.

His mother (79) has not been well; cancer treatments are eroding her health. Betty, who has never worked, has spent emotional and physical time caring for his mother at home. Unexpectedly, John, not Mom, passes away. At the reading of the will, he has bequeathed his joint holding in the house to Betty.

Surprise, title was never conveyed to Betty by his mother.

Not only that, but the matriarch's medical bills are mounting, and the home will be sold. After thirty years of being a homemaker with little in the way of marketable skills, Betty must simultaneously grieve, find a job, and an affordable place to live.

Four cases, four avoidable tragedies. We work so hard to acquire assets and establish the good life, but never quite finalise the details.

Not to belabour the point, but Why is it so difficult for so many of us to take care of these most necessary financial tasks?

The Avoidance of the Necessaries Can Pile Up.

People neglect to clarify all sorts of financial paperwork:

- They forget they own stock warrants and options which end up expiring on them.
- They earn pensions in other countries, have little to no documentation, can't remember the amounts, let alone where to claim what they are rightfully due.
- They make 'handshake' business agreements with family members (and other people), then never put anything in writing.
- They loan money to others and never collect.
- They get dividend checks and lose them.
- They marry and divorce, never once reviewing life insurance, pensions, wills, annuity contracts, and bank accounts for correct beneficiaries, ownership.
- They stop making payments on life insurance policies, with no idea if the contract is a whole life or term policy.
- They never check their property insurance to see if the face value of the policy will remotely pay for replacement cost if the property disaster occurs.
- They open accounts abroad, and forget how much, where they are, and tell no one.
- They forget to file income tax returns.
- They set up trusts, and never get around to funding them or transferring assets into them.
- They buy investments, have no idea what they bought, letting their broker choose for them.

And the list goes on.

Actually, no one enjoys this type of paperwork. One can try to blame universal financial systems for the indecipherable language, complicated, lengthy, and tedious forms, wending the maze as it were. The reality is that we live in a complex world. It is just not easy no matter how you view it. We are after all, only human, and feel we have an excuse for being overwhelmed.

We Think that we are going to live forever, *** until we don't.

We never know when the Good Lord will call us home. You don't want your left-behind relatives (rels) to start with the refrains of IF ONLY he/she:

- had been more careful;
- taken better care of her/himself;
- put together a simple will;
- established a guardian to take of his/her little son and daughter;
- had filed the papers for the Bermuda Primary Homestead Resident Certificate;
- changed the beneficiary on his/her pension account (instead of leaving it all to that wufless rat of a first husband/wife);
- set up medical directives, and life-support testator wishes;
- had put all those documents in one easy place to locate.

And the even more painful, emotional IF ONLY'S...that make managing all legal and financial matters from the lost loved one, even tougher to manage.

- If only, I had told him/her we loved him/ her one more time;
- If only, we hadn't had that last argument;
- If only, he/she spelled out non-resuscitation wishes for terminal illnesses;
- If only, we had had the chance to say goodbye.

Truly, no one wants to talk about "the end." This is reflected globally, where 45-50% of people do not have wills. A trend that simply has not changed: rich, middle class, or struggling, no one wants to prepare for their own demise.

You! have the courage to break this trend.

If you are very young -

single, with no dependents, very few assets, you may think you do not need a will.

But, even so, if you are employed, you probably do have a small savings account, possibly a term life insurance policy benefit from your employer, and your Bermuda National Pension Scheme.

Make sure that the people you care about are listed as beneficiaries on these accounts!

If you are older -

in a serious relationship, especially with children, other dependents, extended family (divorce, widow(er)hood), a mortgage, a home, and other assets, you **need a will.**

NOW!

Do you honestly want the Bermuda Government to decide who benefits from your assets, and who is assigned guardianship of your children, the residual of your life's work and your plans with your loved ones for the future, you know

---

"the things that built our dreams, yet slipped away from us?" ***

Don't believe me? Then read Michael Mello's wonderful free Bermuda estate planning book, or wade through Bermuda Government estate law, both sourced below.

Then, make a will; be sure to execute your will with an attorney.

It is not enough to write your last will and testament wishes down in a document that provides for your families' needs in a thoughtful, careful, loving and clearly designated manner.

Your will must be executed to be legally binding!

On rare occasions, a holographic will (hand-written, composed and signed by yourself) has been found to be legally valid. You must have your wishes documented, witnessed and placed into private, (sometimes public) domain as a legal document by an attorney.

Store it where it can be found and tell trusted individuals how to locate it!

Your wishes regarding burial with your favourite bottle of champagne - hidden in a high place over-looking the sea isn't going to happen if no one can find your will and its directives.

Dying intestate. The consequences if no will exists.

In Bermuda, the law of intestacy is governed by the Succession Act 1974. Passing to your great reward without leaving a valid will is known as dying intestate.

Since no one at that point (other than you and you are gone) knows what to do with anything, the Bermuda Courts decide for you – from the grave as it were by utilising the Succession Act.

With the exception of very small estates, a more cumbersome process of obtaining a Grant of Probate, or Letters of Administration kicks in to dole out your net estate (after legal and filing fees, liabilities, stamp duty and other costs) according to a set formula that may bear no resemblance whatsoever to how you wanted to dispose of your assets, or care for the needs of your immediate family.

For instance, Bermuda Succession Laws state the following:

One: If you and your spouse have no children, your spouse will inherit your entire residuary estate, but there is a catch.

He/she will inherit all only if your parents, full brothers or sisters, or their children died before you did. If, for instance, your parents are still alive, your spouse will receive your personal possessions, house contents, boat, car and no more than two-thirds of the remaining assets or $150,000 whichever is greater. Your surviving parent(s) will receive the final one-third. If both of your parents have passed away, the final one-third remaining won't go to your spouse but to your surviving brothers and sisters equally or to their children.

Two: If your spouse and your children outlive you, your spouse gets an even shorter end of the stick.

She/he will receive no more than 50% of your remaining assets or $100,000 whichever is greater. The remaining 50% is given equally to your children. This edict creates problems when a considerable fortune is left to minor children, and no one is capable of managing these investments. Another body blow to the grieving spouse occurs when it is learned that transfers to spouses are exempt from stamp duty at death, but your estate may be liable for stamp duty of up to 15% on the taxable assets left to your children – that remaining 50% has just been considerably reduced, and you still have to raise and educate these children.

Three: Overvaluation of the family home.

Under the Succession Act rules, if the family home is worth more than your spouse's entitlement to your estate (that is two-thirds or fifty percent), your spouse can still keep the property, but he/she must pay the difference between what he/she is allowed back to the estate where it is distributed to the remaining beneficiaries. How many spouses have that type of liquidity in land-rich cash-poor Bermuda? We don't know what arrangements the court can or will make if the spouse can't beg, borrow or steal sufficient cash to keep what she/he has considered to rightfully theirs all their life.

Four: Uncle Scrooge and Aunty Meanie become Guardians of your dear children.

Regardless of whether the children like these people or not, if no Will exists, particularly in the case of a Single Mother, the Supreme Court may appoint a guardian who may be considered a more suitable guardian than even the child's biological father. The court takes the position that it is always obligated to act in the best interest of the child(ren).

These types of situations can actually happen, even to people like Princess Diana, who had access to the most brilliant estate planning minds in the Commonwealth. Most of her £21.5 million fortune was bequeathed in trust to Princes William and Harry, but she failed to make a new will after her divorce from Prince Charles, leaving her sons with an £8.5 million inheritance tax bill on her estate.

Not to be outdone, other famous people neglected to plan, as taken directly from probate court filings in the United States which still has a fairly punitive estate tax regime. Marilyn Munroe, Elvis Presley, JP Morgan (the founder of the massive investment firm), JD Rockefeller, and the head of one of the Big Four accounting firms all died without leaving a will. Their estates paid from 55-73% of the value of the assets to US Internal Revenue Service before the beneficiaries received a dime. Even the most well-intentioned…

Making a Will declares your intentions (to your executor)

on how you wish your property to be disposed of at death. Additionally, if your estate held in your sole name (in Bermudian dollars) is above $50,000, it is subject to death duties with only a couple of exceptions: bequests to charity and leaving your estate to your spouse.

What would happen if you were able to suitably restructure the titling of all of your estates so that at death there is an automatic transfer to the beneficiaries (or a trust) of your choosing?

Sharing the Load, also mean giving up some control. Bermuda dollar bank deposits, securities, and other investments may be held with your spouse, partner or heirs or other parties. They may be titled as: joint with rights of survivor, joint, tenants-in-common, as guardian for, in trust and so on.

It is important for you to assure yourself and the family that the assets are titled correctly for your beneficiaries. There is a distinct difference between titling these assets and who will inherit them.

Life insurance proceeds. You, as the owner of the policy, have full authority to designate (or change) a beneficiary while you are alive. This is a legal contract between you, the owner and the insured, and the insurance company. At your death, your beneficiary(ies) receives the proceeds.

Pensions structured under the National Pension Scheme and other older private pensions generally work the same way as life insurance. The Government Old Age Pension does not. Your benefit dies with you, although your spouse may receive a similar sum under the widow entitlement.

Real estate property transfers (of Bermuda property) during your lifetime (known as voluntary conveyances) can legally be accomplished in a variety of ways, the most common being transfers into joint tenancy with spouses and others. Life interests, trust structures, and holding companies are more complex methods of holding real estate for future beneficiaries. There is a transfer stamp tax cost to these processes for real estate, but generally less than the cost of death duties.

The Bermuda Government's Gift to You. How would you like to save all death duties on your primary personal residence for your beneficiaries? Under the Stamp Duties Act 1976 as amended by the Stamp Duties Amendment Act 2005, you can do just that.

By making a formal application to exempt your primary homestead from stamp duty, you can save your heirs (and your home for them) the often-punitive cost of stamp duty due on Bermudian property at death.

Scuttlebutt from readers; Primary Home-stead applications are taking years to be processed according to some readers.

This is simply unacceptable, when originally legislated it took a matter of weeks.

Final Opportunity Arises even after Death.

Even after death, your estate representative may designate your sole property (or one of your properties) to obtain this certificate. There are several caveats, however: if you own more than one property, your executor can only designate the property your lived in. If you pass your last years in an extended care facility and do not receive the exemption prior to this change in residence, your family property will not be eligible at all.

Below is the Schedule of Bermuda death duties for your perusal. As stated above, there are planning opportunities to designate your assets for optimum benefit for your survivors. I highly recommend consultation with a knowledgeable Bermuda estate attorney, such as Michael Mello, QC who can provide expert advice and structure to your estate plans.

Final note: tax, legal, finance laws change without notice. This is not personal advice. Always check with a qualified estate practitioner for current verification of data.

Documenting Your Net Worth (Alive and Deceased). Death Duties to Be Paid

Source: LAW OF WILLS AND ESTATES IN
BERMUDA Ninth Edition
BY MICHAEL J. MELLO QC, JP, TEP
page 82

What you own

- House (your share if jointly owned) (at present market value)
- Car
- Furniture, Appliances and Fixtures
- Jewellery
- Other personal effects
- BD$ Cash
- Bank account (BD$ current & deposit accounts)
- Deposit Company BD$ Certificates
- Bermuda Stocks & Shares, bonds, and mutual funds (at market value)
- Life Insurance (if your estate is the beneficiary what your estate would get if you died today in BD$)
- BD$ Money owed to you
- Any other Bermuda assets you own, company(s), partnership interests, etc.

Less what you owe

- The mortgage on your house (not applicable if you have a Primary Family Homestead
- Exemption Certificate from death duty)
- Overdraft facility at bank
- Loans from the bank
- Unpaid bills
- Credit card balance owing

- Contingent liabilities (i.e. guarantees of loans, etc. and other obligations which do not cease at death)

Deductions/Exemptions deducted from Net worth before death duty calculation

- Any Bermuda personal or real property left to a spouse or charity is exempt the value of any real property interest where you have a Primary Family Homestead Exemption Certificate foreign property of all kinds should be excluded, for example a US$ bank account or US$ de-nominated securities and investments, even if held at a local bank

Net worth (your total Bermuda assets less your total debts)	$_____
Net dutiable estate Bermuda Death Duty calculation	$_____
First $100,000 Exempt	$ - 0 -
Next $100,000 @ 5% (or part thereof)	$_____
Next $800,000 @ 10% (or part thereof)	$_____
Next $1,000,000 @ 15% (or part thereof)	$_____
Everything over $2,000,000 @ 20%	$_____
Total Death Duties	$_____

Healthcare Directive, Advanced Directive Or "Living Will"

A Healthcare Directive (sometimes called an Advance or Medical Directive and commonly referred to as a "Living Will") is either a separate document, or a paragraph in a normal Will in which a person sets out in advance what kind of medical treatment he wishes or does not wish to receive in the event that he subsequently becomes incapable of communicating his own wishes.

A Healthcare or Advanced Directive or "Living Will" is not really a Will in the traditional sense as it does not dispose of property and it does not speak from death. The purpose of a Healthcare Directive is to inform healthcare providers of the patient's wishes when the patient is unable to do so himself and, equally as important, to spare relatives and medical attendants the problem of having to make difficult medical decisions on the patient's behalf.

Basically, a Healthcare Directive sets out which person you want to make health care decisions for you when you can't make them yourself (a healthcare proxy), the kind of medical treatment you want or don't want, how comfortable you want to be, how you want people to treat you and what you want your loved ones to know.

Leaving Specific Instructions and Documentation. Don't Forget!

Internet Access to your social media, email, bank and investments and any other accounts: Passwords, keys, safety deposit boxes, copy of last will and instructions and so on.

Leave these where they can be found.

No point in going to all the trouble of laying out your wishes, then not telling anyone where yours and your family's valuable information is! Not having recourse to retrieve assets may mean the difference between survival and stability for your family!

Huge case in point - Cryptocurrency CEO - dying unexpectedly in Hong Kong leaving no passkey to access millions of Bitcoins. There you have it, a vast fortune, floating anonymously in global vapourware.

A crypto exchange may have lost $145 million after its CEO suddenly died

By Daniel Shane, CNN Business, February 5, 2019

Bermuda Trusts: Relative Thinking Applied to this Complex Area

This section has been included mostly as a reminder to include in your review if you are connected in anyway with Bermuda (or other) trust programs.

Trusts, almost used to be informally operated by trustees who were trusted family friends, possibly including an attorney, and so on. There were fewer requirements to formally conduct a trust under strict reporting, accounting, distribution, and other transactions.

Current trust legislation in Bermuda significantly changed how formal trusts must be administered, one particular legal requirement is that one trustee must be a registered trust company.

There were many reasons for these legislative upgrades, among them, the global tax, legal, financial, and accounting mandates for individuals and businesses, both local and international, through the Anti-Money Laundering, Know Your Client, OECD influences, and large country governments to provide authenticity and transparency to even the most complex of trust structures. The United States, in particular, in enforcing the FATCA (Foreign Account Tax Compliance Act) increased complexity of administration and reporting with respect to any United States connected individuals, businesses, and trusts, themselves.

Noncompliance can trigger draconian monetary and financial constraint consequences through foreign financial institutions reporting requirements and oversight to US Internal Revenue Service. Other country Revenue Agencies have emulated this compliance model, meaning that a trust may face reporting to numerous country tax agencies, depending upon the citizenship,

residency make up of all individuals and entities associated with a trust.

Bermuda families who may have established a trust simply to hold their Bermuda property, have found that the compliance requirements and accountability have decreased the trust cost effectiveness.

Needless to say, as trust structures are a complex topic in and of itself, we can only provide a brief review and reminder of you, the reader's possible potential issues and direct you to consult with an experienced trust officer, an individual with the TEP credentials is advised.

TEP is the Trust & Estate Practitioner designation earned through a rigorous series of examinations and participation in the Society of Trusts & Estate Practitioners (UK/ Bermuda).

Are you the Grantor/Settlor? A Beneficiary?

Are You or Any Individual Connected to the Trust, also United States Connected?

What is entrusted?

Has the Trust Borrowed Funds?

 Listen to Dimming of the Day – Estate Planning

https://tinyurl.com/yf9hrn7g

References
& Resources

MICHAEL J. MELLO QC, JP, TEP Author:
The Ninth Edition of the Laws of Wills & Estates in Bermuda

According to Attorney Mello,

"Of the topics we are most unwilling to discuss, making a Will is near the top of the list because it means making arrangements for our death. Most Bermudians will tell you they want their family and friends to know their last wishes, yet too many have never taken the time to set out in a Will what those wishes may be. For example, in the UK it was found that nearly two-thirds of adults with children in the household did not have a Will. However, the rapid increase in Bermuda's death duties since 1976 has made more Bermudians take notice and embark on estate planning, one of the most important considerations when making a Will."

GOOGLE all below

Bermuda's Executors and estate settlement. They must know their fiduciary responsibilities and act promptly on death of a testator.

Bermuda Administration of Estates Act 1974

Government of Bermuda: How to Probate an Estate in Bermuda

Bermuda Legislation

Bermuda Primary Homestead Certificate

The Administration of Estates Act 1974

The Non-Contentious Probate Rules 1974

The Succession Act 1974

The Wills Act 1988

Stamp Duties Act 1976 (as amended)

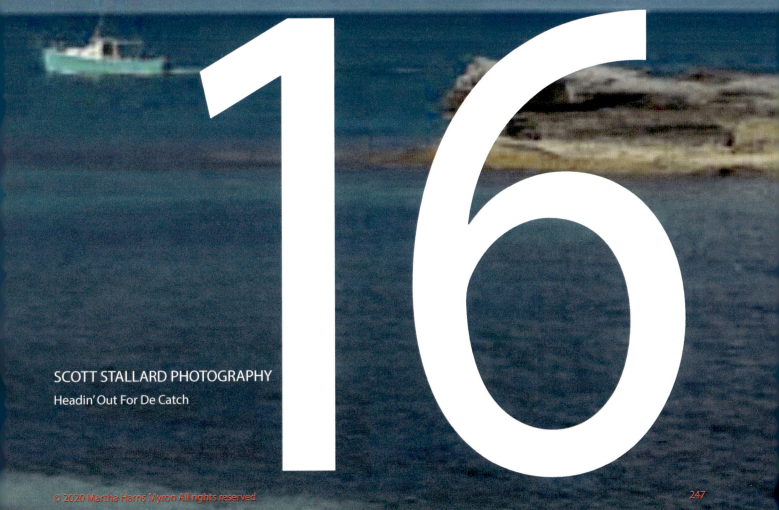

Bermuda Taxation
&
Global Compliance

16

SCOTT STALLARD PHOTOGRAPHY
Headin' Out For De Catch

Taxes come in many forms

	Tax/Fee
NEW	Airbnb surcharge
↑	Commercial lease tax for one year
Current	Conveyance fees
↑	Corporate registration fees
↑	Customs duty, courier services, excise free - wine and beer
NEW	Dividend and interest tax on local company shares
Current	Estate death tax and stamp duty
↑	Financial services fees on banks, local insurers
↑	Foreign exchange purchase fees
NEW	General services tax
↑	Immigration fees
↑	International company fees
↑	Land tax
NEW	Managed services tax
NEW	Notional new salary tax
↑	Old age contributory pension conversion to 'progressive contribution'
↓	Payroll tax decrease for employer*
NEW	Rental subsidy to the BTA
NEW	Rental income tax, commercial and residential - ARV progressive
NEW	Sugar tax
↑	Telecommunications, mobile, government authorisation taxes

Nothing Zero about tax in Bermuda: Martha
Harris Myron 2018Dec07 The Royal Gazette

Step Sixteen - Bermuda Domestic Taxation and Global Compliance Impact

Nothing Zero About Tax in Bermuda's Economy!

All governments across the globe assess some sort of taxes in order to operate a country, if you will. Some countries do have low tax rates - due to high valuations from native and natural products, such as sheer volumes of oil supplies to the world - that have the effect of reducing the need for taxation from the local populace to almost nil. Most countries, however, assess taxation in one form or another on their residents and citizens.

Bermuda is no exception, having just as many taxes as other jurisdictions, working out to a marginal tax rate of an average 22% of GDP (Gross Domestic Product).

Our domestic taxes are not based upon progressive outcomes; consequently, those families in the lower earnings brackets are much harder hit than the more upwardly mobile.

Additionally, the customs tax on all goods entering the island are assessed upon arrival, not at the cash register when the goods are sold, leaving retail at a severe disadvantage when left with unsaleable inventory - that has been taxed at full value upon entry into Bermuda, but now is worth less than wholesale value or nothing. The retailer must absorb these customs duty costs, no matter what eventually happens with ultimate sale of goods. Although, there have been severe complaints and attempts to change this regressive customs tax, all efforts to-date have not succeeded.

Further, our taxes are not based upon an income tax system, although the recent spate of new tax initiatives introduced for the first time, a tax on corporate dividends. How that will be accounted for, without the utilisation of a income tax program, remains to be seen.

International Business companies are exempt from corporate income taxation, dividends, and interest until 2035.

The effect of taxing the already heavily taxed.

A tax, by any other name – fees, tariffs, subsidies, registrations, licenses - is still a tax.

Certainly, a multitude of taxes for a country consistently labelled as a zero "tax haven." Little does anyone realise how incorrect this misnomer is!

Oh, and to top off all these taxes, tariff, fees, etc. increases:

- Health insurance rates set to, or have already, increased upwards of 18% for the year.
- It is unknown at this time, what the "real" cost of the new Bermuda Government single-payer health insurance plan will cost the ordinary Bermuda resident family.

- Home Mortgage interest rate increases announced at end of 2018 by local lending banks.

Taxes, the effect of direct and indirect taxation.

At fiscal year-end, 2018, Government estimated $147 million generated in increased tax collections based upon new and revised taxes - see chart above - over next three years, per the Tax Reform Com- mission Report.

How will said tax increases be utilised?

- Reduce annual budget deficit?
- Government Debt principal reduction – wouldn't that be wonderful?
- Consumed by inflation and laggard implementation.
- Upgrading capital transportation and other infrastructures?
- Increasing the sinking fund reserve?

Better question. With our current uncollected government tax liabilities now standing at 140 Million plus (increasing), what are the chances that these new (or increased) taxes ($147M) will be rationalised?

Your guess is as good as mine.

The Tax calculations. I'm particularly interested in two items:

1. Under the "new" Old age contributory pension progressive changes, will the contributor making larger contributions during work career, at retirement receive the same government pension amount regardless of the size of their work history contribution, or will those who pay in more, receive more?

If this is how the new legislation is intended to work whereby the work contributor pay more, but receive the same as a lower earning individual, is it fair and equitable, or aren't we just looking at another tax?

2. How will the "new" notional (really a dividend) tax) will be assessed against those high-earning professionals who earn a salary, but then receive additional distributions, not subject to payroll tax?

Bermuda employment statistics list an estimated 19% of working population individuals in the International Business senior management and professional categories, assuming earnings in excess of $96,000 per year. Are IB professionals included in this calculation?

But, are these really distributions? What happens if these professionals are already existing, or become, shareholders in their corporate entities? Wouldn't this notional tax actually legally be defined as a real dividend, not a deemed salary distribution? And won't they be doubly taxed?

And, if that is the case as currently, Bermuda shareholders of local incorporated company shares are not taxed on dividends paid.

Will this reclassification change the entire concept of the notional salary tax?

And if it does, will it mean that all local owners of incorporated companies shares, both publicly-traded and private companies, will be subject to double taxation: a dividend and a salary tax?

Could such a revaluation conflict with two opposing tax positions: zero dividend tax for International Business, but a serious dividend tax on all local incorporated entities?

Taxation (both increases and decreases) has a direct and indirect effect on an economy.

Increased Taxation (both new taxes and current tax increases) reduces the direct net income received by ordinary Bermuda resident households while indirect tax- passthroughs to them affects their purchasing decisions for food, clothing, retail products, utilities, health needs, services, and entertainment. Households faced with shrinking purchasing power - in ever increasing numbers - will instinctively cut back consumption, trim other costs, or go without.

Renters, both commercial and single tenant-type homeowners, will raise leases.

Exempt companies are always cited as getting a "free ride" with their legislated corporate zero tax until However, they, too, will experience higher costs across the board for personnel, benefits, commercial space, administration, et al. Public companies have an overriding responsibility to their share-holders and investors. They will never hesitate to trim expenses.

Increasing taxes is never an economic accelerator.

History reminds us time and time again. Tax costs are always passed on, because no one is going to absorb (immediately, or indefinitely) such, some would say arbitrary, tax expenses by accepting small-er profits or no profit at all.

Tax cuts, on the other hand, can (not always) increase household and consumer demand by increasing workers' take-home pay, boost business-es demand by increasing their after-tax cash flow, which can be used to pay dividends and expand activity, and by making hiring and investing more attractive.

Can our community stand the pain of these tax increases?

The supposedly well-heeled will seek alternative methods to transfer assets to other jurisdictions to generate income, completely nullifying their local tax contributions. Those who do not have such choices, Bermuda's middle class, will have to tighten their belts further, while limiting their consumption again, to perhaps nothing but the necessaries.

Tell me, then. How does such a tax initiative help rejuvenate an economy?

Meanwhile, Bermuda government expenses continue to rise: a current deficit budget (more deficits projected for next several fiscal years given the Morgan's Point bailout debacle), credit line and higher debt interest increases, financial assistance levels rising, new authority administration costs, continued capital infrastructure assets/services breakdown, etc.

Shouldn't government be focusing on revenue generation through every means possible?

Bermuda & Her Statutory Global Tax Compliance & Reporting Obligations

Bermuda is globally respected for its leadership and proven record on compliance and transparency. The jurisdiction has more than 120 treaty partnerships with nations around the world.

Notably, the European Union awarded Bermuda full equivalence with its Solvency II insurance regulatory regime; only one other jurisdiction (Switzerland) has that distinction.

Bermuda also holds qualified jurisdiction status from the National Association of Insurance Commissioners (NAIC) in the US diction.

Bermuda's global business hub comprises numerous markets: insurance and reinsurance; captive insurance; life and annuity insurance; insurance-linked securities; asset management; trusts and private client vehicles; family offices and other high net-worth services; shipping and aviation registries; ship-finance and ship-management; life sciences, fintech, insurtech, cryptocurrencies and digital assets businesses.

Bermuda has 41 bilateral Tax Information Exchange Agreements (TIEAs) and more than 125 multilateral treaty partners. The island exchanges information with all G20 nations, European Union members states, and other OECD countries. Bermuda has implemented US FATCA and exchanges OECD Common Reporting Standard (CRS) and OECD Country-by-Country (CBC) information with every country around the world that belongs to the OECD's Convention.

The adherence to global transparency, compliance, AML- Anti-Money Laundering and Terrorist, KYC-Know Your Client and related regulations has generated significant, and often, costly complexity in required documentation for local residents, thousands of whom have multinational, multi-jurisdictional connections to all parts of the globe.

There is no such thing as an individual (or entity) 10-minute bank account opening or a speedy corporate formation (with no underlying beneficiary disclosure) in Bermuda. All applications from individuals and businesses are thoroughly vetted by all Bermuda banks, Bermuda Monetary Authority, financial institutions, and other services providers.

Our reputation is vital to continued success.

See

The Craft of Creating a Lasting Reputation by Martha Harris Myron, 2013Sep21, The Royal Gazette, Bermuda

All readers of this missive who may have connections elsewhere, should carefully peruse the final chapter of this book on

BERMUDA PONDSTRADDLERS' LIFE™ & THEIR INTERNATIONAL CONNECTIONS

for ramifications of

CROSS BORDER PLANNING CHALLENGES, TAXATION AND COMPLIANCE!

Listen to
Bermuda Taxation
& Global Compliance

https://tinyurl.com/ygk59pcr

References
& Resources

Bermuda Department of Statistics

Bermuda Job Market Employment Brief 2018 https://www.gov.bm/sites/default/ files/9370_ EB%20August%202018.pdf

Bermuda Tax Reform Commission http://www. royalgazette.com/assets/pdf/ RG3952681119.pdf

The Following Bermuda Legislative Acts Are Listed on either Bermuda Laws or Parliament Bills by year.

Bermuda Payroll Tax Rates Act 1995

Office of the Tax Commissioner

Bermuda Land Taxes Amendment Act 2019
All homeowners and long-term tenants are required to pay Land Tax twice yearly. You must pay Land Tax if you are: the sole proprietor of a property; a life tenant in a property; a leaseholder for three or more years; a periodic (yearly or monthly) tenant of property owned by the Government of Bermuda. Land tax is assessed on the ARV (annual rental value) of the property.

The Land Tax on Commercial Properties is 9.5%, annually, billed semi-annually.

Bermuda Conveyancing Act 1983
Fees - stamp duty, etc. estimated at around 4% of property sales value. See Conveyancing Act 1983 - Bermuda Laws Online

Bermuda Corporate Taxes for Exempt Undertakings
Bermuda imposes no taxes on profits, income, dividends, or capital gains, has no limit on the accumulation of profit, and has no requirement to distribute dividends. All companies pay an annual company fee, based on share capital levels.

The Bermuda government routinely grants Tax Assurance Certificates to exempted undertakings (i.e. exempted companies, permit companies, exempted partnerships, and exempted unit trust schemes) on application to the Minister through the Bermuda Monetary Authority. These Tax Assurances guarantee that any Parliamentary imposition of such taxes will not be applicable to the company and its operations in future years. Currently, the Tax Assurances being granted extend to 31 March 2035.

Bermuda Rental Properties Listed on Airbnb
4.5% Airbnb-Bermuda Guests who book Airbnb listings that are located in Bermuda will pay the following country taxes as part of their reservation: Vacation Rental Fee: 4.5% of the listing price including for all reservations. For detailed information, please visit the Bermuda Tourism Authority website.

Bermuda Custom Duties - a 450-Page Missive!
25% Bermuda Customs Duty Fees - aka Import Tariffs - average 22.5% - 25% on transaction value of imported goods. Food is lower at 5%.

Vehicles - exorbitantly high almost double the value of the wholesale vehicle cost.

Bermuda Domestic Company Dividends Tax
5% Interest and Dividends Withholding Flat Tax on Local Companies, both Public and Private. $1,000 exemption, annually.

Annual company fees
Varies by size of company

Bermuda Estate Death Tax and Stamp Duty
See STEP Fifteen

Bermuda Financial Services Tax Amendment Act 2019
Banks 00.75%. Domestic Insurers 3.5%. Money service businesses 1% on aggregate income/out-go volume

Foreign Exchange (Currency) Purchase Tax Amendment Act 2019
1.25% of Bermuda dollar value plus bank fees and commissions

Corporate Services Tax
7% on local providers of corporate services on gross revenue earned from exempted entities.

Immigration and Work Permit Fees Various thresholds of work permit salaries imposed on a sliding scale.

Managed Services Tax -
This tax is assessed on companies offshoring work based on gross volume of work contracted - to a lower cost economy - that could ordinarily be performed in Bermuda.

Notional Salary Payroll Tax Increases
- new regime based upon progressive thresholds From 1.75% up to 10.25%

Bermuda Government Old Age Contributory Pension Fee Structure
In process of revision to a "more equitable" type progressive tax assessment.

The Controversial Sugar Tax
5% of Gross Purchase assessed on all sugared drinks, candy and related items.

Telecommunications Tax.
Vacation Rental tax 4.5% of the rack rate

Vehicular and Oil Taxes
New vehicle tax - incredibly punitive, at almost 100% of wholesale value Oil / fuel tax at estimated 30% per litre cost

Other Related Taxes Sources:
How Taxes Affect an Economy
US Tax Policy Centre

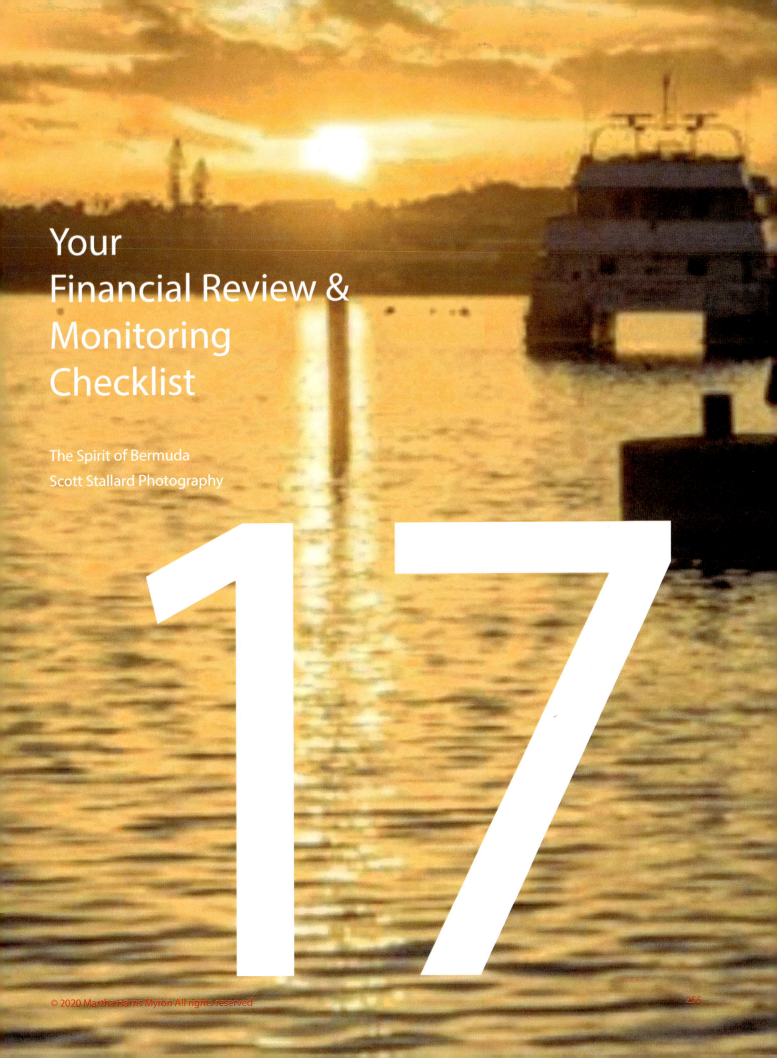

Your
Financial Review &
Monitoring
Checklist

The Spirit of Bermuda
Scott Stallard Photography

17

Step Seventeen - Financial Monitoring Checklist

Dawn Of New Beginnings Financial Monitoring Checklist

Your Bermuda Back-2-Basics Financial Review is Over.

You've reached the Lightness of Being - in Financial Control of your finances, in our unique Bermuda financial environment.

Bermuda's Coat-of-Arms is Quo Fata Ferunt, meaning wherever the Fates will Lead Us.

You do not embrace that motto.

You be in control of your financial destiny!

This is the final step of a long, hopefully exciting, illuminating review of all of your Bermuda financial resources in order to improve your financial Lifestyle

Did you do it?

Congratulations. You've run the course - gone through frustration, boredom, and lack of confidence, now you are just about at the end.

What was your outcome? Were you happy with your financial review? Was it fun, frustrating, or just plain depressing?

Do you feel more in control of your financial life now?

Did you think it was a good idea to review your personal finances, but then never got around to it?

Do it now. It is never too late to start.

The prevailing reception that ran throughout the original 16-week articles in the Royal Gazette (not this 250+ page plus scrutiny) of the original Fundamental Financial Review in 2015 - was positively exhilarating, with more inquiries in personal finance than ever before, and from as far away as New Zealand.

I hope those of you who struggled through the "I Just Don't Know What I Bought That Day" budget category got things sorted out.

We can all learn something from that classic exercise, and it is this.

It is not the big expenses that put us in the Red.

We all fritter away more money on little every-day treats, food, drink, and random purchases that we do not need.

It all adds up – to big numbers at the end of the month. If you have done nothing else but control this impulse spending, you have come a long way, readers.

Just a few financial housekeeping chores left to wrap up your financial review to dramatically improve your financial lifestyle.

You've realised you have some gaps, say in life or property coverage; you saved a bit and now would like to start a small investment fund; or, you know that you seriously need to update your estate plan and will.

Where do you start?

You may consider DIY-do it yourself, or perhaps, you would rather work with a qualified planning professional.

You will be challenged because you must undertake a basic understanding of three items:

- Understand the Bermuda Financial Environment and how it affects you, your budget and your family planning;
- Understand the qualifications of an individual finance person you choose to work with;
- Understand the financial product you may purchase;

And honestly, you must Learn how to USE the Internet to your advantage!

Since February 26, 2000, I have written a weekly Moneywise column - more than one thousand (1,000) articles to date on a wide range of illuminating financial subjects for the Personal Finance section of the Royal Gazette, Bermuda's national newspaper.

My opinions, rants (sometimes) and experience in offshore (and onshore) financial matters, and feed-back from readers, have ranged the gamut. People still ask me how I can possibly find topics of interest.

The answer!

Our finances are the biggest concerns in our lives next to our relationships and our health. There is a never-ending stream of current financial topics to understand. It is my mission always to help with that understanding.

I have a serious personal commitment To You, dear Reader, who may be reading this.

I care deeply about your financial success, and those of the loyal Readers of the Personal Finance column, Royal Gazette, Bermuda

Resources and references have been provide throughout to allow you to perform you own due diligence, independently of advice from friends, relatives like your BIL (brother-in-law) or your aunt who truly care about you and profess to know all things financial (maybe they do), your pastoral counsellors (God love them), an outside visiting "axpert" who is actually a financial salesperson ready to sell you the latest "hot" investment, your local banker, the butcher, baker, candlestick maker and more.

All the best, now it is up to you!

Martha

Wrapping Up the Residuals and Future Monitoring of Your Financial Matters

- <u>Get your Life Goals in Place</u>. Keep them in mind at all times. Biggest goal to buy a home? Paste up pictures of your dream home - everywhere - in your current residence. It will motivate you!

- <u>Continue to Monitor</u> Your Bank, Investment, Pension, Insurance Accounts from your plan review for the next year and the next and the next.

- <u>Set up a reminder schedule</u> that you are comfortable with, particularly if you are on a savings binge.

- <u>Review your cash budget weekly</u>, or monthly, or as best as you. Once you've successfully met your first savings goal, by controlling your expenses, you can back off to once a month.

- <u>Set up another savings goal</u> for the next new thing that you'd like in your life: a home, a new car, a vacation, a growing savings and investment fund(s).

- <u>Review your Bermuda National Pension account immediately after receiving the statement</u>. If the account is deficient, notify the Pension Commission immediately. The faster you react, the faster the contribution deficiencies can be rectified, or at least stopped. Waiting six months or a year to review your pensions statements may be too late to attempt to recoup those late, or delinquent contributions. If you only receive semi-annual statements, then open your pension account online for review, monthly.

- <u>Check on your Social Insurance Old Age Contributory fund</u> by calling or stopping in to the Government Social Insurance department. The warning is the same as the pension scheme. You must consistently keep track of your contributions!

- <u>Reviewing personal investment</u> accounts and the investment component of your pension plan statements quickly once a month, or pull down the current fact sheets of your investment firm's (bank) website. We will be covering investments in a new series in late 2022.

- In the meantime, if you don't understand what you have invested in, send me a current fact sheet. I will review and comment to you.

- <u>Make sure you are protected for contingencies</u>: property / vehicle/ health/life insurance up-to-date, cash cushion in place, work/career ears to the ground - always watching for the next opportunity to succeed, and to plan ahead if redundancy is looming.

- <u>Assure that your life insurance policy(s), will, and pension have the right beneficiaries</u>.

- <u>Make a will, get your health care directives in place - take care of your family</u>

- <u>Finally, take care of yourself: physically, mentally, holistically, emotionally, and spiritually.</u>

- <u>You are important to this world, your family and community.</u>

Repeat.

Stay the course, now.
Don't let things slip.
Remember always.
You control your financial future!

Should You Work with a Qualified Financial Planning Professional?

It also could be - the establishment of a one- on-one relationship with a knowledgeable, experienced, qualified financial planning professional who will, in a fiduciary client interest-first proscribed documented format,

The Alphabet Soup of Financial Advisors Credentials

A. Assess your personal situation (with feedback from you);

B. Review and Analyse your financial, and non-financial data;

C. Present written objective recommendations with strategies to solve financial problems;

D. And provide guidance on how best to implement your financial goals.

Caution for Readers! Scepticism is a necessary investment research component

The Alphabet Soup of credentials. Regrettably, the term financial planning has become a generic commodity these days. It is a marketing hook for all things financial, from selling a mutual fund to purchasing a home; so much so that in many cases, the perception of what planning is, what it can actually accomplish (or not) has become blurred.

Readers, you must be careful to exercise due diligence at every phase in your financial planning to be sure that what you are doing and the advice you are receiving is unbiased from qualified, conflict-of-interest-free financial planners. There are many trusted advisors available, so you have choices in deciding on an experienced qualified person, a fiduciary and one that makes you feel comfortable.

See more details on How to Choose a Trusted Advisor in Book Three of the Bermuda Fundamental Financial Planning Primer Series – Tacking & Turbulence. The First Bermuda Investment Primer.

Does Everyone Need a Plan?

Some in the industry would say, yes, others would argue definitely not always.

Sometimes, a full financial plan is over- whelming in length, depth, and time to implement. It becomes such a hurdle that nothing ever gets done.

Focusing on one aspect of a plan at a time can accomplish more.

This is a new directional trend that people getting their finances up to par find appealing and achievable.

There is no doubt, though, that at some point in life most people will need some sort of a financial plan. Now whether they will admit it or not, and whether it is formalised or not, is another issue – but without some type of financial structure, those who fail to plan, are planning to fail. You've heard this quote many times, I am sure.

How will you know whether you need (or don't) a plan?

Start with the questions below, and if you answer yes to more than a couple, you'll have to think seriously about some professional help.

Then review the Trigger events - many also listed below - that may necessitate working with a qualified planner, or a team (legal, financial, holistic) to resolve your complicated issues satisfactorily.

- Cash Flow Projections: Are you the kind of person who feels your finances are totally out of control?

- Do you have neither time nor inclination to refine management of cash, accumulate savings, and start a serious long-term investment program?

- Do you have a savings allocation for contingencies and liquidity?

- Assets – Are your investable assets producing for you, or are you wasting opportunities. Don't forget, you are your most valuable asset.

- Liabilities - do you have high debt?

- Do you want to restructure your loans to be more manageable?

- Are you struggling with reducing credit card debt or education needs?

- Risk management: Do you have any life insurance?

- Property and casualty?

- Do you have any idea how much you should spend and what coverage you really need?

- Investing:

- Do you want to invest?

- Any idea how to invest?

- Do you know what your investment knowledge level is?

- Or do you just want to pass the entire job over to your advisor.

- Do you have any retirement savings?

- Do you have any idea how, where, when, and with what you will consider retiring?

- Estate and trust planning:

- Do you have a will?

- Have you protected your property with the Primary Homestead Resident Certificate?

- Do you have a medical health care directive, or a power of attorney? We won't live forever, you know! Of course, we are very sure that we will never leave this dear earth as a young person, either.

- Personal Goals: do you have several financial goals that you wish to achieve and need guidance and counselling.

Significant Impending Life Event Triggers:

Are you experiencing significant changes, such as any of the following life happenings?

- Annuity distribution decisions, domestic, foreign pensions

- Retirement

- Redundancy

- Deferred compensation payment, stock options and benefits

- Significant changes in lifestyle creating demands on investment portfolio, which will require an objective review

- Divorce, marriage, extended family support issues

- Serious disability, special needs, or illness in family of child, or breadwinner, etc.

- Recently widowed, loss of partner in relationship or business

- Beneficiary of an inheritance

- Proceeds from sale of, or investments in, real estate, securities / investments

- Mortgage finally paid-off!
- University financing
- International / domestic tax connections and liabilities
- Property investments abroad
- Obtaining another citizenship, e.g. United States, Canadian, UK,
- Expatriation - US citizen, US green card holder
- Lump sum Settlement of an insurance policy, lawsuit, lottery winnings, bonus
- Investment knowledge upgrade, choosing an advisor
- Starting a business, incorporating, selling a business
- Organising an estate, making a will, settling a trust,
- Immigration to another domicile
- Personal relative Eldercare, and accompanying long-term maintenance of real property

Should You Pay Fees -

If you need professional planning guidance? The debate regarding the method of compensation for obtaining a plan remains largely unsettled, with basically two opposing methods. The first group feels that financial plans should be free, but that statement is a complete misnomer because the client will pay a fee to purchase a financial product, be it investments or insurance, or another investment structure.

This method may work quite well for the client whose ultimate goal was to simply purchase an investment anyway.

But what of the client who has

- a specific life issue,
- or financial problem that cannot be solved by buying an investment product,

- or one who is not at the stage where they even feel comfortable investing,
- or a person who has multinational, multi-jurisdictional personal and business connections,
- or even a person who has as many investments as they absolutely need, but still desire some very personal financial consulting?

These clients (and many more) fall into the advocates of the second financial planning camp, those who provide separate-from-any-financial-product independent financial advice for a fee.

How much for an independent financial planner, that is the real question?

Fees will range according to needs assess- ment, amount of analysis and consulting needed.

You may only need an hour of a qualified advisor's time to a full plan for your entire profile. What you pay should be declared upfront and provide a clear-cut value for money.

And if you think that paying fees for financial planning seems expensive, consider two things:

1. Just about every security transaction (touting free financial planning) charges a fee that may be obvious, or may be embedded in the purchase price, e.g. every mutual fund investment purchase may have a commission attached, i.e. invest $10,000 in a mutual, 5% ($500) of that pays your advisor. Annuity fee and commissions may be even higher.

2. Secondly, no planning at all may ultimately generate huge fees to 'fix' the mistakes in say a portfolio of losses, a completely incorrect handling of a foreign tax issue, or to sort out an estate.

How do you know if paying a fee for financial planning is worth it?

In the final analysis, what you receive in terms of any described financial plan, should be advice that is specifically tailored for you.

- It should be easy to understand, but not so generic as to have little relevance to your life needs;

- short and simple to read, not 10 – 50 pages of pie charts and numbers - bet you never thought your financial life could be so extensive;

- easy to implement by yourself – or if more complex tied to the planner/advisor working with you along the way to be sure that the recommendations for various phases all correlate;

- provided by a fiduciary, a planner that must put your interests first: and

- gives you a comfortable feeling, a feeling of real serenity that your personal financial plan structure will get you to where you want to go.

It's time to plan for the future!

Trust, but Verify should be your new mantra.

All of the above types of financial planning professionals are, in general, well intended, but a basic cynic like me, under my professional fiduciary standards, must independently verify all information provided to me including an individual's credentials who may be holding out as an "advisor."

Disclosure. This verification has credibility - I no longer am practicing as an international financial planning practitioner and have no conflict of interest.

- Get the facts, no embellishments.
- Either your advisor is qualified, or he/ she is not. Ask for the credentials!
- Always get the truth.
- You too must be prepared to verify before making your own informed decisions.

Why do you need to do this? There is a literal massive alphabet soup of financial representatives out there, most legitimate, but some with nothing more than a six-week course touting a business card and certificate that is intended to represent far more knowledge and investment experience than these individuals actually have.

Additionally, nefarious scammers, hackers, misrepresenters of qualifications, and fraudsters are all lurking thereabouts to take advantage of your trusting nature, limited knoweldge of complex financial products, your feelings of intimidation, subliminal peer pressure, and or misunderstandings of how our economy affects your financial interests. Keeping current on financial issues and being aware of how to detect threats to your financial existence (even on a small scale) is extremely important.

No one else can do this for you.

Case-in-point,
a true scammer story.

"But he was a nice-looking gentleman wearing an expensive suit.

She came to see me a number of years ago. "I invested most of my savings with this man, who came to one of my social circles in our church. He seemed so nice; some people seemed to know him. I thought he had credibility and the return he offered on this investment was really good.

So, I gave him more money than I could really afford. I haven't seen any interest payments and now, I cannot get any reports from him; the phone just goes to voice mail; he has never called back, and of course, he lives in another country.

Can you help me get the money back?"

My regretful answer. PROBABLY NOT.

Probably not, this is person long gone with the money, too.

A quick Internet search revealed criminality, tax fraud, and indictments linked to this individual.

<u>Use the Internet to your advantage.</u>

Many people still don't want (or can't) enter the Internet Age. Yes, I realise that not everyone can afford a home computer, the monthly cost, and all of those related items. But, you probably can afford a smart phone – the next best thing to a standing computer. It will work to your advantage to stay informed.

Overall, though, the toughest part for many is actually learning how to use these electronic devices to the fullest extent. Yet, they can be your best protection against misunderstandings of financial products and outright fraud.

In today's hacker environment, waiting 30 days to review an investment portfolio or bank statements allows Internet theft to happen long before you ever find out, certainly, or can have the transfers stopped!

For instance, in suspected credit card fraud, the cardholder must notify the credit card company within 48 hours. **After that, your chances of reimbursement are almost - nil.**

Internet search engines, such as Google, are your friends. If you cannot find adequate information on a product or a service to make an informed decision, write to me. I will help.

References
& Resources

Alphabet soup of financial registrations: Some legitimate, some may not even have a six-week course in finance. It is vital to be CONSUMER BEWARE.

Research these work-permit holders frequently employed in Bermuda - home country national web-sites for information on your advisor. See below.

Also note, that Bermuda does not license or register financial salespersons, planners, brokers, and so on. It is up to the finance company as employer to verify the credentials of their financial advisors.

Bermuda Investment Business Act 1998

Bermuda Investment Business Guidelines 1999

Professional Designations

Verifying a financial advisor's credentials: you can write, call, or research online for these various categories.

The Alphabet Soup of Financial Certifications Google investopedia

Certified Public Accountant and Chartered Accountant License

United States: search individual state boards of accountancy, if known where the individual was licensed, e.g. Martha C Myron NH#1929, current licensee through June 30 2024

Canada. Chartered Professional Accountant: CPA Canada

Bermuda. Chartered Professional

Accountant: CPA Bermuda Chartered Account: United Kingdom

UK. Institute of Chartered Accountants in England and Wales (ICAEW)

Certified Financial Planner designation

Certified Financial Planner CFP® – US CFP Board of Standards

Certified Financial Planner, CFP™ – UK Chartered Institute for Securities & Investment 2020 Brokers; Investment Advisers; Investment Managers; Wealth Managers; Financial Planners; Financial Advisers; Discretionary Fund Managers; Private Bankers and Portfolio Managers

FP Canada Institute – CFP® QAFP CIFP

Chartered Financial Analyst designation CFA®

CFA Institute Inc. US – global certification, search by country, or name to locate a member

CFA Society of the UK CFA Societies Canada CFA Society Bermuda

Security Licenses: Investment brokers and more specialized categories.

United States. FINRA Financial Industry Regulatory Authority Credentials:

Securities Industry Essentials(SIE), Series 3, 4, 6, 7, 9/10, 14, 16, 22, 23, 24, 27, 28, 30, 31, 32, 34, 39, 50, 51, 52, 53, 54, 57, 79, 82, 86/87, 99

Broken into levels: FINRA- representatives and principals, municipal securities (MSRB), national futures – NASAA 63, 65, 66

Canada. Canadian Securities Institute A Moody's Analytical Company

Credentials: FCSI® PFP® CIM® CIWM MTI®

United Kingdom. FCA Financial Conduct Authority - Chartered Institute for Securities & Investment 2020. Brokers; Investment Advisers; Investment Managers; Wealth Managers; Financial Planners; Financial Advisers; Discretionary Fund Managers; private Bankers and Portfolio Managers

Insurance Licenses

US. NIPR National Insurance Producer Registry CPCU ChFC

UK. Chartered Insurance Institute

Canada. Insurance Institute CIP® Chartered Insurance Professional FCIP® Fellow of prior.

BERMUDA

Pondstraddlers' Life™

Cross Border

Complexity

18

Scott Stallard PHOTOGRAPHY

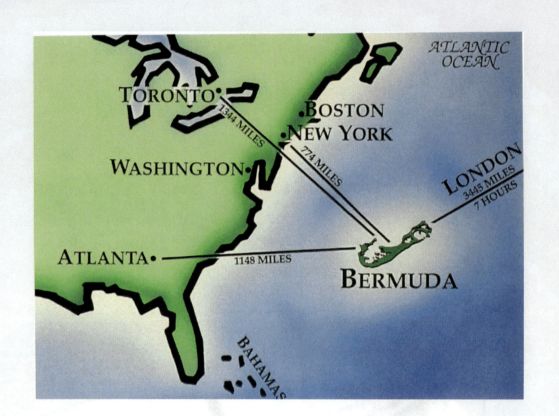

Step Eighteen - Bermuda Pondstraddlers' Life™ Cross Border Challenges

Cross Border Financial Planning Challenges, Taxation and Compliance

A Pondstraddler is a person with one foot on each shore whose heart resides in both countries.

Heads Up for Bermuda Pondstraddlers and Their International Connections

Bermuda Residents are Perennial Pondstraddlers, so many of us have International Connections. We have uniquely sophisticated lifestyles

Where are we?

Remote, beautiful, Bermuda Island Living instils independence, determination, and flexibility. Such qualities derived from surviving and thriving on a tiny dot of an extinct volcano fed by the warm Gulf Stream in the middle of the North Atlantic Ocean - the fourth most remote habitat in the world.

Who are we?

Adventurous and innovative far beyond Bermuda's limited population size, our Bermudian forebears and now contemporaries ventured aggressively into the outer spheres of global commerce for sheer economic survival: pioneer builders of the fast rake-masted, 'Bermoode' rig sloop that dominated the sailing world in the seventeenth century; aided large young countries in domestic strife and world wars; established an export food production business to the Eastern seaboard, northward, and south to the Caribbean; then, reinvented ourselves again as a tourist destination and currently, as the premier offshore financial risk centre.

Today, the Modern Bermuda International Finance Centre is the third largest global (Re)insurance capital in the world, along with being the largest captive insurance market, investment funds, maritime shipping industries, fintech, and trust administration in international commerce.

Why are we Bermuda islanders Perennial Pondstraddlers?

For more than 400 years, Bermuda residents have been habitual border crossers. You can label us "puddle-jumpers" "Pond- straddlers", "nomads," "global explorers" or "inveterate wanderers," but the fact remains that there is no unequivocal choice.

We physically have to leave this dot of a re- mote island to get to where we want to go. While there may be a few Bermudians who have never left the dear island in their entire lives, we can assume that almost everyone travels elsewhere, building relationships, investments, business and links of all sorts to countries with different regulations and tax regimes.

And are we connected!

United States, United Kingdom, Ireland, Canada, Caribbean, Mexico, Brazil, Honduras, Guatemala, Aruba, Germany, France, Italy, Spain, Greece, Australia, New Zealand, Hong Kong, Switzerland, Eastern Europe, Ukraine, Croatia, Philippines, Thailand, Sri Lanka. Can you name more?

Every border crossing has a consequence.

Mobility affects one's finances as each country that considers you a resident - if you have stayed there for a legally-defined time period (or over-stayed as a "visitor") - wants to tax you for the benefits you are presumed to have received.

Mobility is not limited to physical activity transitions.

Finances of all sorts are incredibly electronically mobile today, too. Open an investment account in your home country; the security assets may be derived from or sited in a second country, while the custodians may be located in third, fourth, and fifth country.

Other mobile circumstances generate tax accountability.

Moving abroad for a lengthy career — under Canadian tax regulations, certain of your assets are deemed to have been sold with the tax assessed, then remitted to the government's revenue agency. Leaving a country permanently while also relinquishing US citizenship in the process, could also find you facing a exit tax (if above certain ordained financial / legal /immigration thresholds) computed on phantom sales of your current and future assets (ie pensions, etc) as well as your estate. Multinational families / dual-triple citizens with residences and assets in multiple jurisdictions just added an additional complexity multiplier to the tax equation.

Every government is eager to collect Taxes from every source for its coffers.

The United States citizenship-based taxation structure still tends to receive criticism for its world-wide tax and reporting positions.
However, in the age of global information exchanges, along with implementation of various cooperative reporting schemes between countries (i.e. FATCA and its emulators, EU Directive, CRS-Common Reporting Standards, etc.), the taxation of non-resident citizens and residents of a country has become more exact, fluid and relentless. Cooperative agreements of various types have given global taxing authorities tremendous jurisdictional reach and ability to monitor, analyse, compare and track the financial lives of their residents and citizens wherever they may be!

The global migration effect on Bermuda islanders and their families.

A local family may have in the past appeared to be purely Bermudian, domestically situated. This family picture is deceiving.

Reality may be far different.

Generations of families have grown, migrated abroad, and returned to Bermuda, changing their entire family structure, irrevocably. The resident Bermuda population then may contain many nationalities, all of whom whether migratory career professionals, finance and risk management executives, hospitality and related service foreigners, local Bermuda families with longevity ties, or migrant construction / agricultural workers have certain ties and provenances to elsewhere.

Domestic families, with hundreds of years old Bermudian family ancestral lineage, now have international relatives, assets, and business interests that need complex legal, tax, immigration, and cross border financial planning.

Families cannot plan complacently as was done in the past if they wish to continue to build, maintain and preserve their global assets for the future.

March 2020 - Update on Bermuda Residents' Relocation to Other Jurisdictions

More frequently now, according to local social media, and anecdotal commentary, individuals and families have already left Bermuda or are contemplating moving to other jurisdictions. While actual relocations numbers are not quantified, a substantive drop in the resident population has been noted by local industries: health-related, retail, entertainment, real estate volumes, insurance, utility and telecommunication usage decreases, grocery consumption, and others - are also affected by COVID safety measures

Globally, people are more mobile than ever before.

Bermuda residents are no exception. One can only speculate on the various reasons for temporary or permanent relocation, such as: schooling, work permit termination, career development, eg. secondment, individual and family opportunities, cost-of- living challenges, and a comfortable retirement.

All relocations, particularly permanent ones, are a wrenching decision process, an emotional, exciting, overwhelming experience for anyone, but particularly for Bermuda residents detaching permanently from generations of left-behind family members, the community they have always known and their beloved island home.

An illustration of a homesick Bermuda is- lander springs to mind. On one memorable occasion when working at a local Bermuda investment firm, I placed a call inquiry to a United States bank's investment department.

The analyst answering the phone had our distinctive Bermuda accent, we know you can't miss it. Before there was a chance to state the inquiry, he said: "You're calling from Bermuda. Oh, my wife and I are Bermudian — we're here on a three-year secondment. We miss Bermuda so much!"

At that his voice broke as he choked up (this is a true story, no exaggeration). Then, he said: "We get so homesick sometimes that we play recordings of tree frogs after workdays to remind us of home."

Relocation emotions aside, realistic move planning should be at the forefront.

There are many, many decisions to be made practically, and financially to assure that the family emigration is as stress-free as possible, with the financial planning aspects at the forefront.

Regardless of where (and when) your new lives in a new country will begin, there are numerous primary items that planning a premove will provide a smoother passage.

The alternative of no planning, say, just walking in and overstaying in your new country, has the potential to torpedo any pre-planning protective measures.

Why?

Let's say, for example, that a family has decided to emigrate abroad. Their choices are:

- United States,
- Canada,
- or the United Kingdom.

The defining factor for all three countries are significant income tax regimes, administered by each country tax and revenue agencies. Resident individuals are mandated to file and pay tax liabilities on their domestic income as well as, in most instances, on their worldwide income, meaning including income, capital gains, etc. on assets derived from Bermuda.

Understand that this is a very simplistic version of the tax complexity of the three countries mentioned above.

Bermuda does not have an income tax regime, nor do most Bermuda islanders understand other countries' tax, immigration, and legal responsibilities.

Further, there are only a very few Bermuda tax treaties for income, estate or gift tax with other countries.

Oh, yes, Bermuda taxes her residents, more so than ever before, (see Taxation above) but generally, these taxes or stamp duties do not constitute an income tax regime. The closest the Bermuda Government came to that idea was the introduction of a rental income tax, that was not implemented — to the relief of every homeowner relying upon a studio apartment income to manage the home mortgage.

Consider that this Bermuda family group has worked hard for many years to acquire a home, savings, investments, pensions, insurance and the like on an income tax- free basis - may or will possibly face taxes imposed by their new country on their Bermudian-based income and assets — all that was earned (and saved long) before moving abroad.

Hardly seems fair, does it, to have to face the financial dilemma of allegiance between two (or even more) countries. However, a planning review implemented prior to an emigration move, or an application(say a US green card) and the like before the family is considered resident and subject to tax in another country can mitigate these consequences. Such a review will detail every aspect of you and your family's legal, tax, and financial positions.

The Cross-Border Data Discovery Checklist below was developed by the author from a culmination of 30 years of client domestic and international financial planning. Even so, this list is a general overview, not all-inclusive and does not (or cannot) address individual positions.

The CB Checklist is meant as a guide for emigrating families to start the process of planning — before they walk into taxation surprises.

Readers: Cautious due diligence is required, however, to discover "dormant" international contexts in what appears to be an ordinary Bermuda domestic family.

The full documentation and explanations for cross border financial planning is beyond the scope of this first in the Bermuda Islander's Fundamental Financial Planning Series Primers, but will be featured in a future primer.

This list below is strictly an overview, never comprehensive; it is well to remember that there are always information and adverse circumstances surprises!

- Residency, Domicile and Citizenship(s) compounded
- Country Connections and Familial Relationships: Social, Emotional, Cultural and Physical Ties to Two or more countries
- Multi-national businesses, marital multiple citizenships, global employment
- International and Domestic Tax Compliance FATCA, CRS, AML, KYC, etc.
- Immigration and Customs Regulations in Crossing Borders

- Duelling Economies, Trade & Business Interests Complications
- Cash Management, Currency Exchanges
- Investments, International and Domestic Allocations, Passive and Active, tangible and intangible, foreign and domestic, tax efficient and tax compliant and non.
- Insurance and Risk Management for Multiple Jurisdictions.
- Retirement and Pension Complexity Constraints
- Estate Planning for Multinational Families in more than One Jurisdiction
- Regulatory Quagmires, Conflicts of Laws, and Inadvertent Financial, Legal and Immigration Planning Traps

CAUTION:

I've been warning Bermuda residents of these inevitable tax regime complications for many years. Therefore, it behooves any Bermuda island resident individual / family with international connections to seriously plan for the financial, tax, legal, immigration, insurance, retirement, and estate planning impact of any or all of the following criteria on each financial decision.

If you have these complex family situations, you should consult first with a qualified internationally experienced professional (knowledgeable in all aspects of the international financial / legal connections that you or your family are exposed to) before implementing any financial plan.

For instance: Where Is your residency, domicile, and citizenship(s)?

A person's residency (and domicile), or a business or trust entity's place of central control and management, is the most critical attribute because where a person is considered resident is where the person will be subject to taxation. Residency determination will override citizenship, generally, except for the US model.

Residency is defined in taxation terms by the OECD Model Treaty that is used by most countries in the world today; it is based upon the number of days of residence, generally 183 days or longer in a year. Residency may also be defined by facts and circumstances test, and reference specific country residency definitions: US Immigration and IRS. HMRC — the UK has a different definition of residency and domi- cile; Canada Revenue Agency residency regulations, legal definition of a resident — different again.

Complications of Relocation

Relocating to another jurisdiction is not necessarily the panacea for all ills.

Every single country on the planet has different government regulations, customs, legal hurdles, residency/citizenship obligations, cost-of-living, insurance, immigration constraints, inheritance.

Almost all (oF 244 countries and territories) have income tax regimes. See Wikipedia International taxation

Another primary concern, "free" health costs elsewhere while often cited as a reason to leave, is a misconception.

Health costs in Canada and the United Kingdom are paid for by everyone through their tax liability deductions and income tax return assessments.

Employers in the US are not legally obligated to provide health insurance at all, leaving it up to the individual to fund their own healthcare. Government subsidies exist, but US Medicare for retirees is paid — long in advance — through one's entire working career, in addition to income taxes.

The overwhelming planning for the family here is how to manage the assets they currently own when transitioning from Bermuda's income tax-free environment to a fully integrated tax regime system country.

Also, keep in mind that all financial institutions as well as other bureaucratic offices in these three jurisdictions have just as many tedious bureaucratic compliance forms for opening bank, investment and other accounts as Bermuda does.

Each family's case will be as unique, depending upon the family circumstances, nationality, citizenship ties, financial holdings, relatives, careers, businesses, retirement logistics and so on.

Here is an illustrative example.

A long-term Bermuda resident family is considering emigration, but with no connections to any of the three primary Pond- straddler countries: US, UK and Canada.

The hypothetical family's financial holdings:

- A couple, both fully employed at mid-tier positions.
- British Overseas Territories Citizen Bermuda passport holders.
- Savings accounts and term deposits.
- Small investment accounts, locally provided mutual funds.
- One spouse is a large minority share-holder in a small Bermuda company; the other owns another 10 per cent.
- Home owned for 20 years; little equity, large mortgage due to renovations to rent to supplement their retirement abroad.
- Two mid-size, whole life policies.
- Basic health insurance provided by local employers; couple pays additional benefits.
- Decent individual pensions, accrued from more than 30 years of employment.
- Old age contributory pensions eligible — unknown how much.
- Family trust for two children, both minors.
- Possible, but you never know, small future inheritance.
- Bermuda wills.
- No affiliation with foreign investments, etc, at least they don't think so.

Emigration.

Space does not permit addressing how this family will legally migrate abroad or their choice of country. Egress may be obtainable through various sponsorship programmes to either Canada or the US, or perhaps ties to the UK through Bermuda.

Timing date of residency is absolutely critical to their pre-immigration cross-border financial planning, while there are numerous other pitfalls relative to domicile, citizenship, tax, immigration.

Income and other taxation.

Residents of Canada, the US and the UK are subject to tax on their worldwide income. Each country's tax laws are complex, involving federal government, provinces, states and/or municipalities, relative to types of income, dividends, capital gains, wages, active or passive income and so on.

All three countries employ somewhat similar progressive tax systems with each new income block threshold, the tax rate increases.

We take a look at the 2019 income tax regimes for Canada Federal and Province of Alberta combined that can readily be found by researching the Internet.

An individual with up to $47,630CAD will be taxed at two rate thresholds, rates increasing again over two more thresholds.

Simple (not-all inclusive) observations.

The income generated from family assets may all be taxable in the new country, once they are resident:

- Interest earned on savings and term deposits.
- Dividends paid by the local Bermuda company, investments and mutual funds.

- Rental income on home.
- National Pension distributions, either draw-downs or an annuity choice.
- Government pension distributions.

Additional taxation and regulatory questions arise:

- Are Bermuda life insurance premiums, cash value, or settlements taxable?
- Are the policies transportable, or need to be reissued as new policies?
- Can they operate the Bermuda company from abroad? If so, will it be categorised as controlled foreign corporation (or other) with taxability of undistributed income?
- Are Bermuda mutual funds, National Pension Scheme portfolios transportable in entirety?
- Can a Bermuda trust granter/beneficiary structure, such as attribution of income to granter trigger tax events, or a non-recognition of trust?
- Possible family inheritance taxable?
- Eligible for social insurance in new jurisdiction?
- Are Bermuda wills and trust document not recognised elsewhere?

Investment property low-cost basis tax traps.

Relocation families may keep long-term owned real property, and foreign investments, intact. If these entities have low original costs and are sold after relocation-to-new-country transition is complete, the family may be subject to large capital gains on sale profits, payable to their new country's treasury.

Relocators have touted cashing out as the easiest way to move, but expert professional advice should correlate with this opinion:

- Liquidate all assets;
- wind up life insurance policies, but not before qualifying for new jurisdiction-approved policies;
- convert Bermuda dollar cash to currency of choice, say positively capturing the low current Loonie rate, but taking a penalty for pound purchases.

But even the cash-out method may not cover future Bermuda pensions, trust, or other distributions where the family may be forced to pay income tax on assets earned tax-free far, far away before relocation.

Currently, its Bermuda pension law (for both) has been updated - for the Bermuda National Pension Scheme - to allow for a premature or at retirement lump-sum distribution (25%), an ideal situation for those leaving permanently.

This is a challenge that the family will have to investigate in great detail.

One rule — get qualified professional plan- ning before you go. Readers, I remind you again that this is not specific cross border or any other financial planning advice for you - it is simply an illustrative hypothetical overview to demonstrate the complexity of the cross-border decision process.

These observations cannot be relied upon for your individual situation and the author makes absolutely no representation as to the appropriateness or reliability of said observations.

Research and Plan - Extensively - before Relocating

CupMatch. Scott Stallard Photography

Bermuda Cup Match weekend is a tradition for the ages, and it continues. But this year may be the last Cup Match good time (if it is held physically at all due to COVID) for those planning to leave this precious place.

No matter the reason for going, for those of us with deep roots of limestone and the sea to our iconic island embedded deep into the core of our lives, "parting is such sweet sorrow," à la Shakespeare.

Plan first!

The decision to emigrate requires serious considerations. Individuals and families need to have a very clear cross-border financial plan and timeline in place before the big transition.

- Start with internet research.
- Social network with those gone before;
- allow adequate time for decisions, changes and implementation in your financial strategies.
- Seek qualified credentialed international professional advice if you cannot find answers.

I emphasise this heavily — reliance on friends and family narratives do not encompass you or your financial situation.

Get it right the first time. It will be stressful enough relocating without having to deal with inadvertent, expensive tax and financial mistakes.

Here are some key planning factors (not inclusive) and references for the five most affinity-linked countries. Space does not permit links to Costa Rica, Panama, Florianopolis/Brazil, Australia, New Zealand and Europe, which are all popular places where many Bermuda islanders have resettled communities. Costa Rica alone has more than 150 former Bermuda families.

Where will you relocate?

- The big question. Do they want you? Countries have immigrant quotas, some more generous than others.
- Can you live there, permanently?
- Avoid disappointment. Research everything: language, culture, taxes, legal rights, healthcare, retirement/pension benefits, property ownership, finances and banking, licensing, transportation, cost of living, estate planning, and many government regulations.

How will you get there?

- Entry into new country via government programmes, relatives, employment, business connections?
- What visas/permits needed?
- How, or are you being sponsored?
- Have the applications already been filed, when, and where? Timing for entry/residency acceptance is everything here— relative to taxation (or not) by your new jurisdiction.
- Entry/Exit. Can you come back if you change your mind?

Will your status be different?

- What is your residency, domicile and potential citizenship status?
- Have you been in and out of the new country intermittently already?
- Are you tracking stays for how long and when? Tax revenue agencies may use prior visits and time spent as part of a tax liability assessment. Be very careful here.
- Residency categorisations vary by country, e.g. Canada uses a combination of points including day counting, significant connections and attachments and others.
- Domicile. Keeping your original domicile or renouncing — not clarifying can affect income and estate planning.
- Connections and path to citizenship ties: Parent(s), grandparent(s), marriage?

Finances — review all current positions carefully.

Research the new country's tax structures that will impact your pre-emigration earned income and assets.

- Cash. Convert, compliance, new country account openings, foreign exchange.
- Investments: prohibited, low-cost basis, market timing for liquidation.
- Real property; renting, selling, settled in foreign trust.
- Pensions; leave, liquidate, transportable.
- Insurance: non or compliant life, and possible annuities.
- Wills and estates. Not recognised, wind-up, or two-country wills execution.
- Foreign trust treatment by new country tax authority.
- Local debit/credit cards: keep, close out — possible AML complications from transferring monies held in Bermuda to another jurisdiction, if not reported.

- Business: sell, keep as shareholder, for- eign company tax issues?
- Leaving income-generating assets in Bermuda? Reporting worldwide income is mandated by all of these countries.

Why emigrate?

The 2020 Royal Gazette survey says it all. The cost of living according to more than 76 per cent of the 3,000 survey takers.

And currently, the change in the economic environment due to social distancing, COVID-19 mandates and future employment considerations.

Here are some useful references for a number of popular relocation destinations. All references were considered to be current as at date of publication.

One more thing to keep in mind.

Emigrating to another country means that not everyone says, "Good morning!"

You are in their country now — YOU are the foreigner.

Listen to
Bermuda Pondstraddlers'
Crossing Border Challenges

https://tinyurl.com/yzbyeyx5

References
& Resources

UNITED STATES use Google research

Immigration: How to Enter the US.

Residency: Green Cards and Permanent Residence in the US.

Citizenship: Guide to Naturalisation Process.

How to apply for US citizenship.

Taxation. US Internal Revenue Service.

international taxpayer section

UNITED KINGDOM

Residency and domicile rules defined. Citizenship. Citizenship and living in the UK Immigration. Visas and immigration.

Taxation. Welcome to GOV.UK.

HMRC Revenue & Customs

* EY 2018-19 Worldwide Personal Tax and Immigration Guide — UK.

CANADA

Residency. Determining residency status.

* Applying for permanent residence.

Domicile. Home is Where the ... Domicile is? September 2018 | Dwight D. Dee, Kath- ryn Gullason.

* Immigration to Canada.

Citizenship. Apply to become a Canadian citizen.

Taxation. Canada Revenue Agency

* EY 2018-19 Worldwide Personal Tax and Immigration Guide — Canada.

AUSTRALIA

Residency. Apply for permanent residency Domicile. The Australian Domicile Test.

Citizenship.

Immigration.

Taxation. Australian Taxation Office.

EY 2018-19 Worldwide Personal Tax and Immigration Guide — Australia.

AZORES (PORTUGAL)

Residency. Applying for residency in Portugal.

- Living in the Azores.
- Domicile and succession.

Citizenship. Seven changes in Portuguese nationality law.

Immigration. Official Website.

Taxation. Portuguese Tax Authority.

- EY 2018-19 Worldwide Personal Tax and Immigration Guide — Azores/ Portugal.

Broader References

Wikipedia for all countries under taxation, immigration, domicile, citizenship and residency.

Readers, the firms and individuals listed below are for information purposes only and are not to be considered endorsements by the author.

Always consider locating and working with a licensed qualified international or US Attorney, or a CPA, Certified/ Chartered Public Accountant, a mark recognised worldwide.

PLANNING AND TAX ASSISTANCE

TAX TALK Virginia La Torre Jeker, J.D. — US tax matters affecting international clients

UK. The Fry Group

US. Planning and taxation. Robert Baldwin, CPA, Baldwin & Associates, Charleston US
http://baldwincpa.com/

Canada. Michael Atlas CA

Portugal. Forth Capital

Bermuda taxation accountants: EY, KPMG, Deloitte, PricewaterhouseCoopers.

The Spirit of Bermuda Training Ship at Dusk's Fading Light

Scot Stallard Photography Bermuda

A

About

2019

Martha Harris Myron is a multinational (Pond-straddler) citizen of Bermuda (native), the United States, and the United Kingdom.

A Pondstraddler is a person with one foot on each shore whose heart resides in both countries.

Born (and raised) on the remote island of Bermuda at a time of tourist-filled activity, and parochial economics, all filtered with quiet, picturesque, elegant, and sun-filled sea-sparkling charm, her indigenous Bermuda background and personal experiences as a qualified international financial planner and perennial Pondstraddler between Bermuda and the United States have given her a unique perspective on the challenging financial environment for Bermuda islanders and international residents and their families living, working on island while connected across the Great Atlantic Pond between the border points: United States, Canada, United Kingdom, Europe, and Bermuda, the premier international financial centre.

Her Bermudian grandmother Agnes White-cross Harris is a tiny part of local history with her ancestors appearing in Bermuda church records around the late 1700's, arriving as indentured servants during the long-term impetus to build the Dockyard. Her grandfather, William Stanley Harris was a career British army bandmaster in the Royal Fusiliers, serving in Bermuda and for more than five years in the devastating First World War I.

Her father, Cecil E Harris, was the Bermuda Sewing Machine Man for more than fifty years. Her mother, Anna Clarine Sawyer, arrived in Bermuda during World War II with the influx of the United States Air Force Engineers who built our first airport 80 years ago, wholly modernised in 2020.

Martha is a popular Saturday financial columnist, for more than twenty years (and 1,000 articles), to the Royal Gazette (established 1796), Hamilton, Bermuda, various news aggregators, and US publications. With a passionate mission to provide financial information that relates specifically to the people of her ancestral island home, Bermuda, she writes extensively about domestic and international finance, taxation, economics, law, investments, immigration, risk management, constitutional interpretations, retirement, and a myriad of related topics in plain understandable terms and concepts.

Her articles reach a broad spectrum of Bermuda island readers, as well as aggregated in international publications.

See Managing Finances in a Globally Mobile World, The Royal Gazette by Martha Harris Myron. A contemporary article written, February 28 2015:

She is the Principal/Owner of the Pond-straddler™ Life Consultancy that provided cross border financial planning on international tax, immigration, investment, retirement, legacy, and related financial challenges to the lifestyles of Bermuda islander, their families, related internationally mobile individuals and their businesses residing, working, crossing borders, and straddling ponds in the North Atlantic Quadrangle.

She is the International Financial Consultant to the Olderhood Group Bermuda Ltd.

Finance columnist to the Royal Gazette, Bermda's National Newspaper since March 2000.

Accreditations and Licenses

Master of Laws: International Tax and Financial Services, Summa Cum Laude. Thomas Jefferson School of Law, San Diego, 2013

Certified Public Accountant (USA) New Hampshire 2024

Certified Financial Planner (USA) retired

Member of Society of Trust & Estate Practitioners (UK/Bermuda)

United States Series 7 and 63 Securities License (inactive in Bermuda)

Bachelor of Science in Accounting: Franklin Pierce University, USA

Contributing Technical Author:

Personal finance columnist to The Royal Gazette, Hamilton, Bermuda since February 26, 2000.

Encore Age, A Royal Gazette monthly digital magazine

The Bermuda Islanders Fundamental Financial Planning Primer Series One - Eight. Publishing dates. Mid - summer 2020 for Book One, Winter 21-22 Book Two.

Bermuda Chapters:

LexisNexis® Guide to FATCA Compliance, 3rd Edition (William Byrnes & Robert Munro, LexisNexis 2015).

Company Law & Analysis: Wolters Kluwer: International Trust Laws and Analysis (ITLA) 2014-5 Bermuda Company Law

Various other domestic and international publications and journals.

The Bermudian Business Magazine

Google News Contributor since 2016

Disclosures

Martha Harris Myron, JSM, CPA is a Bermudian/ American finance journalist with an extensive background in cross border and comprehensive international financial planning: cash management, investments, insurance, retirement & pensions, taxation, immigration, estate, trust, and legacy positions.

THE AUTHOR does not recommend, hold, buy or sell local Bermuda, or related international investment products offered on island, nor make recommendations for, nor advise personally on financial planning issues, or on any other specific investment products offered domestically or on an international basis.

The Bermuda Fundamental Financial Planning Primer Series Books are written for information and educational purposes only and are not to be taken by any persons as personal advice, or relied upon, as specific individual legal, tax, immigration, retirement, insurance or any other personal financial planning advice.

The author has no responsibility for financial decisions made by any individual or entity for personal financial planning – based upon the general information provided herein.

The author, Martha Harris Myron is not responsible for inaccuracies, missing, incorrect, obsolete or any other errors of information from third-parties or websites, nor does she receive or pay any remunerations to any individual, company, or website producers.

Information and references are considered to be current as of date of publication. Other individuals' work, photos, etc. is always attributed/referenced.

Martha Harris Myron does not endorse, remit, or receive payment for any third-party information, nor is responsible for any information sourced or provided by third party sources.

Country laws in all matters as well as topics included in the above content are subject to change without notice and it is you, the reader's responsibility, domestically, and/or with multinational connections, citizenships, domiciles, etc., that are cautioned to seek current individual professional advice from experienced, internationally qualified legal, tax, immigration, retirement, insurance, investment and financial planning professionals with verifiable credentials and backgrounds for your personal financial planning issues and positions.

Appendix A

Where to get your financial information

by Martha Myron, Moneywise Published May 4, 2019 and May 11, 2019 in the Royal Gazette, Bermuda.

Readers of The Royal Gazette often write to me about Moneywise column topics and how my answers and resource links have helped them find answers to their finance questions. I am incredibly appreciative, and thank you all, every single one of you who has taken time from your busy lives to contact me.

These special comments are hugely motivating to me to provide as factually, and comprehensively as possible, more financial information relevant to Bermuda islanders' lives.

We tend to forget that Bermuda itself, while outwardly appearing as a gorgeous, tropical, simple life-style jurisdiction in the middle of the North Atlantic Quadrangle, is as financially sophisticated as any other significantly larger-in-scale global financial centre.

Our geographical location and our polyglot of nationalities, citizenships, domiciles, family, cultures, and residency ties means that we have to be cognisant of the financial constraints, requirements, reporting, and regulations of not just our domestic regime, but also those countries closest to us that trade with us: US, United Kingdom, and Canada.

So, these lists are some, but certainly not all inclusive, reference sources that I use and that may be financially useful to you all. These websites are chock full of information, which will almost always require research and digging to find your personal answers. Note also, that I do not receive (or pay) compensation, from any agency or individual for these listings.

Taxation

US, Canada, UK connected dual-triple citizens, investors and others

US Internal Revenue Service, International Section

Canada Revenue Agency: Lists all contact information for individuals, international tax and non-resident inquiries, businesses, etc.

Britain, Her Majesty's Revenue and Customs: international tax manual lists non-resident landlords and/or NR trading in the UK,

And living, retiring or returning from abroad

Additional assistance with cross-border tax planning with expert professionals in legal, tax, and finance:

Bermuda, The Big Four auditing, tax, financial advisory and related services professionals:

Deloitte Bermuda

EY Bermuda

KPMG Bermuda

PWC Bermuda I

International US tax specialist for US citizens abroad and foreign persons investing in the US

Virginia LaTorre-Jeker, JD,

is a US attorney with more than 30 years' experience in US/international tax law. Virginia's blog (US-Tax.org) excerpts/white papers have been cited in the US Congressional Record.

Us & International Taxation for US ex-pats, non-US persons and multinational families

Bob Baldwin, CPA/PFS, AEP, CGMA, Bald- win Associates. http://baldwincpa.com/ South Carolina.

Canada

John Richardson, Canadian attorney with US dual citizenship, specialises in working with US citizens abroad, Canadians abroad and/or with US tax issues, and related matters

UK

The Fry Group: moving overseas or moving back to the UK, tax, wealth and estate planning — wherever you are in the world.

Immigration and Emigration

Bermuda. Government of Bermuda Department of Immigration includes Bermudian status, work permits, naturalisation, employment, travel documents, land licence permissions, permanent residency, etc.

US Citizenship and Immigration Services:

Canadian Government Immigration and citizenship

UK Visas and Immigration

Visiting the UK after Brexit

Investments: Stocks, Bonds, ETFs, mutual funds

The following websites and research groups are still free and quite comprehensive.

Some sites are not included because, while very good, are no longer cost-effective for individual investors.

The Bermuda Stock Exchange: All publicly traded domestic companies are listed on the Board along with hundreds of international securities. The BSX is the largest repository for ILS (Insurance-linked securities in the world).

United States

Yahoo Finance, still my favourite, free, and the most comprehensive: watchlists, "My Portfolio", screeners, markets, industries, videos, news, personal finance, tech covering stocks, bonds, mutual funds, ETFs, cryptocurrencies, commodities, trends, analysis and incredible amounts more

TDAmeritrade. Free, comprehensive, education, research sections, trading platforms, and more

Morningstar Research: daily news, articles, videos, rankings, stock screeners, mutual fund comparisons, etc.

360Financial Literacy

Canada

Yahoo Finance Canada

Morningstar Canada

The Globe and Mail Global Adviser

United Kingdom

Yahoo Finance UK:

Morningstar UK

The Top 60 UK Investment Blogs And Websites for UK Investors in 2019: last updated April 18, 2019

Worldwide

Investment research and very good reading, if you like lots of finance details!

- Bloomberg News — a great favourite of mine, fully comprehensive, worldwide inclusive, and incredibly up-to-the-minute timely, finance and political, global information!

- The Street, Inc — I've followed this investment research and commentary website since its inception in 1996. Jim Cramer, star of CNBC's Mad Money, wrote for them then, and continues to do so now.

- American Association of Individual Investors is a 40-year old membership organisation (with more than two million real individual members) that follows market trends, stock ideas, investing, events, and free reports.

A modest cost of $29 per year allows you to track their model portfolio, which has out- paced the market, and use their tools and resources: "My Portfolio", asset allocation models, investor guides, investor classroom and review articles on getting started, investing, financial planning, stocks, funds/ ETFs, and bonds.

AAII Investor Sentiment Survey is voted on by the individual members. The American Association of Individual Investors is famous for their weekly AAII Investor Sentiment Survey that has become a widely followed measure of the mood of individual investors.

The weekly survey results are published in a number of financial publications including Barron's and Bloomberg and are widely followed by market strategists, investment newsletter writers and other financial professionals.

- TDAmeritrade's The Investor Movement Index is a fascinating, illuminating bit of monthly research on real individual investors and their investing sentiment demonstrated by tracking a randomised sample of their own stock market investing (see chart) above.

TDAmeritrade says: "Introducing an index with a pulse: The Investor Movement Index works by using data from one of the nation's largest online investment communities, the IMX gives you a snapshot of investor sentiment. It does this by analysing and averaging the holdings/ positions, trading activity, and other data from real portfolios held by real investors each month and boils it down to an index. You know where small investors think the market is going.

Have fun with these sites. Be motivated to start your future financial success plan now.

Research and resources of financial planning for individual financial success.

Before progressing readers, please keep in mind that this is general information, some sections or statements may not exactly apply to the Bermuda finance marketplace as they tend to be US focused, but for the most part, mathematics and its offspring, geometry, physics, chemistry, economics, statistics, and so on are a universal common language utilised the world over.

Numbers and math never lie.

Money skills in general

Practical Money Skills, Khan Academy 360 Degree of Financial Literacy

These are two of my free favourites. Everyone needs to brush up on money concepts from time to time. Many of us who have never been great maths people, need good references for verification. Readers, I'm just like most of you, some days maths is a struggle. The old saying if you don't use it, you lose it is so true.

Practical Money Skills, Khan Academy, sponsored by Visa and free

Khan Academy, a non-profit US organisation, originally started in 2008 when Salman Khan tutored one of his cousins in mathematics on the internet using a service called Yahoo! Doodle Images.

Mr Khan, a former hedge fund analyst, is American educator, mathematician and entrepreneur with master's degrees from both MIT and Harvard. Positive responses from other relatives and more followed with later tutoring videos being posted on YouTube. Today, Khan Academy lists more than 20,000 videos in five languages. Funding comes from philanthropic organisations, such as Bill Gates, an early supporter, Google, AT&T, the Carlos Slim Foundation for Spanish versions and many others.

The website lists hundreds to thousands of brief to more expansive videos, breaking down maths concepts for adults and students from Grade 1-12, economics, inflation, mortgages, accounting and financial statements, stocks and bonds, mutual funds, options, and many more topics.

The section on finance is terrific.

And, most if not all of these little courses are available on YouTube, so no need to even go to the Khan Academy website. A sampling and hint — use the closed caption function on the videos, it helps in following the numbers:

- Introduction to Compound Interest
- Rule of 72 states if you divide 72 by the interest rate, say 4 per cent to get 18 years, that is how long it will take you to double your money. The video explains how that number is correct. The Rule of 72 is often used to explain the difference between term deposits and security (stock) appreciation.
- Introduction to Mortgage Loans.
- What it means to buy a company's stock.
- Even Basics, Multiplication and Division. Finding a percentages and Decimals.

We use maths every single day, yet at times, we tend to be challenged by even the basics.

360 Degrees of Literacy

is a non-profit fully transitional life-planning website supported by the American Institute of Certified Public Accountants.
https://www.360financialliteracy.org/

The site has numerous supportive articles on managing your finances, including a clever one on saving by bringing your own lunch to work, using an accelerated principal mortgage pay-down schedule, getting help with the savings on paying down your

credit card, starting a financial plan as well as more than a hundred other calculators for just about every circumstance:

The Home Budget Analysis is very good.

Credit Card Payoff

Lunch Savings, how much can you save by brown-bagging it.

Personal Finance for College Students on YouTube.

Readers, give me your feedback on this one. Very illuminating.

There are lots more besides, and links are all on the 360 Degree website.

Emergency Savings — figure out what you need for a rainy day

Accelerated Debt Payoff — plan to accelerate paying off your mortgage. Here is a calculator to help you with the amounts and to demonstrate what the principal balance should be after every transaction.

Adjustable Rate Mortgage versus Fixed Rate Mortgage. New to home buying? This calculator helps in deciding which contract will work for you.

Benefit of Spending Less — looking for the simple life? This is an eye-opener.

Certificate of Deposit Calculator. Know exactly what your compounded interest balance should be.

Some other financial planning focused websites.

Insurance

How health insurance works. Health insurance: Wikipedia explains how healthcare works, provides comparisons of health systems in 14 countries, among them Australia, US, UK, Canada, Japan, New Zealand, etc.

Life insurance. How it works. Nerd Wallet

Retirement

What is your Rise score? The Retirement Income Security Evaluation Score is a different take on the classic retirement calculator.

Hosted by Alliance, it focuses on practicality in retirement and whether your current income and savings will cover basic living expenses and healthcare. Be sure to reduce the taxation section to zero per cent, since Bermuda does not have an income tax regime, although it can now be argued that there are now plenty of other tax substitutes.

Annuities calculator. Use this calculator to get an idea of your monthly payment when you are ready to retire with your pension under the Bermuda National Pension Scheme.

Ballpark E$timater Interactive Online

This estimator is geared toward a United States audience. However, instead of trying to enter US social security - enter what you think you will receive in Bermuda Government Old Age Contributory Pension payments.

Estate Planning

Michael J. Mello QC, JP, TEP, a member of Appleby's Private Client and Trusts Practice Group and practises primarily in the areas of trusts, wills ad estates. He has over 40 years' experience and is the author of The Law of Wills & Estates in Bermuda, now in its ninth edition, and numerous articles on trusts, wills, powers and estates.

His free book (with updates) is extremely detailed and is a tremendous help to Bermuda islanders planning their estate documents.

Atty Mello is now retired, but his colleagues at Appleby can provide experienced assistance.

In Appreciation

My Gratitude and enduring love above all to my dear husband, Paul, who stepped up to the plate to finance my university education in way-past-the-usual college age (I attended night school - at age 45- after my day job); listened endlessly and patiently, encouraging me not to give up those education dreams when frustrated with the mountainous study burden and qualification exam requirements for financial planning and Master in Laws credentials; and for his willingness and caring to embark with me on a totally new culture journey and career experience on the Island of Bermuda, my family home.

Paul J Myron, RPh, came to Bermuda with me having more than forty years of extensive experience in the pharmaceutical industry as well as the Registered Pharmacist retail trade in the United States, to then serve as the Senior Registered Pharmacist at Somerset Pharmacy, Mangrove Bay for more than fifteen years. He successfully wrote the requisite Bermuda Pharmaceutical Board's pharmacist licensing exam, further developing a comprehensive knowledge of four countries (USA, Canada, UK, and Bermuda) Pharmaceutical Formularies in order to provide professional guidance to every customer at the pharmacy.

There are so many other wonderful people to thank along the way, all of whom provided support, and shared knowledge with me:

My Royal Gazette Editors:
Business Editor: Jonathan Kent, a patient boss and brilliant journalist; Scott Neil, a very supportive colleague and great, dedicated journalist;
Managing Editor, Dexter Smith, an editor with formidable qualifications - who barely knew me, yet basically gave me carte blanche to write passionately on our Bermuda economic/financial environment.
Royal Gazette former editor, Bill Zuill – an amazing journalist, and historian who originally hired me, encouraged (pushed) me to write like a real columnist.

Roger Crombie, FCA, a factual, brilliant international re/insurance journalist and a great financial satirist who generously gave me the first start by sharing his column on the Royal Gazette Moneywise Saturday pages.

Julie A. Hendrickson-Simons, B.Sc., AAPA, QPA, my greatest partner in investment successes and an innovative international financial planner in her own right.

The late Heather A. Jacobs-Matthews, JP, FCPA, FCA, CFE, Auditor General of Bermuda 2009-2016

Heather Thomas, CPA CFE CGMA, the current and third Auditor General of Bermuda

Henry Perren, Vice Chairman, Cidel Asset Management Inc. Canada
The Hon. E.T (Bob) Richards Former Deputy Premier & Minister of Finance of Bermuda
The Hon. Sir John W Swan, KBE JP former Premier of Bermuda (1982-1995)
The Hon. N.H. Cole Simons, JP MP, Bermuda Leader of the Opposition
Dwayne Outerbridge, CFA Head of Global Asset Management, The Bank of N.T. Buttefield & Son Limited
Charlene Asphall, former Head of Retail Banking, Bank of Bermuda
Terry Faulkenberry, Head of Management Information, Aspen Reinsurance Bermuda
Robert Stewart, Former CEO of Royal/Dutch Shell Group of Companies Bermuda
Michael J. Mello QC JP TEP, Author of The Law of Wills & Estates in Bermuda and Consultant to Appleby Bermuda
Juliana M. Snelling, Director/Partner of Canterbury Law Ltd. Bermuda
Shantel Deshield, CEO Pocketchangebda, financial introduction for young adults

Keith Archibald Forbes, Editor/author- for more than thirty years of the detailed, wonderful, exclusively Bermudian website, https://bermuda-online.org/

Bill Storie, FCA, FACHT and Robin Trimingham, FACHT, the Founders of the Olderhood Group Ltd Bermuda, Olderhood Productions International and authors of The Third Journey, offering life transition consulting and coaching services including: financial literacy webinars, retirement preparation workshops, and retirement readiness assessments, now with more than 100,000 loyal followers. www.olderhoodgroup.com

Scott Stallard, Photographer extraordinaire, who so generously allowed me to use numerous gorgeous photos from his voluminous works of Bermuda photography of Bermuda. Beautiful, beautiful photos reflecting all facets of Bermuda life, particularly, the influence of the sea, that we all love so well. https://scottstallard.com/

Ryze Photography - thank you for your wonderful photographs

Ralph Richardson, Author: The Bermuda Boater; Owner of Winsome Tours and Consulting Limited, Director of the Tall Ships, Bermuda; Executive Director of the Bermuda Hospitals Charitable Trust and Past Commodore, the Royal Bermuda Yacht Club

The Late Oda Mallory, the Real-Life Blondell, with her historic radio show and Facebook presence keeping "Bermuda Living Memories" alive.

Paul Shapiro, Vice President/Creative Director, Brimstone Media Ltd. Bermuda, a media designer and writer extraordinaire.

Dr. Edward Harris, MBE PhD FSA, Retired Director Emeritus National Museum of Bermuda, who achieved global status with the invention of the 'Harris Matrix,' a vital component of archaeology. His Book - Principles of Archaeological Stratigraphy - and the Matrix has stood the test of time for almost 50 years, now in twelve language translations.

The anonymous Luminaries – who graciously consented to wade through this missive and provide productive feedback and encouragement. Thank you all.

And to you, dear readers of the Royal Gazette Moneywise column, my thanks to every single one of you for reading, commenting, and writing to me. I greatly value your critical contributions – they inspire me to write more, research new topics and continue to present financial facts with humour, positivity, (sometimes critically ranting when readers have reported financial adversity and finding no recourse) and in everyday language.

I am so grateful as well to have had the support and opportunities provided from so many more kind, generous people who requested anonymity.

Made in the USA
Middletown, DE
02 December 2022

16799210R00166